US

AND

THEM

HBR PRESS

2014

US AND THEM

AN AMERICAN FAMILY SPENDS TEN YEARS

WITH FOREIGNERS

By Bill Meara

The opinions expressed in this book are those of the author and do not necessarily reflect those of the U.S. government.

This book has undergone pre-publication review by the author's employer, the U.S. Department of State.

For Elisa, the person at the heart of all these stories, the heart of our family, and the owner of my heart.

CONTENTS

"We and They"
By Rudyard Kipling

Father and Mother, and Me,
Sister and Auntie say
All the people like us are We,
And every one else is They.
And They live over the sea,
While We live over the way,
But-would you believe it? --They look upon We
As only a sort of They!

We eat pork and beef
With cow-horn-handled knives.
They who gobble Their rice off a leaf,
Are horrified out of Their lives;
While they who live up a tree,
And feast on grubs and clay,
(Isn't it scandalous?) look upon We
As a simply disgusting They!

We shoot birds with a gun.
They stick lions with spears.
Their full-dress is un-.
We dress up to Our ears.
They like Their friends for tea.
We like Our friends to stay;
And, after all that, They look upon We
As an utterly ignorant They!

We eat kitcheny food.
We have doors that latch.
They drink milk or blood,
Under an open thatch.
We have Doctors to fee.
They have Wizards to pay.
And (impudent heathen!) They look upon We
As a quite impossible They!

All good people agree,
And all good people say,
All nice people, like Us, are We
And every one else is They:
But if you cross over the sea,
Instead of over the way,
You may end by (think of it!) looking on We
As only a sort of They!"

Achilles Heal

From the Merriam Webster Dictionary:

Nationalism: *loyalty and devotion to a nation; especially: a sense of national consciousness exalting one nation above all others and placing primary emphasis on promotion of its culture and interests as opposed to those of other nations or supranational groups.*

Patriotism: *love for or devotion to one's country. Synonym: nationalism.*

As I sat in my hospital bed with my foot newly encased in a heavy cast and my head still groggy from anesthesia, I wondered aloud about what I would do during my convalescence. The answer came from Elisa: "Write that book!"

Good idea! I got out a pencil and, on the envelope of an X-Ray, we started writing the outline.

It was May 2010, and I was in a small hospital in Rome, recovering from the minor surgery that put my Achilles tendon back together after a little accident involving some kites, an approaching thunderstorm, and a concealed gopher hole. Charming and friendly nuns – most of them from Italy, but one a homesick young woman from Chennai – came in and out of my room, offering encouragement, and asking about my dinner preferences. Nurses popped in from time to time to jab me with needles. One was from Romania, the other from Honduras. People from the American Embassy (my employer) called in to see how I was doing. We were waiting for a call or a text from our ten year-old daughter Maria, who was up in Umbria on a class trip, accompanied by her teacher from Scotland, her Principal from Haiti, and her classmates from, well, everywhere. Our twelve year-old son Billy was at his twice-weekly fencing class, dueling it out with adolescent members of the Italian elite. He'd be taken home by Gunna, a math teacher and poverty refugee from Sri Lanka who now parks cars in the garage in our apartment building, and who helps out in situations like this. Seated with me, and adding as many items to the outline as I did, was my wife Elisa. She is from the Dominican Republic, but after living in four other countries, she, like many of the other people

1

in this book, is pretty much from everywhere, and from nowhere in particular.

There was nothing really special or noteworthy about our day in that hospital – this was typical family stuff: coping with a minor injury, a class trip, an extracurricular activity. But we were doing these ordinary things in a foreign environment, far from home. That had been the story of our lives for the previous ten years: ordinary family life in extraordinary international settings. We had left the United States in 2000. We'd spent three years in the Azores islands of Portugal, four years in London, and three in Rome. The injury that put me in that hospital came just as we were getting ready to pack up and head back to the United States.

That day in the hospital of captures the way we had lived during the previous ten years. We had lived a very international life. This international life has changed us, changed the way we look at the world. Ten years earlier we had departed the United States filled with the triumphant flag-waving American nationalism and patriotism that marked the years immediately following the end of the Cold War. Yes indeed, we were Number One, and my wife and I had gone out into the world with a bit of a patriotic chip on our shoulders. As the end of our decade overseas approached, as we prepared to return to the United States, we often commented on how much our way of looking at the world had changed.

This change came about slowly. It was not the result of exposure to any academic theory or political ideology. It was more of a result of our experiences as a family than from my work in embassies and consulates. It was the result of living abroad, of raising our children abroad. We'd been given the opportunity to experience the world in a way that very few families can. We'd learned a lot. We'd grown. We'd picked up a lot of the kind of insight that only comes through long experience, and perhaps a bit of wisdom. Conscious of the fact ours had been a very high-priced education, with most of the costs paid by our Uncle Sam, we often found ourselves thinking that we should share our experiences and our insights with our fellow Americans – even with those who might find our conclusions distasteful.

Most of this book was easy to write; the stories about our lives in Europe flowed easily onto the page. But when I started to write about the lessons that we had learned from these stories, the writing became difficult. I found myself writing about some very sensitive, emotional topics, about deeply ingrained beliefs about country and nation and patriotism. It would have been easier just to write a travel book about our excellent ten year European adventure, but I think we owe it to our fellow Americans to be honest about the lessons we took away from this experience.

2

US
SOME INTRODUCTIONS

"Us, us, us, us, us…
And
Them, them, them, them…
And after all, we're only ordinary men."
Pink Floyd, 1973 "Dark Side of the Moon" album

New York City circa 1964. Left to right: author, Eugene, author's brother Ed

Before I tell you about our ten-year trip, some brief introductions are in order.

I was born in New York City, on Manhattan Island. We moved out to the suburbs (Rockland County) when I was seven. I am the oldest of five children. I went to Catholic school. My dad was a New York City policeman, and many of my uncles and cousins were New York cops and firemen. Baseball was very important in our family – my grandfather had played for the New York Yankees, and my father had played in the minor leagues. But I inherited none of the baseball genes. I was a truly terrible baseball player. But it didn't really matter – I was more interested in technology, especially radios. My grandmother declared that I was electrically inclined. I was ten years old when they landed on the moon –

3

I was a huge fan of the space program, Neil Armstrong was my hero, and I wanted to be an astronaut. Political awareness came early – at age six I helped my father and uncle distribute campaign literature for William F. Buckley's doomed campaign for mayor of New York. My earliest memory (that I can put a date on) is of the assassination of John F. Kennedy.

At Manhattan College I majored in International Studies and Economics. During summer vacations I helped teach English to Indian kids at a school run by the Christian Brothers in Huehuetenango, Guatemala. After graduation I became an army officer, and spent a lot of time in Central America. After five years in the army, I took the test for the Foreign Service. I think it is safe to say that up until then, no one in my family even knew that the Foreign Service was. My dad had serious misgivings about me leaving the military – he thought I was doing well there, and he feared that diplomacy was an upper class pursuit "not for us." But when they told me I had passed the test I decided to take a leap into the unknown. After a few months of training, the State Department sent me right back to Central America, to Tegucigalpa, Honduras where I was soon up to my eyeballs in the final round of the tropical portion of the Cold War.

After Honduras I was sent to the U.S. Consulate in Bilbao, Spain (in the Basque Country), and then to Santo Domingo, Dominican Republic. In my book about Central America ("Contra Cross"), I had groused a bit about an Army security rule that prohibited romance between U.S. military personnel and Salvadoran women. But I added an important footnote: "As it turned out, this rule had no real impact on my life, because the girl I was hoping to meet was about 1500 miles to the north-east, in Santo Domingo. I met Elisa Ruiz Castro in July 1992."

It was on the 4th of July. I had just gotten finished with the stuffy and formal Independence Day reception at the Embassy, and had headed out on the town. Elisa had not planned on going out that night, but her girl-friends had coaxed her to accompany them. At one point, one of them had said, "C'mon Elisa, who knows? Tonight you might meet the father of your children!" Prophetic words, indeed. I was sitting at the bar in a restaurant called "Esquisitos" in the Naco neighborhood of Santo Domingo when Elisa and her friends walked in. She had this amazing smile, and was wearing this beautiful floral dress. Using the skills that come with being single too long, I threw a line and eventually got her phone number.

I called the next day and asked her to lunch. She told me that first I'd have to meet her parents. She thought I'd balk at this, but I didn't. I guess I passed muster; we started going out. We had a wonderful courtship. The Dominican Republic is a beautiful place, and I had this beautiful girl by

4

my side, teaching me how to eat mangoes, dance to merengue and to speak like a Dominican. Every week-night her mother made me a sandwich for my dinner. On weekends we'd go to the beaches east of the capital, or into Santo Domingo's colonial zone for Spanish tapas on the plaza in front of the house built by Columbus's brother Diego. We'd ride around in my black BMW-325, listening to Bob Marley, Ruben Blades, or Juan Luis Guerra. Life was good. I'd never been happier. I loved Elisa and I loved being in the DR. The assignment had been for two years, but I extended twice and stayed for four. That's what you do when you find yourself assigned to paradise – you try to stay as long as you can.

Elisa's dad is a medical doctor. He came from a struggling family of

thirteen children. The Dominican Army had been his ticket to medicine – they had sent him to do a residency in Spain. By the time Elisa and I met, he had retired from the army as a colonel, and had gone into private practice. He has a very stern, serious demeanor. Whenever he leaves the house, he carries a chrome-plated .45 caliber pistol (and he is not averse to using it). But he has a heart of gold – he has a soft spot for kids, and much of his medical work is done for free for people who can't afford to pay him. He's always been very kind to me.

Elisa's mom is from Puerto Plata on the north coast of the Dominican Republic. She has an identical twin sister. Many Dominicans have nick-

names: Elisa is Kiki (but I call her Elisa). Elisa's mom is Yuya. Yuya's twin is Mate. Elisa is Yuya's only child, but Elisa's dad has five other children from previous marriages. When Elisa was nine she and her parents moved to a new neighborhood where there weren't many kids. Elisa was lonely – her only playmates were her dogs. She is very fond of animals – this explains the presence in our house of Cappuccio, our "Flying Cream-Cheese Latino Retriever."

Elisa was just twenty years old and still in college when we met (I was 33 – it was a bit of scandal). While on the surface it might have seemed that we came from vastly different places, in fact our families had a lot in common. We were both from middle class families, both of our dads had had public service careers. When I met her, Elisa was working full time, and studying full time. She was a very diligent student and worker, but it was a struggle for her. To get from school to work she, like most everyone else in Santo Domingo, made use of the Dominican Republic's extremely rickety system of multiple-passenger taxis ("carros publicos") and, for shorter journeys, "moto-conchos" – motor-bike taxis with the passenger on the back. Soon after we started going out, I put an end to her use of the moto-conchos and carros publicos. I arranged for a trusted driver to be on-call for Elisa's trips

to and from work and school. Most of the time I was there to pick her up – I'd go to her house early in the morning to take her to work, and in the evening I'd be waiting outside the university when school got out.

Elisa grew up on American rock-and-roll and movies (she was a huge fan of *Grease* and *Footloose* and would sing all the songs without knowing what the words meant). She dreamed of one day setting foot on foreign shores (little did she know that she'd be stepping onto quite a few of them). For her first trip to the U.S., we went up to New York to visit my parents. It was in January. Elisa had no clothing or shoes suitable for a northern winter. The weekend before our trip we scoured the stores of Santo Domingo for winter-ish apparel. I warned Elisa that it would be cold, but, never having experienced cold weather, she just didn't get it. Our plane landed in New York on a very bright sunny afternoon. Looking through the window, Elisa saw sunshine and associated it with warm weather. "This won't be so bad!" she said. Stepping out of the plane, she was pleased to announce that she was handling the winter weather just fine. It was my sad duty to point out that we were still inside the terminal. When we stepped outside, the cold air took her breath away. She was really shocked. She kept telling me that she didn't think it possible for human beings to live in those conditions.

My parents loved Elisa from the start. My mom had met her during a visit to Santo Domingo. On the night of their first meeting, after I dropped Elisa off at her house, I returned to my house to find my mom waiting up for me. Her opinion was quite clear: "You have to marry that girl!" My dad met Elisa during that first winter visit to New York. He too loved her from the start. It was really kind of surprising because during his years as a New York City cop, he had not been very fond of the Dominicans who had moved into his precinct. But wow, he really loved Elisa.

We got married in 1997 in Elisa's parents' living room (right where I'd eaten all those sandwiches). Elisa's aunt Anelsa (who is a judge) officiated. A few days before the wedding, Elisa's dad said he wanted to talk to me – he asked me to come to his office. I was kind of concerned, but as it turned out all he wanted to do was to warn me that Elisa had never learned to cook. "I don't know what you are going to do... maybe you could just go out to restaurants a lot." He was really worried about this. I told him that we'd figure something out.

We moved to Falls Church, Virginia. Almost immediately Elisa was dealing simultaneously with culture shock, a new husband, English language lessons, home-sickness, and... morning sickness. Billy was born in November 1997. It had been a rough pregnancy and the little guy arrived about six weeks ahead of schedule. Because he was premature, all the medical attention was focused on the baby. I went with him to the neo-natal ward, leaving Elisa in the delivery room with her mom. It turned out that I should have focused on Elisa. Soon after delivery her blood pressure soared to dangerous levels. We could have lost her that day.

Elisa is very perceptive about the feelings of others – this makes her a much better diplomat than I am. Friends are very important to her, and she will do anything she can to help a friend in need. She is passionate about gardening and she is a very good artist – she has done portraits of Billy and Maria. Elisa is very Dominican, and she misses her homeland. Sometimes, if I put on some Dominican music, it will stir up some nostalgia and make her sad – she'll ask me to turn it off.

Billy is a real Foreign Service kid, a real citizen of the world. He is pleased that his birthday coincides with England's Guy Fawkes Day – the celebration (with blazing bonfires) of the foiling of the gunpowder plot. He took a very early interest in technology – as soon as he could walk he'd stand by the window and watch cars and truck go by. One of his first words was "car." On his very first trip to the beach he was building sand castles; he still does this – he seems to have some engineering instincts. He is more of a science and technology kid than a sports guy, but in Italy he got into fencing, and in High School he has joined the Cross Country team. Billy swung a cricket bat before he ever used a baseball bat. When he was younger, he started writing an adventure novel featuring a young guy named Reddy Firestone (I hope he finishes it). He recently built his own computer. He is passionately interested in politics – one of his favorite books is Orwell's "1984." He has a deep dislike for the dictator of North Korea. He is deeply skeptical about organized religion, but is interested in Buddhism. He is a connoisseur of Root Beer. He recently turned our car port into a weight room. He is thinking about joining the Peace Corps. In college he'd like to study computer technology and business, in the hopes of joining forces with some friends to become an enormously wealthy technology entrepreneur.

Maria was born in Virginia in March of Y2K, so during Elisa's pregnancy with her, we were worried about the possible effect of the feared computer meltdown. During that pregnancy I had been going through some difficult negotiations with the State Department about our next assignment. We wanted to go overseas (life in the D.C. area was too expensive). For a while it looked like we'd be going to either Monterrey, Mexico or Madrid, Spain. We tried for Madrid, didn't get it, and in the process lost out on Monterrey. For a while our future was up in the air. But just days before Maria was born we got word that we'd be heading to the Azores islands of Portugal. We joked that it seemed that Maria was waiting to hear where we were going before officially joining the team. She too is a real Foreign Service kid. Some of her first words were in Portuguese, picked up from the cook and housekeeper who worked at the official residence of the

American Consul in the Azores (our place). People always say she looks (and acts) like me. When she was little she found this quite confusing – she couldn't figure out how a little girl could look like her father (she expected to be told that she looked like her mother). Over the years she has spoken with the accents of Sao Miguel island (in Portuguese), London (cut glass, BBCish accent), and Rome (Romanesco – the street talk of Trastevere). She has a taste for exotic and unusual food combinations. You'd never know it from looking at her, but she is a big fan of gangsta rap. In Rome, she was into gymnastics, but switched over to figure skating when we returned to the USA. She is deeply devoted to the violin. Her favorite book is "To Kill a Mockingbird." She is thinking about becoming a pediatrician. She sings to herself, and, when she was younger, couldn't sleep well unless I tucked her in. Sometimes she sleepwalks. She doesn't like scary movies.

Shortly before we headed to the Azores Elisa had been sworn in as citizen of the United States. Enthusiasm for her new country was reinforced by the very nationalistic worldview that she got from me. We were both registered Republicans and would vote for George W. Bush for President in the 2000 election. (Billy and Maria were, I suppose, still independents at this point.) We were a very patriotic couple, believers in American exceptionalism, and convinced that our American citizenship was a very important, very distinguishing characteristic, something that set us apart from the rest of the world. Off we went...

WHERE WE LIVED
HOUSES AND 'HOODS

"To me, it seems a dreadful indignity to have a soul controlled by geography." George Santayana

I wore an uncomfortable business suit on the flight to the Azores. I had been told that being the Principal Officer at the U.S. Consulate there implied VIP status and possible press interest. So that first trip required planning not only for car seats, baby bottles, and dirty diapers, but also for some rapid fire questions (in Portuguese) from the local media.

Maria seemed to cry for all of the 900 miles that separated the islands from mainland Portugal. For a good portion of the trip I stood in the aisle with her in her favorite position: tummy-down on my forearm. This won me admiring glances from the family-oriented Azoreans on the flight. Wow, I thought, we're winning points with the locals already!

Elisa was looking out the window on final approach, and the contrast with big-city Lisbon was already quite apparent. Ponta Delgada was obviously a very small town. Bright green pasture land came close to what looked like the city center. There were only a few tall buildings, and the place seemed to be a collection of small, red-tiled houses. Elisa is a city person; growing up, she had developed an aversion to small towns and the countryside. She later told me that her hick-town alarm bells were going off even before we touched down. We had picked up some warning signs about this: During our week of consultations with the U.S. Embassy in Lisbon, it seemed like every time we found something that we liked – a shopping center or a restaurant – the Lisbon folks would quickly tell us "Well, there's NOTHING like this in the Azores." Elisa had befriended a couple of the Portuguese women working in the Embassy. At first they thought we were newly assigned to Lisbon. When Elisa told one of them that we were going to Ponta Delgada, the lady kind of gasped and put her hand to cover her mouth. That was a bad sign.

The business suit proved to be totally unnecessary – the local press apparently wasn't interested in our arrival. But the staff of the Consulate was there to greet us – these were people who would play an enormous role in our lives for the next three years (and beyond).

The Consulate's driver, Mr. Silva, guided us to our somewhat decrepit "official vehicle." My first task in the Azores turned out to be wrestling not with the press but with the kids' car seats. (Even with diplomatic

11

status, those horrible little metal H clasps are hard to adjust.) So I was sweating profusely as we headed to the house.

It probably would have been a bit better if Mr. Silva had opted for a more scenic route. Instead he went the quickest way, which took us through some of Ponta Delgada's least attractive areas. Elisa's internal alarm bells were almost audible at this point.

On arrival we met the two women who worked at the house: Ana Paula Santos Furtado and Margarida Matos. Both had been working there for many years, through the tours of many American Consuls. But I was the first to bring small children, and that obviously made this arrival special. Margarida (who was already a grandma) barely looked at me. One quick "Welcome Mr. Consul" and she was diving into the backseat of the car to pluck little Maria from her seat. Paula focused on Billy (she has a son his age). Back in Virginia we'd been very cautious parents, yet here we were, with less than an hour on the ground in a foreign country and these two foreign ladies who we'd barely met were carting our kids away.

We'd seen pictures of the "official residence" but they did not really prepare us for the enormity of the place. Even harder to grasp from afar was the tremendous contrast between this gargantuan house and the tiny Azorean homes that surrounded it. This contrast was one of the things that made living in this palace, well, uncomfortable.

It was huge: Spanish Colonial style, built around an outdoor swimming pool with a big private garden in the back. Eight bedrooms on two levels. Sauna. Garage and work-rooms below. Rumor had it that it had been built during a period in which the hyper-Catholic Azoreans were toying with the idea of independence from a communist-leaning Portugal. The original owner may have had political ambitions – the house was suitable for affairs of state.

The master bedroom was so far from the kitchen that if I forgot to bring Billy's sippy cup, well, going to the kitchen was sort of like having to go out to the store. A previous consul had actually kept a bicycle in the master bedroom, using it for trips to the kitchen. (This apparently really freaked out the locals – the residence had big windows and the neighbors reportedly saw someone bicycling through the house late at night.)

The swimming pool was more trouble than it was worth. The weather in the Azores is BAD, and there were very few days in which we could swim in the pool. With toddlers in the house, I was rightfully paranoid about the pool, and had insisted that the Embassy put a very tall fence around it before we arrived. In an example of how even obvious things can become very difficult, I had to push hard and make some legal threats

to get the fence installed – apparently there were some who thought the aesthetics of the garden were more important than the lives of my children. Later, we discovered that Luis the gardener (who cleaned the pool) couldn't swim, so we ordered him to wear a life jacket while working around it. We followed up on this by telling Margarida that as the next step we were going to get scuba gear so that she and Luis could clean the pool without having to drain it. We had her believing us for a few minutes. Halfway through our tour we got word that a particularly difficult U.S. congressman was planning on visiting the island. The local staff warned that on previous visits he had insisted on using our pool for his morning exercise. I did a quick evaluation and decided that the pool needed to be drained for maintenance – right at the time of the Congressman's visit.

Billy and Maria were the first children to live in the house. In addition to getting the fence built around the pool, I had to do a lot of other child proofing. Thinking about the earthquake risk, we had all the tall furniture bolted to the walls. Worrying about all the glass, we had them put Mylar anti-blast coating over all of it (sometimes living with a terrorist threat yields some advantages). On the long elegant ceremonial staircase, I put a layer of plastic garden mesh along the inside of the banisters so that that no little heads could get stuck. It took a while, but eventually I started to feel that the kids were safe in that big house.

It was a palace, but – and this seems amazing in retrospect – it was a palace with no central heating system. It was cold. It was so big that we seemed to rattle around in it. There was nothing cozy about it. When you walked in the front door, you were greeted by an American flag, and the flag of an American Consul – this made it seem more like an office facility than a home. We quickly became very close to Ana Paula and Margarida, but at first it seemed more like their house than ours: Elisa would be walking down the hallway in pajamas and would suddenly cross paths with an unknown man. "Who is that guy?" she'd ask. "Oh, that's just Joao the plumber – he's here a lot!" would be the response. "Homey" it was not.

On our first Saturday in the new place, Elisa decided to take a walk around the neighborhood while I played with the kids in the backyard. After a short and somewhat distressing walk (lots of stares from neighbors) she decided to return to the house. But as she reached the top of our pedestal-like front steps, with multiple stares focused on her, she realized she'd forgotten the keys. Ringing the doorbell didn't help, because in this place the front door and the backyard were practically in different zip codes. In desperation, she walked down the street a bit and found a bakery that was open. In Spanish, she explained that she'd been locked out of her house (not mentioning which house, or who she was) and asked to make a phone call. The owner put a phone on the counter and said she could call. Then Elisa realized that she didn't know the phone number. She started frantically looking through the phone book, hoping to spot the name of my predecessor. Seeing this, the bakery owner closed the phone book, calmly turned the phone around and – to Elisa's shocked amazement – dialed our number. She already knew who Elisa was.

Over the next three years we'd have many events like this, little reminders that we were seen as being very different, reminders that everyone knew who we were. Elisa would go to get her hair done. All would seem normal, but as soon as she spoke, all conversations in the room would stop and all the ears seemed to tilt in Elisa's direction. At social events, Ponta Delgada's small group of "paparazzi" sometimes acted as if we were movie stars. We did most of our shopping at a big supermarket on the outskirts of Ponta Delgada. After a while, we started playing a little game. As we pulled into the parking lot, we'd each try to predict the number of friends and acquaintances we'd meet while shopping. (It was usually around seven.) We knew that the number of people who knew who we were was much larger. Coming from the total anonymity of being a mid-level government employee in the Washington, D.C. area, our new-

14

found prominence took a lot of getting used to. Big fish, small pond... We didn't like it.

Transitions to a new home are always difficult, but in spite of the palatial house and the wonderful kindness of the Consulate staff our arrival in the Azores was especially hard. The island and the town were claustrophobic. On one of our first weekends there, I got the idea that it would cheer Elisa up if we took a long ride over to the other side of the island. So we spent some time loading the car with all of the baby accouterments and paraphernalia. Off we went. Elisa had turned around to adjust Maria's car seat as I went up the on ramp onto the island's one and only highway. In the rear view mirror was Ponta Delgada and Sao Miguel Island's south coast. Suddenly, as Elisa continued to fidget with the car seat, I saw, through the front window... WATER! The north coast was visible. And close. Of course we had known the dimensions of the island (roughly 30 miles by 10 miles) but, I guess having grown accustomed to the continental scale of the United States, well, we just kind of figured that a trip to the other side would have taken more than a few minutes. Wow, this island was small!

And it was remote. Lisbon was two and a half hours away on a jet airliner. We were one third of the way from Europe to North America. One day Billy trotted into the living room with a question. He'd been watching American TV via satellite and had heard a phrase he didn't understand. "Daddy – where is 'the middle of nowhere'?" I couldn't resist. Before explaining it to him, I pointed down to the ground and said, "Right here son! Right here!"

Like our first trip to the other side, our first shopping trip was also somewhat traumatic. Again we struggled to load the car, and I maneuvered to get the car out of the garage of the official residence and onto the very narrow, canyon-like one way street (Rua do Contador). Opening or closing the garage door had involved 12 bolts and latches. When I finally got the car out, thinking of all the things I'd heard about what a safe place Ponta Delgada was, I decided to leave the garage door open for the hour that it would take us to shop. As we were pulling away, Daniel, the rather high-strung administrative assistant at the Consulate, happened to drive by. He pulled up alongside of us yelling out the window, and waving his hands wildly. Obviously he thought leaving that door open was an almost insanely reckless action. So much for Ponta Delgada's safety and security.

While a bit over the top, it turned out that Daniel's reaction wasn't really inappropriate. A few weeks later, our belongings arrived from the United States. We happily filled the backyard with the kids' yard toys. Billy's favorite was a big yellow car that my mom had bought for him. In our

15

backyard in Virginia, Billy would sit in the car and drive as I pulled him around, towing the car with rope. We looked forward to do the same thing in the Azores. But the next day Billy's car was gone, stolen from our yard. Meara family morale plummeted. That was a bad day.

Each of our transitions has had its difficulties. But each time we moved we seem to find a theme, sometimes a musical theme, for the transition. In the Azores, that theme was the song "Who Let the Dogs Out?" by the Baha Boys. I don't know how we selected it – it may have had to do with the fact that our Vice Consul Jay Barry had been attacked by an Azorean neighbor's dog soon after we arrived (it was scary but he was OK). But whenever we started feeling down, we'd fire up the Baha Boys CD. Billy would jump around to the beat, Maria would try to dance, and we'd all, somehow, feel a bit better.

Ponta Delgada is probably the smallest city in the world that has a U.S. Consulate in it. The population of the island was around 130,000, with 20,000 in Ponta Delgada. Like almost all Azorean towns, it is coastal. It lies on a gentle, bright green volcanic slope that rises from a port dominated by a large man-made breakwater. Two volcanoes are visible from town. When the air is very clear, the island of Santa Maria is visible on the horizon. The main street is the cornice. There was a little shopping mall, a Baskin Robbins (they are ALWAYS out of vanilla), a few hotels, and an almost complete lack of restaurants. (When we arrived, I'd asked an American who'd been living out there for many years to recommend three good restaurants to which I could take contacts for lunch. "Well, there's the one in the hotel... Then there's the one in the airport..." He couldn't come up with a third.) There were two movie theaters, but one was uncomfortably close to the prison and the other was adamantly opposed to the concept of eating Baskin Robbins ice cream while watching a film.

The streets were very narrow with tiny cobble-stoned sidewalks. Cars would zip by you so close that people were frequently injured by side-view mirrors. (As we drove around, we'd often be startled when our own side-view mirrors would hit a telephone pole or a wall.) The locals had apparently developed a sidewalk protocol for who had to yield to whom. We think it was based on age, because in one early sidewalk face-off, an old Azorean lady had yelled at a terrified, wall-hugging Elisa. Our house was only about 600 yards (meters) from the ocean-front avenue, but the streets were so dangerous that Elisa simply could not walk down there with a baby carriage – she would have to put the kids in our too big American mini-van and then struggle to find a place to park near the ocean front. The post had been sold to us as being "baby-friendly" but one look at the

16

streets made us realize that whoever said that had probably never pushed a baby carriage.

The weather also made strolls with the baby carriage seem like a bad idea. People seem to associate islands with warm weather. Very often, upon telling people we lived in the Azores, they'd sigh and remark about envious they were of our wonderful life in the tropics. We'd have to correct them. There is nothing tropical about the Azores. It is North Atlantic, not Caribbean. It never snows there. (This was one of the first things that Billy learned about the place. As we got ready to move there he would frequently say, "No snow in Ponta Delgada!") But it gets cold and it is remarkably cloudy and amazingly windy. Sometimes it seemed that for months on end we'd be covered by a think, low layer of slate grey cloud. (Elisa hated the clouds and whenever we flew out, as soon as our plane broke through the cloud layer, she'd see the sun and remark about how sad this all was – the sunshine was so close, yet so far.) The cloudy gloom was accentuated by very strong winds; all night long you'd hear it whistling through the wires, rattling shutters all through the neighborhood.

There was another, much more serious reason why Ponta Delgada wasn't really a "family friendly" place: the deportees. There is a long tradition of emigration from the Azores to the United States. It reportedly started back in the days of the whaling ships – Azoreans would sign on with a ship, end up in the Boston area, and then settle there. Fall River, Massachusetts has a large Azorean population – it is sometimes referred to as the tenth Azorean island. Most Azoreans succeed as immigrants in the United States. Others do not. U.S. immigration law says that if a person who is in the United States illegally or as a legal permanent resident (green card holder) commits a serious crime, that person will, upon completion of his prison term, be deported back to his country of origin. There are many people in the Azorean communities in the United States who have been living there most of their lives, but who have never obtained U.S. citizenship. If their parents never did the paperwork for citizenship, then the Azorean-born children of these immigrants remain Portuguese citizens. If as young adults they run afoul of the law, they are in for a big shock. The jail sentence they get might not be a long one, but it comes with a much longer follow-up: deportation. That one year jail sentence for drugs carries with it a sentence of lifetime exile from the only country that these people have ever known.

By the time we got there, there were several hundred deportees in Ponta Delgada. Almost all of them had grown up in harsh urban environments and had recently been released from U.S. state prisons. Most had left the Azores as infants or as very young children. Very few of them spoke

17

Portuguese, and most had no strong family ties on the island. They stuck out like sore thumbs – you could see them swaggering through innocent little Ponta Delgada with their outsized U.S. sports clothes, urban bling and tattoos. They were ominous and they caused a lot of trouble. The Azoreans feared and disliked them.

They were a special problem for us, because I was the representative of the government that had exiled them. They would show up at the Consulate, often intoxicated, demanding assistance or repatriation. Sometimes they would be violent and we'd have to call the police. One day very early in our tour, as little Maria learned to crawl and as Billy played with his toy trucks, I stepped outside to get something from the yard. As I opened the door, I found three of the most dangerous deportees out in the street. Through a toothless grin, one of them looked at me and said (in English) "nice house." At that point I KNEW that Ponta Delgada should never have been advertised as a "family friendly" post.

We took steps to protect the Consulate and our families from the deportees, and we were able to prevent any serious incidents. But they were always out there, and we always had to keep an eye open for them. They put the "hood" in our neighborhood, and they made life significantly more difficult for us. Many Americans think that terrorism must be the big security problem faced by Foreign Service families. But more often the big concern is crime. And in this case it was a crime problem imported from the streets of U.S. cities.

In response to one of our scarier encounters with the deportees, Elisa decided to get a dog. A neighbor had some Black Labrador puppies, so we soon had one of them tearing up the house and the backyard. We called him Cosmo (he was as dark as the night, I was an amateur astronomer, and we'd been big fans of Cosmo Kramer on the "Seinfeld" show). It seemed like Cosmo was cute for a few weeks, then he suddenly became enormous. Maria was toddling by this point, and that dog would knock her over like a bowling pin. So Cosmo was soon banished to the backyard. And then he was banished to the side yard (where we never went). Luis the gardener became Cosmo's caretaker, and we all grew emotionally distant.

Out in the Azores, we also had parakeets. Several sets of parakeets. In addition to his deep love for the Benefica soccer team, as a hobby the Consulate's driver, Mr. Silva, also bred parakeets. This was totally in keeping with his very gentle character. Soon he was leaving parakeets for Billy and Maria. These birds had a captivity half-life of about one week: Billy or Maria would forget to close the door, and off they would go. Mr. Silva would soon be back with new birds. This went on for some time before we all decided that we might be causing eco-system damage by

18

introducing an invasive species to the island of Sao Miguel. Every time I see a parakeet or bird cage, I think of Mr. Silva and how kind he was to our kids.

Obviously we faced some difficulties in the Azores. But to be fair, I should point out some of the many great things about the place. The islands are spectacularly beautiful, like an Atlantic Hawaii. It was a unique and interesting place to live. We lived on an island in the middle of the Atlantic Ocean! There is a distinct culture and history out there in those islands and it was a lot of fun to learn about them. But most of all, as I will describe in the pages to come, those islands are populated by wonderful giving people. Getting to know them was the best part of living there.

After three years of life on that small island, we moved to a much larger island. We went directly to London, postponing the normal month-long "home leave" trip to the U.S. It was breakfast in Ponta Delgada, lunch in Lisbon, dinner in London.

Our theme for this transition turned out to be a line from the movie "The Godfather": Michael Corleone is meeting in Havana with fellow gangster Hyman Roth. (The scene was actually filmed in the Hotel El Embajador in Santo Domingo, where Elisa and I used to go for lunch.) Corleone gets a bit melancholy and reflective, and asks the older Roth if all the bloodshed was really worth it. Roth kind of grabs him by the lapels and tells him to snap out of it. "Remember Michael, THIS IS THE LIFE WE HAVE CHOSEN!" Whenever one of us would get a bit down about the transition, one of us would chime in with that line. I think the kids were unaware of the irony: THEY had not chosen this life. I had chosen it for them. (They are now quite aware of this, and remind me of it any time the possibility of moving away from their beloved cul-de-sac comes up.)

Elisa's first year in the Azores had been very hard on her, and I was concerned about her initial reactions to London. Would she like the place? On the ride in from Heathrow Airport, I began to suspect that she would. While the Azores seemed to be constantly on the verge of taking a nap, London buzzed with activity.

The Embassy put us into a townhouse in the very posh neighborhood, pretentiously called, "The Royal Borough of Kensington and Chelsea." Our area was known as South Ken. The house was small and very vertical: four floors with a staircase effectively functioning as the central hallway. The staircase wound around a small open area making it possible for a small person to fall from the fourth floor all the way down to the ground. I took one look at that and my baby-proofing instincts kicked in. I immediately headed out the hardware store and, perhaps thinking of something I'd seen in an Azorean school, bought a big spool of rope. Soon our new house had a safety net arrangement on the stairwell that resembled Watson and Cricks' double helix. That rope arrangement had British visitors scratching their heads for the four years that we were there.

I later found out that at one point the house had been home to a small publishing company, and later something of a center for occult activity in then-bohemian South Ken. (I held off on mentioning this to Elisa and the kids.) It was crammed in amidst taller apartment buildings. (The house seems to me remarkably similar to the U.S. Embassy house described in Paul Theroux's novel "The London Embassy.") It had a tiny carport that seemed too small for our soon-to-arrive mini-van, and an even smaller, concrete-covered "garden," but Elisa loved all of it from the start. It seemed cozy. We could make it ours from the beginning.

As soon as we dropped our bags in the London house, Billy and I went out to take a look at the new neighborhood. At first we walked one block north. There we found an amazing little park. With swings! And lots of kids! Wow! Then we went half a block south to Fulham Road. As we turned the corner (on which there was a movie theater!) I saw a cluster of shops, boutiques and restaurants that, on that corner alone, seemed to represent about 200% of the retail capabilities of the entire Azores archipelago, including a fantastic book store (Pan Books). Knowing how happy Elisa would be, Billy and I didn't even fully turn the corner – instead we turned and ran back to the house to report our discovery to Elisa. She loved almost everything about London from day one.

South Ken was very international. We estimated that only about a quarter of the people there were British. Another 25 percent were French (the French school was nearby), another quarter were American (many of

20

them worked in "The City" – London's financial district), and the rest seemed to be from everywhere else (many from Britain's former colonies in South Asia and elsewhere). We must have seemed like real hicks during those first days in London – upon hearing an American accent (something that NEVER happened in the Azores), we'd greet our compatriots with a cheery: "Hey, are you from the States? Us too!" This always drew puzzled, annoyed "Yea, so what?" New Yorker-ish responses. There were so many Americans in the neighborhood that only bumpkin newcomers and tourists found it remarkable.

In London, people often mistook Elisa for a South Asian. People from India asked her where in India she was from. When she told them she wasn't from India, they'd sometimes get annoyed. One Indian lady scolded her about denying her heritage.

The French added a definite element of savior-faire to the neighborhood. Because of them, we had some great bakeries. And every morning, as I waited for the 14 or 414 bus outside the South Ken tube station, I'd watch with amazement as French high school boys got a couple of good-morning cheek kisses from just about every female classmate who crossed their paths. British kids don't do that. I found myself feeling envious – believe me, my school day in Clarkstown High School did not begin with hugs and kisses from every girl in class. I found myself wishing I'd been French. Occasionally, Liberte, Egalite and Fraternite seemed to just spill out into the streets of the neighborhood – the election of Nicolas Sarkozy brought enthusiastic supporters bearing the tricolor into the streets of South Kensington. Even at age five, Billy was aware of the distinct features of French culture – one day during dinner, he looked up from his plate and said, "Dad, you know what the problem with the French is? They're so FRANCY!" Indeed. But hey, Vive la différence!

South Ken was also a place of movie stars, celebrities, and billionaires. In the months prior to our transfer, in an effort to get ready for our next assignment, we'd watched a lot of the London movies of the actor Hugh Grant. On our second day in town, I went down to Fulham Road to get us some coffee and donuts. As I stood there on line, I got the feeling that the fellow standing next to me looked familiar. Hugh Grant! I'd forgotten my cell phone, so I ran home to get Elisa. Madonna was (or had been) in the 'hood. Also, the singer Kylie Minoghe, and the Sultan of Brunei.

The London "Blue Plates" on many of the houses revealed that celebrities of days-gone-by had also been there. Agatha Christie had lived one block over (appropriately, very close to the venerable UK "Society of Authors," an organization that I had the privilege of joining). The infamous spy Kim Philby lived in the apartment building directly in front of our house; he reportedly walked his two dogs (snidely named MI-5 and MI-6) down our street (*he* didn't get a blue plate). DNA pioneer Rosalind Franklin had lived across the street. Henry VIII had had a little place down by the Thames.

Our neighborhood was also known as the museum district. Within a kilometer of our house was the Natural History Museum, the Science Museum, and the Victoria and Albert Museum. The wall tiles of the South Ken tube station features dinosaurs and other museum themes. There is a long tunnel from the station to the museums – that tunnel became part of my route home from work—it kept me out of the rain for part of the trip. The Natural History museum was our favorite. The exterior of the building is amazing – if you look closely you can see figures of monkeys and dinosaurs and exotic birds in the masonry. Billy and I developed a little routine that we'd follow every time we went there: We had to go to the little area in front of the main entrance and – perhaps emulating the pterodactyls on display – we'd put our arms out (as wings) and pretend that we were flying around. He grew more and more embarrassed about this as he got older, but he was always a good sport and he never broke the tradition – not even when we went back for a visit in February 2010 (he was 12).

We (well Elisa) quickly developed a support network of friends in the neighborhood. Adjacent to our house we had Sir Jeremy and Belinda Morse – the best next door neighbors you could possibly hope for. (Billy thought it was amazingly cool to have a real Knight right next door to us.) Across the street (in Philby's old place) there was Raj the doorman (from India). Raj kept an ear to the ground and knew what was going on in his area.

Around the corner was the kiosk of Mrs. Amin (from India). Every time we went in there, she'd give our kids free candy, and give us great information about happenings in the hood. Sometimes it would be details on some recent crime – from her we learned that the British police were not allowed to pursue thieves onto the rooftops (health and safety!). This explained the frequent presence of police helicopters. Mrs. Amin once got us into a Bollywood movie as extras. (The film was called "Cheeni Kum." The cast included Indian superstars Amitabh Bachchan and Tabu. They were looking for passers-by. Elisa and the kids were selected to be extras, but I was asked to step aside. I sulked off to a nearby Starbucks while Elisa and the kids did their passers-by thing with their fancy new Bollywood friends. But they ended up on the cutting room floor, while I made it into the movie: the film has a few frames showing me sitting in a window seat at the Starbucks, sulking.)

The development of this neighborhood social support network had its up and downs, and a few moments of social terror. One evening soon after we arrived, as we were having dinner Elisa told me – very pleased – that we'd received an invitation from neighbors. She said that a couple living nearby (I'll call them Jerry and Jessica) had called inviting us over for English tea.

For some reason this struck me as a bit odd. Jerry was an older fellow who lived – part-time it seemed – in the block of apartments near to us. He was living with his sixty-something "girlfriend" Jessica. We'd been warned by the previous resident that Jerry would quickly move to use the space in front of our small driveway to park his car. And we'd already spotted poor Jessica kind of weaving her way down the sidewalk in the late afternoons, apparently en route home from a long visit to the local pub. Our ability to distinguish between British social classes was not yet as developed as it would eventually become, but even in those early days my "class radar" made me doubt they were from the segment of English society that would invite neighbors to high tea.

"Are you sure it was Jerry?" I asked. Elisa came back with the kind of "Yes, I think so" response that meant she was not really sure. Of course it wasn't her fault. She was dealing with a rapid-fire phone call in a completely new accent. And – and this is the part that caused the social terror – we had neighbors with very similar names: to the side we had Jerry and Jessica. Behind our house we had Jeremy and Belinda. Oh no! Who invited us? What do we do now?

Elisa was really concerned – she had visions of us showing up all dressed up with flowers in hand at the wrong front door. And we couldn't very well call up the couples involved and say, "Hey, were you the ones who invited us over for this tea thing?" So for a while we lived in a state of social terror.

I got us out of this predicament. The evening before our tea, I met Jerry in the street (he was probably trying to park in our driveway). In the midst of the neighborly chit-chat, I suddenly commented that the night before we'd received a phone call, but that Elisa had been tired and hadn't quite understood who was calling... "Did you call us last night Jerry?" He said he had not called us. Mystery solved. We had a wonderful tea with Sir Jeremy and Belinda. (Jerry did continue to try to use our driveway. Several times I asked him nicely to stop, but this didn't work. When his parking antics started making it dangerous for Billy to get into his school bus, I switched to a more coercive approach. I told him that if he ever parked there again, I would send the "diplomatic security service" after him. That took care of that.)

Much of our London shopping was done on Fulham Road. On one nearby corner there was a convenience store called Cullens, that later morphed into a branch of the omnipresent TESCO chain before finally turning into a store that sold bathtubs (how many could they possibly sell?). We became friendly with the Bengali and Sri Lankan guys who worked in the TESCO. Early on, Billy learned to greet the Muslims with "Salaam Alaikum" (from the Arabic "peace be upon you"). When the 2004 tsunami hit we feared the worst; we later learned that one of the fellows working in that store had lost everyone – his entire family, his entire Sri Lankan village was swept away.

Up the street was Farmer Brother's, surely one of the most expensive hardware stores on Earth. I guess the high prices were justified – if people in the neighborhood were willing to pay eight million dollars for dilapidated townhouses, why not charge them five dollars for a light bulb? The proprietors – Londoners with roots in Pakistan – made up for the price gouging by being friendly with the kids, and by helping us with our rather bizarre projects: "We want to make bows and arrows. Do you have something flexible that could serve as a bow?" Soon we'd be down in the basement, digging about for the perfect piece of plastic.

We traveled around the neighborhood mostly on foot, during our early days Maria was still in her little stroller. We made efforts to use mass transit, but London – and especially its bus and train system – is not at all kid-friendly. So very often we'd start out on foot, but then it would start to rain. Or start to get cold. Or start to get dark. Or the kids would have to go to the bathroom. Or all four things at once. The solution was always right at hand: London's venerable Black Cabs. Wow, what a liberating discovery that was! We'd be "out and about" as they say, when suddenly, we'd find ourselves with an urgent need for transportation. BHAM! A Black Cab would appear out of nowhere. With one quick wave of the arm, it would be ours. They are big and roomy – they reminded me of the big yellow Checker Cabs we used when I was a little kid in New York. The drivers came equipped with "The Knowledge" – an encyclopedic familiarity with London's streets. And because they were under the supervision of the Metropolitan Police (aka Scotland Yard) you could be reasonably certain that the drivers were trustworthy. What a deal! Perhaps because as the youngest member of the crew she was the focal point for most of the emergencies, Maria quickly became the member of the family most enamored of the Black Cabs. She HATED mass transit. She would scream and cry at the mere suggestion that we take the bus. By age three she had learned how to hail a taxi. We'd be on our way to the bus stop, and she'd be frantically straining against her stroller seat belts, desperately trying to hail a passing Black Cab.

South Ken is very nice, but it is definitely an urban place, with big-city grit, urban crowding, traffic, and noise. Our house was on a narrow two-lane street, but during rush hours, we'd have a traffic jam right outside our front window. On off-peak hours, the cars would zip by at reckless speed (London drivers know where the automatic speed cameras are, and our street didn't have one). Our American minivan barely fit into the car port, so we usually parked on the street – this sometimes required several orbits of the neighborhood in search of a spot. Noise from the street and from drunken pub clients made it impossible for us to sleep with a window open – we ran fans to generate white noise to drown out the urban street sounds.

Additional noise was provided by the neighborhood's sports enthusiasts. The home stadium of the Chelsea Football (soccer) Club was within earshot. Whenever they played a home game we'd find out about it when Fulham Road would start to fill with fanatical-looking people in blue shirts emblazoned with advertisements for airlines that take you to Dubai. We called it "The Blue Flu." The fans sometimes had a whiff of hooliganism about them. The World Cup would add a strong dose of nationalism to the football fanaticism – the Brits would start riding around with the English flag flying from their car windows. The police were always trying to identify dangerous football hooligans so that they could prevent them from travelling to matches in other countries. There was a joke that said if you had three or more English flags on your car, you really *should* have your passport confiscated.

Driving in the UK posed some special challenges. Our steering wheel was on the left, while most everyone else had theirs on the right. This isn't as much of a problem as you might expect (but toll booths do require either team work or good aim). Moving past a slow vehicle requires some extra caution, because your view of the oncoming lane is limited (you are passing on the right while sitting on the left-hand side of the car.) The real adjustment involves just getting used to staying on the left hand side of the road, and – and this is very important – remembering which way to go in the ubiquitous "round-abouts" (traffic circles). Elisa made the adaptation very quickly, and, because she was driving every day, got very proficient. I, however, soon became a real threat to British lives and property.

You see, I didn't drive during the week. I went to work on the 14 or 414 bus, and I walked home. Some weekends we wouldn't use the car. So every time I got behind the wheel, I was, in essence, starting the left-side-of-the-road adaptation process all over again. Elisa would sit, terrified, in the right seat, fearful that at any moment my 30 years of driving on the right would kick in and send us hurtling into oncoming traffic or counterclockwise into the Brits' clockwise roundabouts. It didn't take long for Elisa to become our permanent designated driver. I became the navigator.

We really needed a navigator, because getting around the UK in a car is not easy. I heard that during World War II the Brits took down all the road signs to confuse the feared German invasion force. It seemed to us that they never really put them back properly.

Driving in central London is stressful. It is a bit like New York in that everyone is under time pressure and struggling with traffic. We found Londoners to be prone to angry outbursts and the use of the middle finger. Road rage was common and often resulted in fist fights, head butts and broken noses. We jokingly attributed all this to England's well-known shortage of hand guns (the possibility of gunfire seems to discourage road rage fisticuffs in the US). One Sunday morning as I was walking along a nearly deserted Old Brompton Road, holding one kid with each hand, an angry Londoner honked his horn and gave us the finger when we didn't get through the cross walk quite fast enough for him.

Things didn't get much better when you got outside London. It seemed to us that the British traffic authorities took real delight in the enforcement of any regulation that might require the total shutdown of a major traffic artery, especially on long weekends. There would be some minor accident and four drops of motor oil will have spilled on shoulder of the road. Result: M4 motorway closed for hours. Thousands of people trapped in their cars. "Health and Safety! Musn't grumble!" Sometimes we'd go to France just because it was easier to get around.

And of course we had to deal with the British weather. It is, in fact, quite bad. There were days in July when I had to wear my ski jacket. The winter skies had the same slate grey clouds we'd lived with in the Azores, but now we were much further north; London is nearly at the same latitude as Moscow, so those winter days are very short. It was really quite shocking at first. In mid-December cars would start putting their headlights on around 3:30 pm. Elisa loved London, but she didn't like the darkness – in an effort to cope, she got herself a Scandinavian "happy lamp." I too seemed to focus a lot of attention on illumination: I found an online calendar that included sunrise and sunset times for London and posted it on my office door. I remember December 12 being the day with the earliest sunset. In June, sunshine would come blasting through your windows at 4 am. London is just too far north!

We had convinced the kids that Cosmo the Azorean Labrador really needed to stay on his home island. This was good move, because he just would not have fit into our London house. Everything seemed copacetic on the pet front, but soon the kids started to ask for a dog. I struggled mightily against this, but eventually compromised by agreeing that we could get a cat. Delighted, Elisa and the kids began visiting animal shelters. One cat seemed especially interested in them. His cage had a big sign that said "ANTI-SOCIAL." Coming from British cat-lovers that was obviously a warning to be taken seriously, but they still decided that this one was for us.

They thought we'd just bring him home, but, no! What were they thinking? We were in the UK, land of animal lovers and the nanny state. We had to go through a vetting process. There were interviews. I think they may have actually come to visit the house. They may have asked for references. Finally, we were approved and Elisa and the kids went down to pick up the cat. And they were turned away. The basket they had hoped to use to carry the cat home was simply not up to specifications. They had to go back the next day with a "proper" cat basket.

The new cat already had a name: Tyson (we don't know why, but we suspect it may have been related to the "ANTI-SOCIAL" thing). He soon settled into life in our house. After a while, Elisa started letting him out into the micro-yard. He went AWOL a few times, and, on one adventure, he snuck into Sir Jeremy's house just as Jeremy and his wife were leaving for two weeks in the country. We didn't know where he was, and launched a search in the neighborhood, complete with Wanted posters. Fortunately, Jeremy and Belinda came back early, and a somewhat thinner Tyson emerged from their house.

Eventually we adopted something of a musical theme for our new English home: It was the song "Werewolves of London" by Warren Zevon. The lyrics mentioned places that were all around us. Billy was especially taken with the song:

He's the hairy, hairy gent, who ran amok in Kent.
Lately he's been overheard in Mayfair.
You better stay away from him, he'll rip your lungs out Jim.
Huh, I'd like to meet his tailor.

Well, I saw Lon Chaney walkin with the queen,
doing the werewolves of London.
I saw Lon Chaney Jr. walkin with the queen,

doin the werewolves of London
I saw a werewolf drinkin a pina colada at Trader Vic's
And his hair was perfect.
ahhhooooo, werewolves of London
Draw blood

There were no actual werewolves, but there were hints of big-city crime. The windows on the bottom two floors of our house had bars on them (raising scary questions about the fire escape procedures). I was kind of concerned when I saw graffiti gang tags in the 'hood. Apparently South Ken is the turf of the "NRG." It took me quite a while to find out what that acronym stood for: "The No Remorse Gang." With a word like "remorse" in their gang's name, well, these guys were obviously a long way from the Bloods and Crips. For me, the NRG thing seemed to capture the essence of our neighborhood. South Ken was reminiscent of New York City, but kind of toned-down, sort of a kinder-gentler New York, a bit more articulate and literary...

****

Rome turned out to be even softer. We moved there during the summer of 2007. There we lived in a neighborhood called Trastevere, which is sometimes described as Rome's equivalent of Paris's Left Bank. Trastevere (which means "Behind the Tiber") is just across the river from the heart of Rome, just opposite the area that contains the Coliseum, the Pantheon, the Roman forum and all the main attractions of the "Eternal City." It is a place of really old buildings and winding, narrow streets and alleyways. In places it has the feel of a medieval village. Like Paris's Left Bank, it is a somewhat bohemian place, with artists and writers and film makers. It is also one of Rome's centers for night life and partying, with lots of restaurants and bars.

We had gone to Rome via home leave and some language training in the United States. There, specifically in Virginia, Maria came up with the catch phrase for this move, a slogan that would also cover our subsequent return to the U.S. One day while I was away learning how to say "Buon giorno," Elisa and the kids decided to walk to the local supermarket for supplies. Bad move. It was really hot, and Northern Virginia is not made for walking. As they struggled back to our temporary apartment with bags of melting and leaking groceries, suddenly Maria (at that point seven years old, with an understandably confused Spanish-English-Portuguese vocabulary) blurted it out: "Gosh this is hard work and.... poultry!"

28

Maria was just searching for a word, and somehow poultry seemed to fit. So whenever things got tough, we'd all acknowledge that we were indeed going through a period of "hard work and poultry."

At Rome's Fiumicino airport we were greeted by my boss, Tom Delare. He took us in an Embassy van to our new apartment. The entrance was kind of unsettling – it was at the end of a dead-end street. There was graffiti on the walls of the building. The entry door was very narrow and seemed to be encumbered with a lot of security devices. Inside we squeezed into an elevator that was a tight fit even by British standards.

I was exhausted and decided to take a nap. Elisa and the kids decided to go out to have a look around. Their initial exploration was a bit distressing. They found a neighborhood that seemed a bit down at the heel, and, even more worrisome, largely devoid of people. Most of the stores were closed. The only people on the streets seemed to be homeless. It took us a while to realize that this was simply a matter of timing – Elisa and the kids had gone out during the time of the mid-day meal when Rome really does shut down. A few hours later the neighborhood came back to life and our concerns about our new neighborhood disappeared. There were kids to play with and new neighbors to meet. There was pizza. And gelato. And coffee. It was wonderful.

As with London, Elisa loved Rome from the start. She loved the light, the weather, the pastel colors of the buildings. She even liked the chaos – t reminded her of the Dominican Republic. One of her favorite things about Rome was the gracious way in which Romans complimented beauty – she would get three or four "bella" comments from passersby each day. There was nothing creepy or lurid in these comments. It was Roman graciousness – bella figura – and it made her feel special, and very welcome.

In addition to Maria's catch phrase, we also had musical theme for this transition period. It came from an Italian rap group Fabri Fibra. Their song "In Italia" was very popular during the summer of 2007. Our Italian language skills were very weak at that point, so we couldn't understand most of the lyrics. But the kids liked the beat and would go around repeating the "IN ITALIA" refrain. Later, we came to understand the lyrics, and the social problems they were describing:

In Italia...
Ci sono cose che nessuno ti dirà…
ci sono cose che nessuno ti darà…
sei nato e morto qua
sei nato e morto qua

nato nel paese delle mezza verità

In Italy...
There are things that no one will tell you about
There are things that no one will give you
You are born and die here
You are born and die here
Born in the country of the half-truth

A couple years into our tour, one of Maria's Italian classmates was in our apartment on a play date. Maria showed the visitor the YouTube video that accompanies this song. It was filled with the kind of dark images that you'd expect with this kind of refrain – lots of images of corruption and organized crime. After watching the whole thing, Maria's little friend sat back, sighed, and said, "Yes, most of it is true."

South Ken had urban grit; Trastevere had urban goo. The streets of our Roman 'hood always seemed to be covered with a thin layer of dog dirt (in Rome, pooper-scoopers are NOT part of the social contract). In London putting your car's tires a few inches over a parking space border line would get you a ticket, but in Rome most sidewalks were seen as semi-legitimate parking spaces, and if a policeman did approach with ticket book in hand, he could usually be dissuaded by a good explanation. ("Hey! I had to go to the pharmacy! My kid has a sore throat!")

We couldn't say that driving in Rome was easier than driving in London, but it did seem softer. The Italians were a lot less prone to road-rage than the Brits. They would honk their horns and there would be a lot of hand and arm signals, but they didn't seem to get as worked up and angry as the British did. The Brits would give you the finger and would seem to want to break your nose. The Italians would throw their hands in the air in an exasperated "mama mia" gesture, but they never seemed willing to punch anyone over being a bit late for work. The roads outside Rome were a lot better than the roads outside London, so getting around Italy was quite easy. But on the highway the Italians all seemed to have been taught to tailgate at high speed any car that they found in the left (passing) lane. If for any reason you moved into the left lane, the nearest Italian driver would instantly place his front bumper inches away from your car and would then start flashing his lights. It happened so consistently that it seemed like it must have been an obligatory requirement. I asked some of our Italian friends about this – all of them admitted to doing it, but none of them could tell me *why* they engaged in this life-threatening practice. They just did. One book shed some light on it. It pointed out that for Italians, the right lane on a four lane divided highway is known as "La via della vergogna" (the lane of shame).

Trastevere has LOTS of graffiti, and this often alarms visiting Americans. But my kids pointed out that it is not "scary" graffiti. Most of it seems to be about… well AMORE! Livia ti amo! (Livia I love you!)

Trastevere has a large contingent of homeless street people. They seem to be drawn to the 'hood by the pan-handling opportunities afforded by the tourists, and by the free meals doled out by Rome's charitable Sant'Egidio group. Many of these folks seemed to be from Eastern Europe. They were often drunk or stoned. Some seemed psychotic. And they did hang out near the kids' playground in the piazza. But somehow, they never seemed to cause much trouble.

One of the reasons the homeless drunks didn't cause much trouble was probably the fact that the people of Trastevere would react harshly. Before it became chic, the neighborhood was working class, and, unlike the posh areas of London, most of the working class families have stayed on in the neighborhood. You'd find out that the guys working in the tobacco shops and hardware stores were living upstairs in family apartments that were worth more than two million dollars. In London folks like this would have cashed out and moved to Oxfordshire, Malta, or Florida, but in Italy moving is unthinkable. The end result is that the streets and piazzas of Trastevere are filled with a lot of working class folks who wouldn't hesitate to beat the hell out of a purse snatcher. And any perceived threat to children could easily provoke a lynching. So, even in an area covered with graffiti, dog pooh, and whacked-out Ukrainians, Elisa always felt quite safe in Trastevere. She always felt that she was being watched over by the omnipresent network of neighbors and shopkeepers. And she knew that they would help her if there was any trouble. Little Maria however, was not so sure. She REALLY didn't like the homeless. They scared her. She would ask us to cross the street to avoid having to walk near them and she would frequently come up with innovative proposals for dealing with them: "Let's put them all on an island and let them farm for their food!"

Maria's views on the homeless – along with her long-evident aversion to mass transit – supported Billy's suspicions that his little sister is a Republican: "Maria would be the world's worst communist," Billy would declare, "she's all about PROPERTY!" Billy is definitely far to the left of Maria, but he showed some capitalist instincts himself while in Rome: After a summer-time stint as a bagger at the check-out counter of the U.S. Embassy commissary ("Wow dad, these people buy a lot of booze!"), Billy realized that the American candies in the store – unavailable in Italy – would be a big hit with his classmates. So he got into the black market and

31

became a schoolyard pusher of Snickers bars and other high-octane American candies. I became his supplier, often raising eyebrows at the commissary with my bulk purchases of tax-free Tootsie Rolls. Sales were so brisk that Billy had to take on a business partner. Of course, it didn't take long for the school authorities to find out what was going on. I suppose in the US they would have called in a SWAT team and dragged Billy off in handcuffs, but tolerance is still seen as a virtue in Italy. Demonstrating strong diplomatic instincts, negotiating skills, and cultural insight, Billy convinced the Principal to allow him to stay in business by pledging to donate a portion of the profits to poor kids in Haiti. (The Principal had been born in Haiti.)

Reading the comics in "Stars and Stripes"

We made occasional use of the commissary, and I'd stop by there most days to buy Billy and Maria the U.S. military newspaper "Stars and Stripes" (they liked the comics and the personal advice column), but we did most of our shopping in Trastevere – there were three little supermarket branches close at hand, and six days a week there was a beautiful open air market on Piazza di San Cosimato. In the supermarkets we often had to play "dodge the drunks," but we got used to it. The people who worked in the open-air market became good friends, and were an important part of Elisa's day. There was also a small, family-run food shop very close to our apartment. I used to like going in there to shoot the breeze with Alberto and his son Roberto.

After we got back to the States, as part of sixth grade project, Maria put together her own book about her life in Rome:

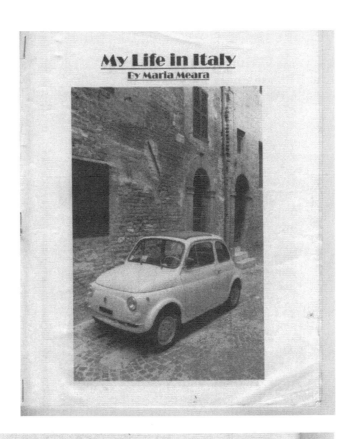

My Life in Italy
By Maria Meara

Dedicated to
The children of the
Foreign Service.

'Free?'

My mother and I used to go to the market very often, and this is something that used to happen a lot.

'Ciao!' Says my mother to Alfredo, the market man. Alfredo is an old, but strong man, and all of his years on the farm show in his hands and face, and the way he shows pride in the things he sells. 'Ciao! Come tu stai?' This means Hi! How are you? In Italian. My mother and Alfredo small talk for a while, and then my mother starts collecting the things she needs for dinner that night. I sneak away to say hello to the cheese man, all the while trying not to get too close to the back of the market (witch is actually a black market)

Finally, after my mom has collected every thing she needed, she hands it all to Alfredo. 'Ten seventy eight' said Alfredo. My Mom looks disappointed. 'I only have eight Euros.' Alfredo shrugs. 'Just give me what you got.' By this time I'm skipping back nibbling on a whole piece of free cheese. My mom doesn't have to say thank you because Alfredo knows she is grateful, and we both start walking home.

Chilin' in The Hood

'Fresh fish! Buy some fresh fish!'Music from Trastevere is playing, and its one of the most beautiful music ever. Stores are packed, with both locals and tourists. The café is buzzing with the game on the television. A dark cloud that was blocking the sun moves away, and the bright light hits the old, crumbling yet beautiful apartment buildings.

Screams from children are coming from the playground, and yells of joy from the café (Roma scored a goal) A couple is arguing at the end of the block. If you closed your eyes, it would be like music from an orchestra playing, and each part of the orchestra would be a different part of Rome. To think, this place was once called the ghetto.

There I am, wishing I had a place to wash the sticky ice cream off my hands, thinking of how fun it would be to roller blade down that hill. I wish I could stay there forever. I felt like the luckiest person in the world. Actually, I think I really was.

This is how the streets of Italy looked like when they weren't historic places. This is the culture in Italy.

A Man in Italy

I see a man sitting at the café. When you first see him, he is a dashing site. He is wearing a pink polo, with paste designer trousers on. He has black sunglasses on over his shaved head. On his feet are leather shoes. He just got off the phone with his daughter, using lots of hand motions. (Italians speak with their hands)

He is sipping on an espresso, being careful not to spill on his clothes, for his wife's sake. Despite his appearance, he is very dear to his family.

He is reading the newspaper. He is as sharp as a knife. A real man of pride. If someone saw him in America, they would think he was girly, but in Italy, he is a cool, cunning figure of respect

Another important part of the day was cappuccino and cornettos. Almost all Italians have, sometime before 10:30 am, a cup of cappuccino and a croissant-like piece of bread known as a cornetto (from the word for horns – the bread looks like it has two little horns at the end), and we quickly adopted this wonderful habit. Italians usually have this little mini-breakfast in their local bar. We tried out several local establishments before settling on one conveniently located on Piazza di San Cosimato. We became regulars, with all the benefits that come with this status.

We found that the words "bar" and "café" meant very different things in the three places we lived. In the Azores, you'd enter what was advertised as a café, only to find that their main product was strong alcohol-based beverages served in thick clouds of cigarette smoke. Even early in the morning. And the main early morning customers seemed to be bus and taxi drivers (who'd claim that they were drinking for medicinal purposes – to ward off parasites). In London bars were pubs, and THE PUB is one of the most important elements of British culture. We are teetotalers so the whole pub things was a bit lost on us. But we did find it annoying that a good portion of the pubs were completely off limits to kids. You'd find a place that looked like it would be a good place for lunch, only to be told that because of some mysterious British bureaucratic formula, even the restaurant portion of the place was off limits for kids. Even at noon. In Rome, "bar" means "coffee bar" and it is pretty much just that. They are very kid friendly. There are bottles of booze on display, but nobody seems to use them. Amazingly, the Italians actually comply with the "no smoking in bars or restaurants rule." This, combined with the absence of customers intent on getting intoxicated (that would be bad form – bruta figura), helped make the Italian bar experience very pleasant – one of the nicest parts about life in Italy. So, in summary: In the Azores, a café is really a bar. In Italy, a bar is really a café. And the Brits have their pubs, which are more like American bars.

I suppose "free housing" sounds like a marvelous benefit, and it is, but in the Foreign Service it comes to you via a very bureaucratic organization known as the Embassy Housing Committee. You do not get to pick your own housing. The Embassy Housing Committee assigns you and your family to a house or (in Rome) to an apartment. We sometimes joked that this system provides American diplomats with a little taste of what life must have been like under communism.

The committee put us in a small apartment on the northern edge Trastevere. On one side our place looked out on the Janiculum Hill (not quite one of Rome's famous seven hills, but a place with a lot of history nonetheless). On the other side our apartment – like most Roman apartments – looked out on the windows of other Roman apartments. We lived in a complex with a central courtyard and garden. As in London there were other foreigners around, but we soon discovered that our new home was an intensely Italian place.

Our apartment house at the end of a typical Trastevere street

The apartment was small by American standards, but quite large from the Italian perspective. Three bedrooms, but – get this: NO CLOSETS: Italy, it turns out is a BYOC country. Bring Your Own Closets. We quickly discovered that a good portion of the 1300 square feet of living area was taken up by IKEA closets supplied by the Embassy.

There was also no air-conditioning in the apartment. Like the Brits, the Italians don't share in our obsession with cold air. And besides, as soon as it gets hot, they go on vacation and don't come back until it cools down. We didn't have this option, so we asked the Embassy for some assistance. They sent over a few "penguins" – these were little R2-D2 like devices that sort of looked like penguins. A short, flexible exhaust tube ran to the window. It was kind of Rube-Goldberg, but the penguin would cool down a bedroom, and the noise of the fan would drown out street noise. (Maria got quite used to this and in her room we'd have to run the penguin fan year-round.) After an incident in which Maria fainted on a very hot day, Elisa pushed the Embassy to install a system that would cool down the living room and kitchen. The penguins couldn't handle this job, so a larger, in-wall machine was installed. The Italian techs who worked in the Embassy were cooperative, but they clearly shared in the national dislike for air conditioning (my Italian teacher considered it unfair for us to dump the hot air from our apartments on everyone else – I guess she had a point). So the installation ended up – as many things do in Italy – being kind of half-way done: They could install the AC unit, but there would be no drain pipe for the water collected by the system. We'd have to use a bucket, and we'd have to remember to empty it. (We frequently forgot).

We were up on the fourth floor (fifth by the American way of counting – the Europeans count the ground floor as zero). The elevator was not much bigger than a phone booth, and it always seemed on the verge of breakdown. In one early elevator ride little Maria had one of those 7 year-old "vocabulary moments." Meaning to say that she was claustrophobic, she instead announced that she didn't like the elevator because she is "lactose intolerant."

The building was very solidly constructed. This didn't seem very important when we got there, but by the time we left we were grateful for the thick walls. On April 6, 2009 at 3:32 am, Elisa woke me up yelling "Earthquake!" in Spanish. At first I dismissed her warning – I thought we were hearing the wind blowing. But then I saw the bedroom door shaking in its hinges and I knew that Elisa was right. The town of L'Aquila, about 35 miles from Rome, had been hit with a deadly 6.3 earthquake. For weeks there were aftershocks. We had some ornamental glass balls hanging in the kitchen – they came to serve as our earthquake detector.

Billy was nine and Maria seven when we arrived, so the grass and the gardens in the courtyard seemed like a wonderful asset for us. What luck! The kids can play right here in the compound! WRONG! One morning the kids and I were waiting in the courtyard for Elisa. We had a little plastic ball with us and we silently tossed it back and forth. The doorman – a grumpy old guy named Fernando – approached and very gruffly told me "NO PLAYING IN THE COURTYARD!" He seemed genuinely surprised and offended by our little game of catch, as if we should have known that what we were doing was DEEPLY WRONG. When I questioned him about this rule, he looked at me as if I were totally nuts, as if I'd been questioning the rules against, I don't know, murder.

At first we couldn't figure out this strict prohibition against play and fun. It seemed so un-Italian. This was, after all, a country that loves kids, and hates rules. But it turned out that this was largely about demographics, acoustics, and child rearing practices. Italy is now a very old country. Many of our neighbors were elderly empty nesters. Italians live very close to each other – the details of family arguments are very frequently broadcast to the neighbors. So noise in the courtyard would definitely be heard in the apartments. And here's the key factor: Italian kids – especially the boys – are raised without a lot of control and discipline. The residents probably figured out a long time ago that if so much as one ball were allowed to be kicked in that courtyard, all hell would break loose and there'd soon be World Cup levels of noise. OK, so no playing in the courtyard. It didn't really matter, because less than 100 yards from our building there was the play-pandemonium of one of Rome's most kid-friendly piazzas: Piazza di San Cosimato.

The view from our window

Italy's age demographics had an almost pervasive influence. We saw another example of this up on our roof. There were spectacular views of Rome from up there, and Elisa immediately saw that it would be a great place for a patio table – the seven families in our building could easily – we thought – share the space, each of them occasionally using the roof for Roman dinners or lunches "al fresco." Six of the families supported the idea. But the elderly couple on the top floor said no. They insisted that the only appropriate use of the roof area was for drying clothes (each family was assigned one day per week for this purpose.) I think they were just bothered by the idea of change, and they couldn't care less about the wishes of their neighbors (especially transient neighbors like us). Billy and I tried to take our telescope up there a few times for some early-evening astronomy, but after a few of these sessions a very officious and unfriendly letter from the building administrator appeared on the access door reminding us that the only acceptable use of the roof was for the drying of clothing on the designated day. It was all kind of sad, and very symbolic of Italy's sclerosis. No al fresco dinners, no enjoying of the view, no gazing at the stars. Above all, NO CHANGE!   Just old drying underwear.

40

One day Elisa took some friends up to the roof for a moment to show them the view. The doorman saw this and tried to scold her in front of her guests (this was the last straw, and led to very loud conversation with the doorman that I made sure ALL the neighbors heard). The doorman could have been nicer about this, but it turns out that he and his doorman colleagues were just not very nice people. At least not to us, and this made life difficult in that Trastevere apartment house. Here too Italian cultural factors were at work. We noticed that with the long-term Italian residents, the doormen were very solicitous, almost fawning. With us they would not even open the door (and yes, we had been generously tipping them on all the appropriate holidays). They obviously knew where their bread was buttered, and knew that those older Italian residents had the power to do them favors, to hire and fire, to approve vacation plans, etc. And the Italian residents were in for the long-haul, for life. In comparison, our three year stay made us seem like complete transients, not worth worrying about, certainly not worth helping. But the meanness of the doormen was more than balanced out by the amazing kindness shown to us by the people who worked in the building's subterranean garage: Pedro (from Colombia) and especially Guna (from Sri Lanka). And it was also more than made up for by the kindness and friendliness of the vast majority of our Roman neighbors.

By the time we got to Rome our kids were at the point where they really needed a backyard. The piazza was OK, but it wasn't quite enough. We noticed that the families of most of their Italian friends had country houses to which they retreated on the weekends. Elisa began scouting around for a country retreat for the Meara kids. Real estate transactions of any kind are notoriously difficult in Italy – even simple short-term rentals like the deal we were looking for can become treacherous adventures in Italian business culture. We found one place up in the mountains that looked OK. The owners seemed charming. But they never mentioned the huge rock quarry just beyond the tree line that would obviously be sending heavy trucks right past the house. (We got that info from Google Earth.) Then there was the lady who wanted to rent us a nice looking little farm. All seemed OK until we learned that she wanted us to agree to carry out ALL needed repairs. (Uh, isn't that they owner's job?) Other places seemed either too far from Rome, or too close. After a while we just kind of gave up. Then, as we approached our last full summer in Italy, an opportunity arose.

It came from our Trastevere friends Michael and Myung. Michael is bearded, free spirited 40-something Canadian lawyer with something of a hippie past. Born in the USA, his Dad took their family to Canada partly out of disgust with the war in Vietnam. While in college Michael made the then-common backpack trip through India.

The 1970's had been far less care-free for Myung. As a teenager she escaped from Vietnam on a boat and eventually made it to Canada via a refugee camp in Thailand. She went on to become a chemical engineer. In Rome Michael worked as an attorney for one of the organizations supporting the U.N.'s Food and Agricultural Organization (FAO). Their son Mateo went to the Ambrit School with Billy and Maria. They had been in Rome for about seven years and had a wide range of interesting friends.

With Michael and Myung in Ponticelli

Among the most interesting were Dan and Pari. Dan is from New Zealand; Pari is from Germany. They met while pursuing graduate degrees at Cambridge University. Their PhD's in economics allow them to live as globe-trotting, big-bucks consultants to the international financial institutions. We considered ourselves very internationally mobile, but we seemed like cautious stick-in-the-muds compared to Dan and Pari. They seemed to handle all the important details of moving across borders – schools, immigration, furniture, cars, housing and all that – with a nonchalance that bordered on reckless abandon. "Pari – are the kids registered in school? You know it opens on Monday." "Don't worry Dan – I'll go over and talk to the principal on Monday... by the way, where IS our furniture?"

Dan and Pari had built a house in the Sabine Hills. Also known as Sabina, this area rises up from the coastal plain on which Rome is built. Legend has it that the men of ancient Rome went to this area, kidnapped a bunch of the local women, and took them back to the city. According to the very biased ROMAN legend, by the time the Sabine men got their act together and went down to Rome on a rescue mission, the women had become so fond of their Roman captors that they no longer wanted to be rescued.

Almost anywhere else in the world this area would be considered spectacular; in the context of Italy's eye-popping beauty, Sabina probably rates as merely nice. But we considered it spectacular. From Dan and Pari's place, in all directions, at a distance of one or two miles, you see rapidly rising hills. Some of the hilltops have towns on them. The lowlands are covered with the same kind of olive groves that have been there since ancient times. If you look to the South, between the hills you can almost look down on Rome. Off to the left there is hilltop town with a castle. That's Nerola – one of the summer places of Emperor Nero. It seems that for the last 2700 years, the region has served Rome as nearby retreat and as source of olive oil.

Dan and Pari's place was near Ponticelli – the Heavenly Bridges. They'd built the house with the same nonchalance that marked their international moves. We got the impression that there wasn't a lot of design or planning in the building process. Pari described one evening in which the builders needed to be told where the windows would go. With a baby slung on her hip, Pari made the needed decisions on-the-spot. "Put one there! And another there!" Electrical wiring was handled in a similar way. Somehow – as often happens in Italy – the chaos coalesced into something beautiful.

One day Michael and Myung were visiting Dan and Pari in their new place. They went for hike after lunch, and, just as Michael was thinking about how nice it would be to have a place out there, suddenly, in the middle of a beautiful olive grove, they met Enrica.

Enrica is a hyperactive septuagenarian. We all soon came to realize that she is from one of the wealthiest families in the region. She owned not only the olive grove, but also many of the hills that surrounded it. Later she'd point to the largest of the nearby hill towns – Scandriglia – and tell us about what it was like to live there under Nazi occupation and allied bombardment.

On the day they met, Michael told her how much they liked the area and mentioned his desire for a place out there. In what must have been one of the most miraculous events in the history of Italian real estate, Enrica responded by saying that she happened to have an apartment for rent on that very olive grove.

It probably didn't take Michael very long to decide. The apartment was in a big, beautiful, top-of the-hill family house surrounded by olives and Sabine Hills. The house had been subdivided – Enrica and her children held on to some of the units, the others were for lease to Romans seeking escape from the big city. The appeal for families with kids was almost irresistible. This was the antidote for Rome's urban crowding and urban goo. There were open fields for running in. The olive groves seemed made for hide and seek. There were tall pines for climbing, and the nearby hills held the promise of mountain climbing adventures. And there was a swimming pool!

The pool was definitely the deal maker. It was on the crest of the same hill on which the house was built, but it was out in the open, with completely clear views of the surrounding terrain. The contrast with crowded, dirty Trastevere could not have been more complete. The thought of the kids playing in that pool, surrounded by olive trees and Sabine Hills, well, it must have sold Michael on the apartment, and it was definitely what brought us into the deal.

At first, we were just going to sublet Michael and Myung's apartment during their summer vacation in Canada. But with relatives coming to visit us, we decided to also rent the apartment next door. Then we REALLY started to enjoy our weekends in Sabina. We got to know people in the closest towns (Ponticelli and Scandriglia).

Our bicycles, my telescope, and more and more of our recreational stuff made its way out to the country house. And before we knew it what had started out as a one month sub-let turned into a year-round experience in country living. The kids identified the best climbing trees. Elisa found blackberry bushes and fig trees and cherry trees. We became familiar with the local wildlife – there were huge green snakes and dangerous vipers and scorpions. Most interesting were the wild boars. In Italian they are called Chingali; they can become huge and they are aggressive and dangerous. Billy was bitterly disappointed when he and I were obliged (by his mom) to abandon our tent and go into the apartment when, at bedtime, we heard a Chingale snorting close to our campsite. As summer turned to fall we even got used to the gunfire that came with hunting season. As the temperature dropped we learned to use the wood-burning stove. Elisa and I found a coffee bar in Ponticelli and became regulars there for our customary cappuccinos and cornettos.

The kids loved the place. Perhaps inspired by the "In Italia" musical theme of our transition period, we worked up our own rap song about beautiful hill towns that surrounded us in our corner of Sabina:

Scandriglia – I wanna see ya!
Ponticelli – Molti belli!
Nerola – Gotta know ya!

Billy and Maria would squeal with delight at the corniness of it all.

I'm proud to say that we out-did the other ex-pats in our exploration of the towns. All of our Foreign Service instincts kicked in and, just as we had done in our other foreign homes, we began to make contact with the locals and find out who-was-who and what was going on. In Ponticelli we were quickly on friendly terms with Patricia, the lady who ran the gas station, and with the fellow who owned the coffee bar. Up in Scandriglia we made friends with the family that ran the grocery store. In Ostia Nuova Elisa soon achieved "regular customer" status at the Fratelli Liberati butcher shop. Through these folks we'd be alerted to the many festivals and other events on the local social calendar. And through them we soon developed a sense of belonging to that little Sabine community.

It didn't take us very long to start feeling like locals. We'd notice that Patricia seemed a bit down. Her eyes would water up as she'd tell us that that her elderly mother was faltering, and that she was worried about her. Elisa would console her. When I went in to pick up the newspapers, Patricia would check to make sure I hadn't forgotten milk for the kids.

One morning Elisa mentioned to Patricia that we'd like to find a place where the kids could ride horses. Patricia pledged to look into it. We went back to the house with our newspapers and milk. A few hours later I heard the sound of galloping hooves. Three magnificent horses and their impeccably attired owners had arrived in our front yard. They spent the rest of the morning giving the kids rides. They did this out of the goodness of their hearts, because it was a nice gesture, because of the Italian sense of "bella figura." Ponticelli was a lot of fun.

All these places were a lot of fun, and, for a time, all of them became our hometowns. Whenever we'd move, after the excitement of being in a new place began to fade, Elisa would start to think back to the place we'd moved from. She'd think of the small details (what were the doorknobs like?) and realize that they were already starting to fade from her memory She'd start to yearn to go home, to go back to the place we were before. Early on, that meant back to the Dominican Republic, or back to Virginia. But later it meant back to Ponta Delgada, or back to London, or back to Rome.   People who espouse a nationalistic view of the world would have you believe that there is something special about the cities and towns that lie within your particular national borders.   Somehow, according to this view, Americans should feel more "at home" in Peoria than in Ponta Delgada, more comfortable in New York than in London, more at ease in San Francisco than in Rome, happier on the Jersey shore than in Ponticelli. This just wasn't the case with us.   Sure, there were difficult periods of adaptation, but even on exotic and remote Sao Miguel Island we came to feel at home.   We discovered that we could feel completely at ease and "at home" in all the "foreign" towns and cities we lived in.

INTERNATIONAL SCHOOL

"God has given you your country as cradle, and humanity as mother; you cannot rightly love your brethren of the cradle if you love not the common mother." Giuseppe Mazzini

Earlier in my career as a diplomat, in those dark, sad days before marriage and fatherhood, my main connections with the local cultures and societies came via the bars that I hung out in, and the friends that I made in those bars. But in this last decade abroad, as a married man with kids, the bar scene was definitely over (thank God!), and my kids' schools took over as the main channel for interaction with the locals.

Our kids went to four – all of them very good, all very different. They ranged from an ordinary public pre-school to one of the world's most expensive private international schools. We loved them all, and in different ways, each of them taught us lessons, lessons that were not on the formal curricula.

These schools varied greatly in their sophistication and worldliness. At one extreme was Ponta Delgada's little Enchanted Castle. The kids there were the sons and daughters of dairy farmers and store keepers, policemen and nurses. It was a very ordinary school, in a very isolated little town. We were – by far – the most exotic people ever to have set foot in that building. In the eyes of the locals, we must have been almost extraterrestrial in our level of weirdness. This was a place in which almost everyone else had been born on the island and – in all probability – would spend their entire lives on that island. We'd just blown in from Washington and Santo Domingo, would only stay three years, and would then go SOMEWHERE ELSE.

London's Southbank was at the opposite end of the scale. Here our kids went to school with the sons and daughters of the captains of finance. We knew that we had gone through a big change when, during our first weeks in London, Billy told us that his best friend in kindergarten would be out for a few days: "Charlie went to Saint Morris!" It took us a while to figure out that it was St. Moritz in Switzerland. In this school, when the kids told you that little Oliver got a helicopter, you'd soon find out that it was a REAL helicopter, and that his Dad had acquired it to beat the traffic.

But in spite of the differences, each of these schools – each in their own way – contributed to the changes in worldview that we experienced over the last ten years.

One of the main reasons we got assigned to the Azores was *because* that isolated region had no English-language school. As a result, Foreign Service colleagues with school-aged kids weren't interested in the job – this reduced the competition significantly. Billy and Maria were, we thought, both far from the time that they'd be needing schools, so I asked to be considered for the Azores job.

We were wrong about the kids not needing a school. As soon as we got to Ponta Delgada, we discovered that my lofty official position gave us a social status that made it difficult for Elisa to re-create the "moms with little kids" group that had been at the center of our social life in Northern Virginia. Suddenly, we really *needed* a pre-school. Bad. Billy was bored and sad and desperately needed social contact. We went looking for a school. At around this time a special variety of flower was blooming – we became quite attached to this flower. This September bloomer is called "Meninos p'escola" ("Children Off to School").

Meninos p'escola -- Amaryllis belladonna

There was a school right across the street, but we were kind of shocked by the physical setting (ancient) and some obvious safety hazards: There was a large, very open stairwell, and for some reason they'd wound rope through the banisters. At first we thought that it was some attempt at art – we were shocked when we were told that it was an improvised safety net

49

for the stairs (but I later built the same kind of DNA safety net at our house in London).

At work, when I asked our local employees about schools they immediately recommended one that was used by the other big cheeses on the island. Elisa and I got an appointment. We thought Billy was a shoe in – after all, in the short time that we'd been there we'd been constantly reminded of how gosh-darn IMPORTANT and ELITE we were. It was, after all that very elite status that had caused the social isolation that caused us to look for a school in the first place! Surely this school would have a place for the FIRST BORN SON of the AMERICAN CONSUL... Wrong again.

The nun who ran the place wasn't impolite. She was frosty, but not impolite. She started out by asking us why we hadn't applied for a spot last year like everyone else. I explained that we got the assignment in late March and had arrived in late July... She was unimpressed. She insisted that we should have applied last year, just like everyone else. (That would have been tough, I thought, because at application time we had never even heard of Ponta Delgada, or Sao Miguel Island.) It was quite clear that Sister wasn't going to cut us any slack. This is the flip side of elite status – there are a lot of folks out there who take delight in stickin' it to the man... Especially, perhaps, when the man represents Uncle Sam.

Our salvation came from the opposite end of the Azorean social spectrum: Ana Paula. She was the cook at the official residence of the American Consul. Her little boy (Ivo) was Billy's age. Seeing that we were struggling with the rich-folks school, she mentioned to Elisa that Ivo's school was quite nice, and would probably take Billy.

It was really beautiful. Perfect. Up on a hill with a view of the sea, the Castelinho Encantato (The Enchanted Castle) pre-school was run by the Portuguese public school system. The building was new and bright. The place had a great feel to it. The kids seemed happy and friendly and the women who worked there all seemed to want to provide Billy with loads of affection, care, and Azorean soup. We looked no further. That was the place.

When at age 2.5 we took Billy into the Enchanted Castle, he didn't speak a word of Portuguese, and there was NO ONE at the school who spoke English. Realizing that our little guy was facing extreme culture shock, we took it easy and limited his school time to 2-3 hours each day. I'd often drop him off on my way to work and then bring him home when I returned for lunch. Of course, he cried and cried when it came time for me to leave him, but I didn't really feel bad about it because of the amazing kindness and tenderness of the Azorean women who worked in that school. Suzette and Fatima comforted him during that difficult first year. Later there was Ana and Concecao. In the early days, I suspect that Billy's little feet rarely touched the ground. As soon as he started crying, whoosh, one of the Azorean ladies would pick him up and wipe away his tears.

The kids in the school were also very kind. At first, I worried that Billy might get some pre-school bullying. After all, he couldn't speak Portuguese and spent most of his time weeping and being carried around by one of the

teacher ladies – he wasn't exactly building up street cred. But there was no bullying. Never. I always thought that this pre-school tolerance and kindness said something very positive about Azorean society.

I figured that Billy must have been really self-conscious about

not being able to talk in school so, one day on our way home, I told him that he shouldn't feel bad about not being able to speak in class. I explained that this was simply because we were new in town – soon he'd learn Portuguese.

"No Daddy, that's not why I don't speak in class!" he said. "I don't speak in class because my teeth are too big!" I didn't argue with him. I guess that was his way of understanding it.

During our time with The Enchanted Castle, I picked up a little book on how to teach your child to read using the phonics method. ("Teach Your Child to Read" by Sidney Ledson.) Billy and I started June 2002; Maria joined in about two years later. It was great fun. We used flash cards and made steady and very satisfying progress. We started with the letter U. "Uh, uh, uh," I would have them say. Then we went to P. "Puh, Puh,

Puh…" Then the two sounds together: "Uh-Puh." UP! That was the big breakthrough. From there we'd go through the rest of the alphabet. By the time we made it to the back of the book, they were reading little short stories. It was wonderful. I got to teach my kids to read.

That little pre-school opened many windows that gave us special insights into Azorean society, but I can't say that we really became integrated into the community of parents. We were part of that community, but we always remained special, different members of the group. I suppose this is inevitable. Billy (and later Maria) arrived in school each day in the Consulate's chauffeur-driven Crown Victoria armored car. (After months of back and forth to school in that armored car, Maria one day asked, "Daddy, *why* does Mr. Silva came to our house each morning and drive us

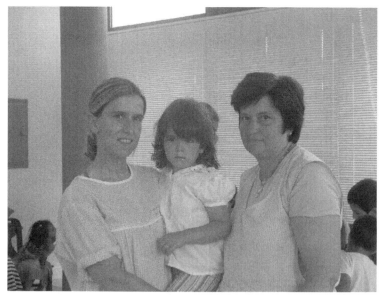

to school in his nice big car?") But even if we didn't become full-fledged members of the Ponta Delgada PTA, during our three years at that school we joined with the other parents in the parental team effort that goes with school. Parents everywhere are involved in this kind of collective effort, this management of play-dates and birthday parties, the shared concern for a little classmate with a bad cold. But we had the experience of doing this in a foreign society. It may have been here that we started to drift away, started to realize that there are basic human concerns that are more important than nationality.

Maria (with the fabulous shades) with classmates in the Azores

London was our first experience in picking a school from afar. Billy would be going into Kindergarten there – the State Department would pick up the tab for private school for him. Elisa swung into action as soon as we found out we were London-bound.

The default solution in this situation is usually "The American School." In most major cities overseas there is a school that is partially supported by the U.S. government. The student body is usually a mixture of rich locals and the children of other foreigners (diplomats, business people, etc.) with the American kids being in the minority. But three years in the Azores had made us accustomed to being off on our own. By this point the war in Iraq was in full swing; we decided to heed the advice of the security experts to avoid large gathering of Americans. Elisa started scouring the internet for other options.

Elisa found the Southbank International School via the internet. We liked the school's inclusion in the International Baccalaureate program. The Embassy had a lot of apartments and houses in London, but most were clustered around the American School. Our selection of Southbank marked us as outliers and seemed to confuse the Embassy administrative staff. They seemed unfamiliar with Southbank's location and concluded that we'd require something far from the neighborhood used by most of the

Embassy staff. Fine with us! Soon we were assigned a little house in the Royal Borough of Kensington and Chelsea.

Maria was still of pre-school age, and Uncle Sam doesn't pay for pre-school. Knowing where we would be living, Elisa started Googling for a reasonably priced pre-school for Maria. Miraculously, she found a state-run school within a few blocks of our house that had a spot for our Maria: The Bousefield School. It was perfect: Just a few blocks from our house, the school was the site on which Beatrix Potter had written Peter Rabbit.

The school-induced sensation of drifting away from our American roots that we'd first experienced in the Azores was certainly reinforced in London, but in a very different way. In the Azores we were in contact with one foreign society, but in London it seemed we were in contact with ALL foreign societies simultaneously. One day early in our tour, I came home from work and found Maria waiting to tell me something: "It's Ramadan Daddy! At school we're celebrating Ramadan!" They also celebrated the Hindu festival of Diwali (which conveniently coincided with England's Guy Fawkes celebration – Diwali is a festival of light and Guy Fawkes is marked with bonfires).

The wounds of 9-11 were still open, and I know that my relatives back in New York (they were close enough to see the smoke) would have been a bit taken aback by little Maria celebrating Ramadan. But in London it was normal, and we always saw this openness and tolerance as being very positive. Sajita, a teacher's assistant at Maria's nursery school class, is Muslim and wore the hijab head scarf. Of course, her hugs and care were every bit as effective as those of the ladies in the Azores.

Bousefield was a great experience for little Maria and for the whole family. It was all very London: definitely English, but with people from all over the world living alongside you in England.

We were reminded that we were living in the nanny-state when the school insisted on a "home visit" (more of an inspection really) before Maria could be enrolled (we passed!). There were lots of rules at the school, and everything was kept very orderly. Everyone was very polite and kind. Maria loved the Bousefield School. Elisa would take her up to the school in her little stroller, through the leafy streets of South Kensington.

We thought that all was well until one day, about three months after out arrival, Gillie, Maria's teacher, asked to "have a word" with me after school. In England, "have a word" usually means there's trouble...

"Mr. Meara, are you considering getting professional help for Maria? You know we could make some recommendations."

I was dumbfounded. "I'm sorry, I don't understand. Professional help for what?"

"Well, for her speech problem, of course."

Gillie was speaking as if Maria's problem was glaringly obvious. But I really didn't have the slightest idea what she was talking about. I briefly thought that she might be referring to Maria's American accent, but at this point Maria had developed a really beautiful London accent, and we were hoping that it would stick.

"I'm sorry Gillie, what speech problem?"

"Well Mr. Meara, it's just not normal for a child to be almost four years old and not talk! I think there is definitely a development problem here!"

At this point I couldn't help but laugh. I pointed out that Maria talked pretty much non-stop from the time she woke up, until the time she went to bed. Sometimes in several languages.

But not, apparently, at the Bousefield School. Never. Not once. Not one word in three months. We were really surprised. It seemed obvious that this was Maria's way of coping with the new environment, with the rapid switch from the Portuguese Enchanted Castle, to Beatrix Potter's old place in downtown London.

We talked to Maria about her not speaking in class. She told us she felt "shy." We encouraged her to speak up. A few weeks later, while calling the class role, they heard a faint but distinct "Present!" when Maria Meara's name was called. The whole nursery burst into applause and Maria was hit with a wave of hugs.

Bousefield School was an amazing place – it was an urban state-run school, and it didn't have the resources of the private schools that Maria would later attend, but this resource deficit was more than made up for by the dedication and creativity of the school's energetic teachers. The school plays were where this energy was most visible. Working with kids from around the world and from across a wide range of the English social spectrum, those teachers had those kids putting on some really wonderful productions. Maria, having overcome her "speech impediment," became an active participant in Bousefield theater. Her portrayal of a snail in the 2008 pre-school class play brought the audience to its feet (well, it was really just Elisa and me).

In an example of the kind of parental team effort that we were involved in, minutes before the opening act of one Bousefield Christmas production, Elisa noticed that Maria's friend Daisy was crying. It seems she'd forgotten to wear a red dress that day. She was the only girl in the class not dressed in red, and she was mortified. Seeing Daisy's distress, Elisa literally sprinted home, grabbed a red dress and made it back to school in time to get that little girl in the proper attire. Up on the stage, dressed in red, Daisy looked down at Elisa smiled, and mouthed the words "thank you." Sometimes it does take a village.

We loved Bousefield so much that we seriously thought of forgoing the fancy, Embassy-funded private school and keeping Maria there for first grade. But we decided it would be better for Billy and Maria to be in the same school.

When it came time for Maria to go into Southbank, we had to prepare a bio for her application. It included this:

At the age of three, Maria asked us to rent Steven Spielberg's movie "E.T." – she then amazed us by watching it from beginning to end. We think she may have become interested in this movie because of her own experiences as a small alien from far away.

Unlike Bousefield, there weren't many British kids in Southbank – the high tuition chased a lot of people away, and the school wasn't really part of the traditional British system. This made Southbank extremely cosmopolitan. In classes of fifteen kids, there might be twelve different nationalities. The kids seemed uninterested in the origins of their classmates: When I asked Billy where little Asaaf was from, all he could tell me was that the new kid spoke Arabic. When I asked again what country he was from, Billy grew impatient: "I dunno.... What difference does it make anyway dad?"

Southbank was located in two conjoined houses in the Notting Hill area of west London. I had expected a school this rich and this expensive to have its own grounds and sports facilities. But this was Central London, where even British Princes like Will and Harry did their gym class in Hyde Park or Kensington Gardens. Southbank had a small playground in what had been the gardens of the two houses, but for most sports the kids were sent to off-site parks.

Southbank was very different from Bousefield, and for me some of the differences were unexpected. I guess my American beliefs in church-state separation made me expect state-run Bousefield to be more agnostic or religiously neutral. But remember, this was England, the home of the Church of England and all that – it turned out that state run Bousefield was more at ease with religion than was privately owned Southbank. Bousefield tried to celebrate all religions (hence little Maria's enthusiasm for Ramadan). Southbank, apparently in an over-the-top case of political correctness, decided to try to IGNORE all of them. There would be no

Southbank International School

mention of any of them at Southbank. Christmas was referred to as "the winter festival." When I first heard this I suspected the school was being run by Druids, but then I remembered that they had also taken steps against Halloween (they changed it to "dress up as your favorite literary character day"). It was all kind of weird, but eccentricity is an important part of British life. It was a nice school and we liked it.

Southbank seemed to have fully embraced the idea of making the child's self-esteem the central focus of the education effort. There weren't a lot of tests. There was a lot of self-esteem. One day, Billy was a bit grouchy and I asked him what was wrong. He frowned and told me, "I don't know. I just don't feel good about myself today." I told him to stop talking like that.

Perhaps because many of the parents were working in the financial sector, the school-yard language was English, but it was English with a strong New York accent. We watched kids from Brazil and Sweden and the UAE arrive with almost no English – within a year you'd have thought they were all from the Bronx.

Every kid in the Southbank School was required to play the violin. On the first day of school the kids had to bring with them all of the normal pens, pencils and notebooks, but they also were expected to bring a violin. I knew the schoolyard culture at Southbank was a bit different from what I was used to when, on a bus trip to a soccer game, I overhead some of the Southbank "tough kids" talking in the back of the bus:

"I'm bored."
"Me too."
"What do you want to do?"
"I dunno... How about some violin?"

That kind of thing never happened in my school.

Unlike in the Azores, in both schools in London we had the chance to be full-fledged members of the school communities. Working in an Embassy wasn't seen as weird or exotic in hyper-cosmopolitan London. Especially at Southbank, just about everyone was, like us, from somewhere else, and eventually heading somewhere else.

AMBRIT SCHOOL

We got into our Italian school in a very Italian way: through connections. Elisa started Googling for Rome schools as soon as we got the very surprising news that justice would not prevail and that instead of going from London to Ouagadougou, for some strange reason we were going to Rome. World events had made us even more wary about security: We'd been in London when the transport system was bombed, and memories of the horrible 2004 terror attack on the school in Chechnya was on our minds. So as we looked at the options for Roman schools, we were looking for something low-profile, something not clearly associated with the U.S. Once again, the default solution "American School" was there, but once again, and for similar reasons, we looked elsewhere. A school called AMBRIT popped up on the screen and Elisa and the kids were immediately taken with it. It seemed very friendly and nurturing.

For this move Elisa and I did a quick recon. In March 2007 we left the kids with Elisa's mom in London, and flew down to Rome to look at schools. After visiting a couple of places that we didn't like at all, AMBRIT seemed to be our salvation. AMBRIT stands for American British Italian School, and the curriculum borrows elements from those of all three countries. It had the low-profile we were looking for. After a meeting with the Principal and a tour of the school, the decision was made. This was definitely the school for us. But, wait – there was a glitch. The staff told us that while they would definitely have a slot for Billy, there might not be room for little Maria. She was being wait-listed.

This was a lot more serious than being wait-listed for a flight or a restaurant table. I immediately started worrying and losing sleep about poor little Maria being shipped off, without her big brother, to one of those OTHER schools. While the actual security threat was probably quite small, as I fretted about this, in my mind all those other schools seemed to move closer and closer to Iraq and Chechnya, while AMBRIT seemed to become more idyllic and secure with each passing night. I had to get both of the kids into AMBRIT!

Perhaps because of her Dominican roots, Elisa instantly understood what we needed: Influence needed to be applied. We started looking around for strings to be pulled. And it turned out that we had some. Through a very strange coincidence, Maria's teacher in Rome, Ms. Darroch, had, years before, taught at AMBRIT. (She is the wife of a senior British diplomat and they had been stationed in Rome.) There was also a colleague of mine who had been in the Dominican Republic when I was there who was now stationed at Embassy Rome and had his son at AMBRIT. His wife was active in the parents' association. Both of these poor ladies were immediately enlisted in our lobbying campaign. Soon the AMBRIT School in Rome started getting e-mails, FAXes, phone calls, letters of recommendation, etc. Little did we know that even before officially arriving in Rome, we were getting things done the Italian way: via the "recommandazione" system – via the system of personal connections. Even before she got to Rome, Maria had become "una racommendata"! It worked! She was IN! For me, this meant no more tossing and turning, no more Chechnya nightmares.

As in London, not only were the classrooms very multi-national, but so were the families. Here too we found ourselves suddenly in the mainstream. In these schools it was very common for mom to be from one country, dad from another, with the kids born in a third. At AMBRIT's "May Fair" party, they had a little booth at which kids could have flags painted on their cheeks (as they do at the soccer games). We got a reminder of how multinational the families were when we saw that most kids (including ours) had mom's flag on one cheek, and dad's on the other. You can see how difficult that little "Nationality?" question on all the forms becomes. The flags on those little faces was a reminder of one of the big ironies of Foreign Service life: the fact that while we work for a national government and are committed to the defense of U.S. national interests, for many of us the most important relationship in our lives is with someone from outside our nation: about one third of us are married to foreigners. National interest drives our every move at work, but in our personal lives, nationalism is set aside and people follow their hearts. Love conquers all. Our common humanity overrides patriotism and nationalism.

As had been the case in London, our selection of the school determined where we would live. In a kind of weird parallel with our London experience, the school choice caused us to be placed in a neighborhood on the south side of town, away from areas in which most American families lived. That's how we ended up in Trastevere.

The AMBRIT School in Rome had much more in common with the Southbank than with the Enchanted Castle. AMBRIT caters to families assigned to the United Nations offices in Rome: The UN's Food and Agricultural Office and the Headquarters of the World Food Program. This meant that AMBRIT probably had a wider range of countries represented than did Southbank. In some ways AMBRIT made Southbank – with its heavy concentration of people from New York, Hong Kong, Switzerland, and pre-crash Iceland – seem a bit parochial.

AMBRIT was very international, but because a good portion of the student body was Italian the school gave us good connections to the local community.

Most of the Italian kids in the school were from very wealthy families. There were princesses. REAL princesses. One kid in Billy's class needed a full time body guard (he was appropriately scary looking – he too came to Billy's birthday party). One of Italy's most famous soccer players had his kids in the school – he'd frequently be on campus, but the kids were under strict orders not to bother him. There were also some kids from ordinary middle class Italian families. These folks were making big sacrifices to give their kids a better education and fluency in English.

Most of the instruction at AMBRIT was in English, but Billy and Maria spent a good portion of each day working in and studying Italian. This was a far cry from the U.S. educational enclave experience that kids get in many American schools overseas. During our last two years in Rome, our kids were the only U.S. Embassy children in AMBRIT.

In spite of its international aspects, AMBRIT was, culturally, a very Italian school. Things were done in the Italian way. Italy has been described as "The Beauty and the Beast" of countries, and even for people who have been through culture shock many times, the initial exposure to

Italian culture can be quite jarring. It was through the school that we got our first taste of some of the unpleasant aspects.

Furbizia is one of the most important words in the Italian lexicon. It is surprisingly difficult to translate, and there really isn't a fully equivalent concept even in Spanish or Portuguese. *Cunning* and *sly* come kind of close, but a simple definition fails to convey the fact that this is for most Italians, almost a way of life. Italians are raised to be *furbo* – they learn very young to do what needs to be done to successfully navigate the complicated and sometimes treacherous labyrinth of Italian life. They learn to get around obstacles, and they learn that rules are made to be broken. The opposite of a furbo is a *fesso*. Fesso translates as *idiot, fool*. Italians admire the furbo and live in fear of ever being considered a fesso.

This explains a lot of things. Everyone knows that Italians are not exactly good about waiting in line. We had heard all about that. But the real world manifestations of this hit us hard during out first school picnic at AMBRIT. There was a long line for the cotton candy. Maria DESPERATELY wanted some. So we got on line. And waited. And waited. More and more children buzzed around us, happily consuming THEIR cotton candy. But the line (which was filled mostly with non-Italian families) didn't move an inch. Maria grew more exasperated. When I finally went to find out what was going on, I discovered that one of the Italian moms, upon reaching the head of the line, had dug in her heels and had started taking and filling orders for the children of her friends. The kids would just run up to her and place their order. Nobody said anything. Furbizia in action! Eventually we gave up and started towards our car with little Maria crying from her lack of fluffy sugar. But – and this happens a lot in Italy – just as we were getting ready to bad mouth the entire place, the Beauty part of the Beauty/Beast duality popped up. An Italian mom who we had just recently met saw Maria crying and came to our rescue. Without using the same dodgy mechanism used by the mom at the head of the line, she went and got Maria some cotton candy.

Outsiders shouldn't be too scornful – this is all deeply cultural. The story may be apocryphal, but a friend in Rome whose wife worked at one of the English-speaking international schools said that the first time they forced the little Italian kids to line up for lunch (and not just all try to mob the lunch counter) the little guys got all upset, and some of them started to cry. They didn't know what was going on. This was not what they were used to.

Sometimes, of course, you get the beast, but without a countervailing beauty – sometimes your integration into the community of the foreign school makes you want to grab the kids, pack up, and head back to the good

62

ol' US of A. I took some time off from work to go to Billy's 4th grade class play. I got to the school a bit early, so I went in to the auditorium where they were setting up, got myself a good seat in the first row, and settled down to read the newspaper while I waited. A few minutes later, one of the workers came up and rather nervously told me that I couldn't sit there. Figuring they needed the front row for the kids, or for the teachers, I moved one row back. As I did, I saw the worker place – on what had been my seat, and on the two seats next to it – signs with the last name of one of Italy's most prominent families (they had a kid in the class). It was as if I had suddenly been hit full force by the Italian class structure, by the system that drives everything in that country.

But even unpleasant incidents like this one end up helping pull you closer to the other parents in the school. This helped us understand the pain of those non-elite Italian families who found their kids being excluded from the birthday parties of the junior division of the rich and famous set. Or who notice that wealthy Italian parents often didn't worry at all about their children's grades, because for them the race was already won (in Italy, you see, connections trump qualifications).

But generally, it was more beauty than beast. Through the people we met at AMBRIT, we got to know Italy. For every jarring collision with the darker parts of Italian culture, there were dozens of little acts of kindness, little bits of the bella figura that Italians are always trying to sprinkle into life. And once again we became part of a community, a community that the folks back home would call a community of foreigners, but that for us was just a community of parents and kids.

****

I found that just being a parent, just having children, made me more aware of the human ties that connect us with people around the world. It also opened my eyes to the emptiness of the rhetoric used by those politicians who seek to fortify the sense of separation and distinctiveness that nationalism is built upon. From all around the world, we hear leaders extolling the virtue of what they call "love of country." Love? Really? Love is a powerful word. I love my wife, I love my kids. I know what love is. Is the emotion that I feel for the country really supposed to be similar? As the Brits would say, that's a bit over the top.

Being a parent and raising our kids overseas obviously deepened my doubts about the us-versus-them foundations of nationalism. Schools often play an important role in imbuing people with feelings of nationalism and patriotism. That's why each school day in the U.S. begins with the pledge of allegiance. That's why our schools always have a lot flags in them. This all seemed very normal to me as I grew up in the United States. But our ten years in foreign schools has changed my views on this. We learned that the communities that crop up around schools have nothing to do with nationality, but have everything to do with humanity. They have nothing to do with the contrived, artificial political connections of nationalism and patriotism, and everything to do with the bonds that arise from the shared human concerns of parents for their children. And we learned that, left to their own devices, kids will not divide themselves up along national lines in a school yard. The schools that our kids went to helped make us realize that there is nothing natural or inevitable about the national divisions that have come to frame so many lives.

MILITARY MADNESS
WAR, BOMBS, AND BASES

"Borders are scratched across the hearts of men
By strangers with a calm, judicial pen,
And when the borders bleed we watch with dread
The lines of ink across the map turn red."
Marya Mannes, Subverse: Rhymes for Our Times, 1959

"Patriotism: The virtue of the vicious." Oscar Wilde

Lajes Field, RAF Lakenheath, RAF Mildenhall, Camp Darby, Aviano Air Force Base, Naval Air Station Sigonella... In all of the countries we lived in there were U.S. military bases. These installations became little islands of America for us. As an Embassy family we had access to them, and we made frequent use of the shopping facilities and the little on-base hotels. For all of us, it was great fun to go through their gates and spend a few days in the good old USA. Our kids were especially fond of the bases. They would always lobby hard for us to put aside plans for tourism outside the gate. "We want a BASE DAY Daddy! Let's go to the PX!"

For the kids, the bases were a chance to have some contact with their homeland, a homeland that they really didn't know. They'd always be full of questions and observations. During one visit – it was soon after the election of President Obama – they noticed that many of the soldiers were African American. They asked about race relations in the U.S. I gave them a quick briefing on our sad history in this area, but I tried to be upbeat and focused on the recent progress. They were shocked when I told them that not long ago in the U.S. some people would have objected to their mom and I getting married. They looked really puzzled at this, so I tried to gently explain.

"Well, you know, because your mom is Latina and I am...."

Maria often tries to think ahead and finish my sentences, and she jumped ahead on this one: "I know," she said with a tone of sad resignation, "it's because mom is a Latina and you are Catholic!"

The bases also provided lots of little reminders of the fact that our kids had grown up far away from the USA. For example, shortly after checking in to the visitors' quarters at the Naval Air Station in Sigonella, Sicily, Billy came running out of the bathroom to report that the toilet was malfunctioning. "It's filling up with water dad!" We laughed as we

65

explained that what he was finally seeing was a normal American toilet in operation.

The kids loved the bases, but I had mixed feelings about them. Considering my background, this is probably a surprising ambivalence: We have a lot of military experience in my family. All of the men of my father's generation had served in the military, most of them in World War II. My dad had been seriously wounded in that war; I grew up amidst battle scars and war stories, amidst American flags and "Love it or Leave it" bumper stickers. At age twelve I went around our neighborhood collecting signatures in support of Nixon's pardon of Lt. William Calley, the U.S. Army officer who supervised the massacre of 500 Vietnamese civilians at My Lai. (I was genuinely surprised when one neighbor refused to sign.) I wore one of those bracelets with the name of an American Prisoner of War being held in North Vietnam.

My own military experience began with army basic training at age 18. I later went through Special Forces School and deployed to Central America. In my book "Contra Cross", I wrote: "As I prepared for the deployment to El Salvador, I frequently felt my father, and my grandfather, and all of my uncles looking over my shoulder... They had all gone overseas in the service of Uncle Sam... I felt like I was following in their footsteps, and I felt a strong obligation to do my best."

People with my kind of background can usually be found on the right-hand side of the political spectrum, tuned into Fox News, and with National Rifle Association stickers on their pick-up trucks. But that's not me. In college, I majored in Latin American studies and Economics because I want to do something for the poor people whom I'd met as a volunteer English teacher in the mountains of Guatemala. I even minored in "Peace Studies." I guess I'd been bothered by the weapons I'd been trained to operate. Claymore mines *should* have a sobering effect on 18 year-olds. This seems to be recognized in an old saying about another particularly horrible weapon, White Phosphorous, aka Willie Peter: "Willie Peter Make you a Believer." Indeed. Later, my experiences with the Salvadoran and Nicaraguan wars wiped out any lingering youthful enthusiasm for war and the military that I may have had.

Ironically, the Special Forces background added to the ambivalence. Outsiders see Special Forces as the arch-typical military guys. But in fact, the Special Forces have always been far outside the mainstream of U.S. military culture. These are the soldiers who learn foreign languages and become immersed in foreign cultures. These are the guys who parachute into hostile territory to work with foreign tribesmen. In some ways this part of Special Forces has a lot of similarities to the Peace Corps – both groups take young Americans and send them out to live and work alongside impoverished foreigners. Indeed, SF has sometimes been described as "the Peace Corps with guns." Conventional soldiers often dislike the Special Forces, seeing them as being engaged in a lot of touchy-feely nonsense. "If you grab 'em by the balls, their hearts and minds will follow" is the bumper sticker that captures the conventional attitude. The scorn is reciprocated: Many SF guys dislike the very "kinetic," blunt instrument, brute force, "bomb them into the stone age" approach of the conventional military.

In the extremely nationalistic "us-versus-them" world of the U.S. military, the Green Berets are often seen as being a bit too close to them, too close to the foreigners. I got an early exposure to this tension when, as a five year-old, my grandmother took me to see "Lawrence of Arabia" at the movie theater at 231st Street and Broadway in the Bronx. In one of the most memorable scenes Lawrence raised Brit eyebrows when, dressed in Arab clothing, he entered the British Army Officer's Club in the company of an Arab soldier. Many years later, looking back on my sojourns with the Nicaraguan Contra rebels, I wrote, "I ate the same food that the contras ate, and after a time, I came to feel quite at home in the valley... I looked forward to escaping the bureaucratic routine, and found the contras more pleasant company than many of my embassy colleagues."

The Special Forces' dislike of the conventional military and their affinity for the locals is captured beautifully in the award-winning Vietnam war novel "Parthian Shot" by Loyd Little. Little, who had served as an SF medic in Vietnam, described an SF team that had been forgotten by the military high command. Over time the team members grew closer and closer to the "indigenous people" they'd been sent out to work with. And they grew ever-more hostile to the conventional soldiers who only seemed to be interested in dropping bombs on people. Little wrote:

"There was some sense of identity between us and the Hoa Hao. The men who volunteered for Special Forces, for jump school, for Vietnam duty, and for A-team assignments were not run-of-the mill soldiers. Each was escaping the regular Army standardization for some reason. And the regular Army attitude toward Green Berets, in spite of the clever public relations, was one of suspicion and dislike. It was easier for us to sympathize with the problems of the Hoa Hao than with the latest coup winner in Saigon."

I'd obviously picked up quite a bit of this SF attitude toward the conventional military, so I always went into those bases with mixed feelings about our hosts.

Our first base was Lajes Field. It was in the Azores, but it was not nearby. We were on the island of Sao Miguel, but the base was on Terceira Island; there were about 100 miles of very rough ocean between the two. There was a little ferry boat during the summer, but it was a long and difficult trip. You really had to fly there. About six weeks after we got to Ponta Delgada, it was time for me to go visit the base. We decided to bring the whole family, and to bring Margarida along (to help with the kids).

The plane ride was rough, with lots of turbulence knocking around the small 25-seat plane. Once on the base we found ourselves getting the VIP treatment. I was briefed by the senior American officers and taken on a "windshield (driving) tour" by the commander.

I had spent a good part of my life on military bases, so I thought I knew how the world looks from inside the wire, but then the base commander did something that made me wonder if I did. We were driving along the runway when the colonel spotted a plane taxiing for takeoff. He grabbed his walkie-talkie radio, instructed the control tower to have the plane hold its position, then drove us out onto the runway, close to the plane. We got out of the jeep and stood on the edge of the strip. The big plane seemed to be struggling against the brakes that were keeping it from taking off. The colonel told the tower to let the plane go. That kind of jet makes a lot of noise – it seems to shake everything as it roars down the runway. Near the point of maximum noise, the colonel (a B-52 bomber pilot who said his one big regret was never having actually bombed anyone) leaned over to me and shouted a question:

"You know what that sound is?"

I suppressed the urge to say, "Uh, colonel, I'm pretty sure that's a U.S. Air Force B1 bomber!"

"FREEDOM! THAT'S THE SOUND OF FREEDOM!" he bellowed.

The colonel's theatrical little war-gasm was an early reminder that things were a bit different inside the wire.

While I was out listening to the sound of freedom, Elisa was being given a tour of the base by the commander's wife. Elisa's every move was covered by the base's protocol people – they'd radio ahead to the various places she was visiting (hospital, school, library, etc.) giving them updates on her precise arrival time ("VIP 2 is two minutes out, repeat, two minutes out, over!"). This was all quite shocking for Elisa – prior to this her only real encounters with the U.S. government had been getting rather brutally rejected for a visa at the U.S. Embassy in Santo Domingo, and, after we got married, waiting on long lines at the Immigration and Naturalization Service office in Arlington, Virginia. Now, all of a sudden she was VIP2!

They even asked her to make a speech at a meeting of the Officers' Wives Club.

We were invited to a pot luck dinner at the commander's house. The senior officers of the base and their families were there. The wives were very surprised to learn that we were living "out there" on our own, without the benefit of a commissary, American school, or U.S. doctors. They really seemed to feel sorry for us.

We were sad to leave the American environment of the base. They had so many things there that reminded us of what we'd left behind in Virginia. And while our hosts offered to share their American goodies with us, we knew that, in practice, that base might as well have been on the other side of the world.

In London, U.S. military territory was much closer at hand. My duties in the UK had almost nothing to do with our forces there, so our visits to these bases were strictly personal. The big bases (RAF Lakenheath and RAF Mildenhall) were several hours away, up in East Anglia, but there was a small logistical support base very close to central London, in West Ruislip. Like most Embassy folks, we saw this base and its PX as one way to escape London's astronomical cost of living. We became fairly frequent visitors. They had a little playground, and there was a Subway Sandwich shop. We always had a good time there, and at the other bases, but we always knew that we didn't really belong there. The bases have their own distinct cultures. They are not just American enclaves – they are American *military* enclaves. Just like military bases in the States, they form their own little worlds, and – while always very friendly to us – they can sometimes have trouble dealing with outsiders. Being an Embassy family definitely put us in the "outsider" category. Being an Embassy family with both American and Dominican roots made us even more exotic.

One day at West Ruislip, Elisa was going through the checkout. As always, she had a huge quantity of stuff. We were stocking up on American products, on things that we couldn't get on the local market. The PX was busy that day, and there were semi-impatient Americans on line behind Elisa. I'd taken the kids outside to the little playground.

Elisa struggled to get through the checkout as fast as she could, conscious of the silent foot tapping going on behind her. She was also conscious of the fact that she was shopping in a store in which everyone knew everyone else… except for her. And that she was shopping in a store established for EXCLUSIVE use by Americans. She is an American citizen, but she knew that her fellow Americans tapping their feet on the checkout line might have their doubts about this, and that this might intensify their impatience.

All was going well until the teenage girl at the checkout asked for Elisa's ID. She quickly produced her Embassy-issued military ID card. This had been all it took to get her through the checkout on previous visits. But not today.

"I need to see your Russian card," said the girl, in between chews on her gum.

"Russian card?" thought Elisa, "What is she talking about?" She explained that she was the wife of an Embassy officer, that she'd been there many times before, and had never been asked for a Russian card.

The checkout clerk dug in her heals. There were audible sighs and groans from the foot-tappers. The clerk reached for the public address system and called for the manager with a message that seemed to say, "Manager urgently needed at the checkout! Suspected-illegal-alien-gate-crasher-claiming-to-be-wife-of-U.S.-DIPLOMAT attempting to buy American Cheerios! CODE RED! CODE RED!"

The manager arrived and was helpful. Elisa again explained that she was the wife of a diplomat. The manager wisely decided to defuse the situation by making up a story and telling the clerk that Embassy shoppers did not require Russian Cards.

Whew! Credit card papers were signed and a flustered Elisa was soon out in the playground with a train of shopping carts, each one propelled by a helpful, uniformed American Boy Scout.

"What the heck were they talking about? What the heck is a Russian Card!? I'm a Dominican, on an American base in England! Why are they asking me for a RUSSIAN card?"

Ration Card. That's what the clerk was looking for. I guess she had never had to deal with anyone who didn't know that the purchase of tax free cigarettes and liquor at the base was strictly controlled to prevent leakage into the black market. (We don't smoke or drink, and other than Billy's schoolyard candy business had managed to stay completely out of the black market.)

On another visit to West Ruislip it was Maria who got into trans-national trouble. She was only four or five years old. She was at that age when kids will often blurt out whatever pops into their heads. We'd been watching "The Simpsons" on TV. Homer Simpson had been ranting about Canadians. As we waited for Elisa to finish shopping, the kids and I wandered the store. Soon we found ourselves in the military insignia section. Maria was examining all the interesting badges when her little eyes fell on the gold leaf worn by U.S. Army Majors. At this point, it is

70

important to note that our NATO allies and their families apparently had access to the West Ruislip shopping facilities. And wouldn't you know it, the fickle finger of fate caused an extremely CANADIAN lady to be walking past as little Maria loudly declaimed (in Homerian tones) "I don't LIKE that leaf! It looks so CANADIAN!" The woman's jaw dropped and her gasp was quite audible. All of her Canadian fears and suspicions seemed to be suddenly confirmed by little Maria burst of anti-Canadian prejudice. "My God what are you teaching that child?" I blamed it all on Homer Simpson. I hope that no lasting damage was done to the North Atlantic alliance.

Aside from the Canadian cosmopolitanism, as we saw in the Russian Card incident, West Ruislip was really quite insular. We soon found that the big bases up in East Anglia were even more isolated from their surroundings. We would go up there to go shopping and to hang out with other Americans, but we'd also want to try to take in some of the local sites. We quickly found out that our fellow Americans were not a great source of info on conditions outside the perimeter. "Is there any place around where the kids can go to a petting zoo or ride ponies or something like that?" "Uh, no, there's nothing like that here on the base." "But how about in the local area?" "Oh, uh, we wouldn't know..." In more exotic climes this kind of insularity would have been more understandable, but we were in ENGLAND!

There was also a very strong "inside vs. outside" feel to the bases in Italy. The first time I went to the U.S. Base in Naples I was there to pick up a new car that we had bought through the PX system. An Italian employee picked me up at the gate and was driving me to the "Automobile Processing Facility." I tried to make small talk and I made some comment about how nice the base was. She instantly pointed out that "Naples is not like this." She wanted to make sure that I knew that the almost antiseptic cleanliness and order of the base ended at the perimeter, and that Naples was, in comparison, a chaotic mess. I explained that I lived in Rome and was well familiar with the differences.

Things were indeed quite different on the bases. One of the base movie theaters had two screening rooms: One was called "Freedom" and the other "Victory." Sometimes it seemed like we were visiting some sort of Fox News theme park. Television was like normal American TV, but the Armed Forces Radio and Television System had taken out the commercials and replaced them with military self-esteem propaganda and "public service announcements." They were incessantly telling the soldiers that they were "the best," and warning them not to drive after drinking, to wear their seatbelts, and to beware of the dangers of mid-summer hypothermia

(I'm not kidding). Often there were ads extolling the virtues of individual military units" ("173rd Airborne Brigade – Death from Above!") or warnings about the terrorist threat ("Force Protection is EUCOM Priority One!"). Perhaps with its propaganda mission in mind, AFRTS was pronounced by the troops as "A-farts." Obviously designed to bolster morale and esprit d' corps, the AFRTS announcements also seemed to encourage feelings of separation from the world outside.

I can't be too hard on military TV, because the truth is we loved it and used it a lot. During our years in the Azores it was one of our family's most important connections to the United States. Billy and Maria had learned American schoolyard slang from the AFTRS transmission of the Rug Rats cartoon show. AFRTS had brought us Sesame Street and Oprah and Orange County Choppers. We didn't have AFRTS in London but when we got to Rome a friend who was returning to the States gave us his satellite receiver. When we tuned in to the network the effects of the long wars were immediately apparent. Instead of warnings about drunk driving and hot weather hypothermia, there were announcements telling soldiers in Iraq and Afghanistan not to put tape on their hand grenades, advising them how to avoid roadside bombs, and urging them help prevent their buddies from committing suicide. Watching ads like this in our Rome apartment as we prepared to head out to the piazza for some cappuccino or pizza reminded us of the very different reality faced by people in those war zones.

At Naval Air Station Sigonella, Sicily – Mt. Etna in the background

Other reminders came whenever we visited the U.S bases in Italy. Naval Air Station Sigonella was our favorite. Located on the eastern side of the island of Sicily, NAS Sigonella had been split into several different compounds. The one we used seemed to be the creature comfort part of the base. There was no military gear around, no fighter jets or tanks or troop barracks. There was the visitors' quarters, the school, the hospital, the shopping center, a bowling alley, and a wonderful swimming pool with a big slide. Beautiful snow-capped Mount Etna dominated the northern horizon. It was as if Uncle Sam had built a little middle class Club Med, right there in the Med!

Of course, it didn't take us long to find reminders that for many of the folks who used that facility, all that Club Med stuff came at a very high price. The snippets of conversation that you'd hear around the pool or at the supermarket checkout were often about deployment, or, in one sad case, about someone from the base who'd been killed in Afghanistan.

We liked the bases and the people we met on them. Having lived on a base (Fort Bragg, N.C.) for several years, I found myself identifying with the troops. Their separation from the host country cultures is – while a bit sad – understandable. When we take large groups of Americans and their families and put them in very foreign environments we shouldn't be surprised or scornful when they – with the full support of the military hierarchy – circle the wagons and try their best to create a home-like environment. The ancient Romans did the same thing, creating little miniature Romes out there in the hinterlands. It is not the soldiers' job to live and work in the foreign culture – that's what diplomats are supposed to do.

But our visits to the bases always reminded me of how artificial and contrived the nationalist thinking that underpins all this really is. We'd be in our room at the visitors' quarters at the base in Sicily. Right outside the door there'd be Mount Etna in all its snow-capped glory, but the military TV system would be droning on about the *special* beauty of our *American* mountains. Movies (in both the Victory AND the Freedom Theaters) began with everyone standing for the U.S. national anthem. The base supermarkets were always stocked with every imaginable American food product – even in Italy you got the impression that the local food was considered a bit of a risk – better to stick with our good ole' American food! Pass the Cheese-Whiz! The bases seemed to be permeated with dozens of little initiatives and projects and programs all intended to reinforce ideas that support the military mission: You are Americans! You are DIFFERENT! And, perhaps a bit more subtly: You are BETTER! Especially in the final years of our decade abroad, we'd breathe a sigh of relief, when, at the end of our visit to a base, we'd head out the gate and back into the real world. In Italy the contrast between inside the wire and outside the wire was especially strong, no doubt because the Italians are well known for their lack of enthusiasm for chest thumping nationalism (their "nation" wasn't even created until 1865, and they had a very bad experience with nationalistic militarism during the 30's and 40's.)

This nationalistic idea of separation, of us and them, really seemed to be the foundation upon which all of these bases were built. And the military seemed to me to be the ultimate organizational expression of our nationalism. There is a mutually supporting cycle going on here: nationalism provides the justification for the military organization, and the military organization in turn constantly seeks to bolster the idea of nationalism. I can still remember the first line of the code of conduct. I learned it as an 18 year-old in Army basic training: "I am an American fighting man. I serve in the forces that protect my country and the American way of life. I am prepared to give my life in their defense." The message is not at all subtle: the Nation is to die for.

And to kill for. As we visited the bases, I was always conscious of the military purpose of these places, of what they were designed to do. But during our first year overseas (summer 2000 – summer 2001) the military mission seemed almost an afterthought. For us (and especially for the kids) the bases seemed to be nothing more than support structures for PX's, bowling allies, movie theaters, and other fun stuff. But our view of that changed very suddenly one fall day.

We were having lunch at home when someone from the Consulate called and told us to turn on the TV. For most Americans, September 11 is remembered as an early morning event, but we were several time zones to the east, so for us the shocking news came at mid-day; I was at home, having lunch with Elisa. By the time we tuned in the second plane had already hit and it was clear that this was no accident. Then all of a sudden there were blurry, jerky images of the Pentagon in flames.

My phone started ringing, with calls from the Embassy in Lisbon and the Azorean government. I had no illusions about our isolated little post having anything significant to do in response to the attack, but at this point it seemed like the thing for me to do was to go to the Consulate. In the car we heard a radio report (which turned out to be untrue) that the State Department had also been attacked, and that the building was on fire.

Back at the house Elisa was really shocked when, suddenly, Portuguese policemen were stationed outside our front door.

There was an outpouring of sympathy from the Azoreans. We kept getting calls expressing sympathy and solidarity. I went on Azorean TV that night to thank people for their support and to make a "justice will be done" statement. Several well-meaning Azoreans asked me to participate in "peace rallies." They were surprised when I told them that with a military response almost inevitable, I didn't think it appropriate for the U.S. representative in the islands to be out rallying for world peace. Speedy victory, OK. But peace? No, not with the smoke still rising from lower Manhattan.

Our thoughts were with New York. I usually don't react emotionally to news reports, but this was different. What really got to me were the accents of the New Yorkers struggling through the smoke and debris, and, later, through the funerals. I'd been away for a long time, but these were voices that I had grown up with. These were my folks. This was a tribal thing. I still get choked up when images of 911 are shown on TV.

There's not much you can do when you are out in the middle of the Atlantic Ocean, but we did what we could. The Portuguese immigration authorities had stopped a couple of suspicious middle eastern men trying to get to Toronto via the Azores on false passports a few days before – we had them checked out (they turned out to be ordinary illegal immigrants). We beefed up security on the Consulate and kept in touch with the U.S. Air Force base on Terceira Island.

In the weeks and months after 9/11 my family had frequent reminders that we were all representatives of the United States. And we were very proud of it. Even Billy and Maria at times got caught up in our official duties. We were asked to participate in many 9/11 memorial ceremonies. One such event was carried out by Azorean firefighters. We had been given the impression that this would be a very small event, just the presentation of a wreath. They scheduled it for a Sunday afternoon, and we decided to simply work it into our normal Sunday visit to the shopping area near the Consulate. We were very surprised when, as we approached the site, we saw a very long parade of fire trucks led by a marching band approaching from the opposite direction. We instantly knew that this would not be a small event, and that we had to go into protocol mode.

All of us responded almost instinctively: Without being asked to do so, little Billy stood at attention by my side as the firefighters' proclamation was read. When I took three steps forward to make my remarks, Billy instinctively took three very military steps and stayed solemnly by my side, at what the military would call "the position of attention." One year-old Maria (in Elisa's arms) helped her mommy accept the memorial wreath (and made the front page of the newspapers). We were very proud of our kids that day.

Billy was old enough to know that something very bad had happened. He would often ask about "the men who crashed the building." For a time, he associated all bearded men with Al-Qaeda and the Taliban. This became a bit of a problem when our new Vice Consul (Robert Farquhar) turned out to be a bearded fellow.

Early in our tour of duty Elisa would sometimes drop Billy off at the Consulate – I'd let him play in my office as I worked. But after the terror threat increased Elisa and I became wary about letting the kids play in our

very vulnerable Consulate, so (sadly) Billy's visits to the office stopped.

Soon I was following the lead of the folks back in Washington by putting on an American flag lapel pin. I think it was an appropriate gesture, a reminder to others that we were closing ranks, that we'd been hurt. But it struck some outsiders as being a bit odd. One of the Ponta Delgada Honorary Consuls told me he found it to be a bit reminiscent of Soviet diplomats.

The Afghanistan operation seemed to come and go quite quickly. Then, during the summer of 2002 it became clear that we'd be going to war in Iraq. Many of our Portuguese contacts were not happy about this. During a social event Admiral Alvaro Gaspar, Commander of Portuguese Naval Forces in the Azores and one of our closest contacts in the islands, pointedly asked me what gave us the right to decide on our own – without UN Security Council approval – to go to war with Iraq. The fact that a guy like this – a submarine commander, a man who had spent his entire professional life in NATO – had serious qualms about what we were getting ready to do, well, it should have alerted me to the possibility that we were on the wrong track.

There were other signs that should have given us pause: Two Foreign Service officers were assigned to the Consulate in the Azores: I was the boss, and a more junior ranking officer took care of the visa and passport work. But there was a third FSO on the island: Jim McGunnigle was a retired Senior Foreign Service officer. He had served in the Azores early in his career. He and his wife had fallen in love with the place and had bought a house there. Jim stopped in one day as the war clouds were gathering. I was surprised to hear him say that he thought that war was not justified.

But like many people, we were willing to accept our government's dire warnings about Iraq's Weapons of Mass Destruction. I actually took a quote from George W. Bush and had it posted in our Consulate waiting room – it was the quote about how we'd rather face the terrorists with soldiers on foreign shores than with policemen and firemen in American cities.

In a sense, we were blinded by our patriotism. A recent article in "The Friends Journal" by Tony White describes this problem very well:

Patriotism clouds our judgment; it hinders objectivity and detracts from our ability to assess political situations rationally. Patriotism biases us towards our own country's perspective, encumbering our desire and ability to consider outside perspectives. Patriotism breeds conformity and closed mindedness. Furthermore, it makes us overly trusting of those in power over us, and susceptible to abuse of that power.

In an effort to help me, Elisa became America's most dedicated and passionate defender in the Azores. She responded whenever we got a snide comment about U.S. policy. Just weeks before the war started, we had our most difficult confrontation. At a going-away party for another senior Portuguese naval officer, after a number of after-dinner drinks had been served, Admiral Gaspar and the senior Portuguese Army officer in the region decided that the time was right for them to criticize our foreign policy. At first we tried to avoid a fight, but when they insisted, we responded. Vigorously. In Portuguese. It got ugly.

Defending U.S. Policy (over dinner)

The Azorean regional government was in the hands of the center-left Portuguese Socialist Party. They were not enthusiastic supporters of the war. My main mission was making sure that the regional government didn't in any way impede our use of Lajes Field. At one point they started making noises about denying access to the base to any U.S. soldiers who had been inoculated against anthrax. (The inoculation was due to biological warfare concerns; some in the Azores claimed – without justification – that the soldiers could transmit the disease.) I had to weigh in on this issue. Regional President Carlos Cesar was a very sensible guy, and he pledged full support, but in doing so he offered a warning that proved prophetic: "You Americans will have no trouble winning the war, but your problem will be winning the peace." Indeed.

Protests started even before we went to war. Most were outside the Consulate, but one afternoon while were out at the beach I got a call from Carlos the security guard reporting that there were demonstrators at the house. Carlos (who always downplayed bad news) called back to say it was all over. But when we got to the house the police (with dogs) and some of the demonstrators were still there. There was no trouble, but as we drove in, five year-old Billy saw the riot police with their mean-looking German

78

shepherd dogs. "Why did they bring those dogs to our house Daddy?" he kept asking. Elisa was also very upset that they had come to our house.

A few weeks into the war, as I left the Consulate after work, a woman turned to me and shouted angrily, "Peace, peace! We want peace." The next day we went to the birthday party of Alejandro, Billy's Spanish friend from school. There she was, the screaming peace activist. She was among the guests. This was a reminder of how small a place Ponta Delgada was, and how difficult it was for us to get away from our official duties.

By spring 2003, things were obviously coming to a boil. But, believe me, when you are out in the middle of the Atlantic Ocean, 900 miles off the coast of Portugal, it is hard to feel connected to these kinds of events. In the Consulate that spring, we were very focused on an official inspection of our little post. Personally, I was getting ready for our upcoming transfer to London. As part of my wrapping up of my Azorean duties, I decided to write a little article about our Consulate for the State Department's in-house magazine. One of the main messages of the article was that officers assigned to the American Consulate in Ponta Delgada have to accept that they will never be in the diplomatic lime-light, that they will never participate in the big events of the day. I recounted the rather sad story of one of my predecessors standing on the edge of the pier, waving forlornly as the ship carrying President Wilson to the Versailles peace conference passed to the south of the island. I had long ago accepted my position on the far outer periphery of American diplomacy. On the day that our inspection ended, I went home to have lunch with my wife. Together we planned a special weekend – it was our wedding anniversary. Then my cell phone rang.

My secretary back in the Consulate was close to hyperventilation: "The President (GASP) of the United (GASP) States (GASP) is coming (GASP) TO THE AZORES (GASP) THIS SUNDAY!"

I would have been incredulous had I not heard earlier in the day that the White House was looking around for a meeting site for a U.S.-UK-Spain pre-war meeting. I knew right away that they had chosen the Azores. Our anniversary plans were instantly scuttled and I started making preparations to go to base on Terceira where the big meeting would be held.

When I got there, the White House advance team had already arrived. I found them having lunch in the Officers' Club. The senior U.S. Air Force officers at the base were coping well, but they seemed to be in shock. And it was all quite shocking. We hurriedly made preparations for the arrival of the President of the United States. Brits were there working on Tony Blair's arrival. Spanish Prime Minister Aznar and Portuguese Prime Minister Barosso would also be there. It was all very intense. Security was beefed up considerably – there was a Secret Service sniper team setting up firing positions.

Ominously, as I moved around the base with the White House advance team, I could see first-hand the preparations for the war to come. The build-up in Kuwait was nearing completion, and Lajes Field was servicing large numbers of troop transport planes. It was a bit eerie to be talking to the staffers about the logistical details of the pre-war meeting, while watching the guys who would fight the war making their way to the battlefield.

I did what I could to help out (which wasn't much – the Air Force guys had it all in hand), but my mind was with my family back in Ponta Delgada. News of the meeting had sparked protests at many locations in Portugal, and we were worried that our house would again be targeted by demonstrators. The Consulate team really pulled together – the Vice Consul, Jay Barry, and our driver/security man, Mr. Francisco Silva, set up operations in our house and made sure that the family was protected.

Soon we watched Air Force One fly in, framed by the sea and the Azorean mountains. The meetings and press conference went off as scheduled. And we all took one more step closer to war.

I was still a true believer at this point. Over dinner with Bush communication adviser Karen Hughes I learned that they would be writing the President's "go to war" speech that night during the flight back to Washington. As they were all getting ready to go, I found myself standing there under the wing of the big blue and white "UNITED STATES OF AMERICA" 747, under the wing of Air Force One. Through the crowd, I saw National Security Advisor Condoleezza Rice making her way to the stairs. As she passed me I said to her, "Dr. Rice! Good luck!" (with the war that is). She thanked me. Later, this little exchange made me feel even more personally bitter about the lies that the people on that plane told us.

Bush at Lajes Field -- Author in upper right

The next day I was back in Ponta Delgada. I wrote up a report on the Presidential visit for the Embassy in Lisbon. In yet another sign of how polarized my thinking on this had become, I included some rather disdainful comments about the Portuguese protesters, and especially about one of the protest leaders who happened to be on the plane back to Ponta Delgada with me. Afterwards, a colleague in Embassy Lisbon sent me an e-mail reminding me that people were within their rights to oppose this war, and that I shouldn't be so scornful of those who did oppose it. He was, of course, correct. The war was launched soon after that Azores summit.

A few months later we moved to London. We'd assumed that the Embassy in London would be very well-protected and were looking forward to a respite from three years of crime-related security anxieties in Ponta Delgada. But we soon found that we had just traded one set of worries for another. And the new set of worries was directly connected to the war.

We were still on leave (I had not yet reported for duty at the Embassy) when I read in the UK newspapers that the Embassy was so concerned about the threat of a truck bomb attack that they were actually requesting that the UK government allow them to relocate – to Kensington Palace. This seemed pretty extreme – only a few steps short of asking for

Buckingham Palace – and got me worrying about the new hazard that we were now facing.

I tried to put this all out of my mind during those early months, but this was not easy. It is always hard to adjust to a new job, and the difficulty is heightened enormously by the thought that the new job might leave your kids without their dad. For me, this was not a remote or abstract scenario: one of my classmates in the Foreign Service's orientation program for new junior officers, Michelle Denny, had been killed by an Al Qaeda truck bomb attack on the U.S. Embassy in Nairobi in 1998. Michelle left behind small children. Fatherhood definitely changes your perspective: I was really surprised to find myself far more worried about security in London than I had been when I was in El Salvador during that country's civil war. To make matters worse, in August, just as we were settling in, the UN Headquarters in Baghdad was obliterated by a truck bomb. We all read the gruesome tale of the senior UN rep slowly dying under the rubble (apparently while in cell phone contact with the outside world).

One Saturday soon after that attack, I took the kids to the park at St. Mary of the Boltons. There I ran into a senior UK Foreign Office diplomat. We got to talking about our work. Suddenly in a sardonic tone he asked me if it was true that we were trying to move into Kensington Palace. I tried to deal with the question by pointing out that a lot of the pressure on this issue was coming not from us, but from our British neighbors in Mayfair. I was hoping that he'd just nod and change the subject, but instead, as the kids played on the swings under the summer sun, he sent me into a bit of a funk by replying cheerily, "Yes, well of course! Those neighbors are all afraid of being blown to bits with you people!"

Sadly, we did end up being quite close to terrorist carnage in London...

It had been a week of highs and lows: on Saturday, July 2, 2005 they had a big rock concert in Hyde Park. 200,000 people gathered on the field that I had walk across each day on my way to and from work. Early on the morning of the concert I had to go into the Embassy, so I had to walk through the crowds a bit. Everyone was in a very good mood. Because the concert was aimed at getting the G8 summit to approve more aid for Africa, this concert had been a part of my work for weeks. A friend from the Embassy and I had gone (uninvited) to the press conference in which Bob Geldof (with Elton John at his side) had announced the event. We didn't go to the concert, but we ended up watching lots of it on television. The kids and I had watched Bono and U2 open the concert. I stayed up late to catch the return (after 20 years) of Pink Floyd.

Then came the G8 summit in Scotland. Many colleagues went up to assist with that event, but I was spared and stayed in London. The President arrived on Wednesday afternoon.

Wednesday was also the day on which the Olympic committee would make its announcement about the winner of the selection process for the 2012 Olympics. London was in the running, in a close competition with Paris. We knew that the announcement would be made at 12:45, but I'd forgotten about it and at that hour found myself on my usual lunchtime walk through Hyde Park. Suddenly the quiet was shattered by the roar of RAF fighters buzzing London, trailing the colors of the Union Jack. "The Olympics!" said a passerby. Elisa and the kids were at that moment on the upper deck of a red London bus, passing through Piccadilly Square – they saw the news announced on one of the big screens. London had won the right to host the 2012 games. The Brits were very happy to have won, and especially by beating the French. Earlier in the week Chirac had insulted British cuisine, making London's win even more delightful.

On Thursday, July 7, I got off to a late start. I walked up to South Ken station and caught a 74 bus – a red double-decker. It was shortly before 9 when I got into the Embassy. In the elevator, British employees were complaining about a difficult commute. One guy commented that the Piccadilly line had been shut down due to smoke in the tunnel. I thought this was just normal maintenance trouble in the ancient tube system.

Around 9:20 I got a call from Elisa. After dropping Maria off at school, she'd gone to the news agent's kiosk on Fulham Road. Mrs. Amin (the wife of the owner) had come running in, in a panic. She'd told her husband that there'd been an explosion at the Liverpool Street tube station. Their daughters use that station to get to school.

I turned on the TV, and saw the reports of trouble in the London Tube (underground) system. Sky News reported that British authorities were saying that it was all caused by a power surge and exploding transformers. So I stopped paying attention. Then, about an hour later, one of our interns walked into my office and told me that a bus had exploded. Suddenly, we knew this was no power surge. We knew that London was under terrorist attack.

America was still sleeping, but I knew they'd wake up to the bad news. So I sent a "we're OK" e-mail to my siblings.

Billy and Maria stayed in school. The authorities decided the kids would be safer staying put. Later, Elisa offered to take kids in if their parents were unable to pick them up – London's tube remained closed through the day and traffic was bound to be terrible.

At work, London suddenly became eerily quiet – fearing an attack on the Embassy, the police had cut off vehicle traffic on all the roads around us. Inside, Marines patrolled the corridors. One young Marine looked quite shaken. He told me he'd never been through anything like this, and that he was worried because he couldn't reach his girlfriend. I tried to reassure him. I told him that the cell phone network very quickly collapsed with all the "are you OK?" calls.

We got through a very sad day. I called a couple of friends in the British government who lived far out of town and offered them a place to stay if they couldn't get home. I walked home at my normal time. I expected clogged streets, but they were relatively empty. Many shops had closed and sent their people home. The tube system was closed down, but even with the wreckage from that ill-fated #30 bus still in the street, the rest of London's buses were already back on the road.

We found the whole thing very sad, depressing. Fifty two people had been killed and more than 700 injured. Elisa, Billy, Mama Yuya and Cousin Juani had been riding the Piccadilly line on the day prior to the attack. Just weeks before Maria and her 30 little classmates had gone into the tube on a class trip. And of course I used those happy, iconic double-decker buses every day. It was very depressing to think that people would go into those trains and buses with bombs in their backpacks. It was more depressing than scary.

On Saturday we went to a barbecue at Maria's beloved Bousefield School. "Were you in London on Thursday?" parents asked each other, quietly, out of ear-shot so the kids wouldn't be reminded of what had happened.

****

During our first months in London we still believed in the war effort. I remember us being very impressed by George Bush's surprise Thanksgiving visit to Baghdad. (When I mentioned this approvingly to a colleague from Her Majesty's Government – a fellow who spoke Arabic and knew the Middle East very well – he just kind of rolled his eyes and shook his head at what I'm sure he saw as sappy American naiveté.)

Part of my job was working with the British on "reconstruction" efforts in Iraq and Afghanistan, so I was in close touch with developments in those countries. Little by little (but, I admit, too slowly), I began having doubts about the war in Iraq. There was, of course, the failure to find the weapons of mass destruction. But also, I began to notice that the people that Washington was sending to Iraq were not very impressive. We got a look at many of these political appointees as they came through London en route to or from Baghdad. Few of them seemed to know anything about Iraq, or the Arab world. None of them spoke Arabic. They all seemed to have some political connection to the White House and appeared to be grabbing for what – at the time – seemed like potentially profitable appointments in the new Iraq.

In one very memorable incident, one of these appointees flew back to London from Baghdad, ostensibly for consultations with the Brits. We set up the meetings – the Brits were taking it very seriously and put together a big inter-agency session at the Foreign Office. Our man from Baghdad may have made some Anglo-American protocol history that day: None of us could recall a visiting U.S. official ever before showing up for a meeting at the venerable Foreign and Commonwealth Office WITH A DATE. Not an appointment – a DATE! A woman! Indeed, this may have been a first. In his introduction to the UK officials, the appointee noted that he had helped the Bush team with the Florida re-count during the 2000 election (the Brits did not seem impressed). Then he introduced the young woman who was with him: "This is my friend Sofia," he said with a coy, Rodney Dangerfield-like smile, "She's traveling with me. She'll just be sitting in on this meeting..." When the session ended, they quickly headed off to see a show. The Brits were amazed; we were embarrassed. The whole thing just reeked of amateurism.

My faith in Bush and in his Iraq war collapsed completely April 2004, a little over one year from the start of the conflict. The insurgency was, by then, in full swing, and our objectives and plans seemed to change almost every day. Then came Abu Ghraib.

I'd seen the shocking photos of U.S. soldiers abusing Iraqi prisoners on the internet before I got to the office, but several colleagues had not yet seen them. We had the British newspapers spread out on our conference table. One senior officer walked in, saw the pictures and immediately said, "Oh well this is in the *The Guardian*... you don't really believe this actually happened do you?" I had to burst her bubble by pointing out that there were no denials coming out of the U.S. headquarters in Iraq. In fact, U.S. Generals were already apologizing, and pledging to punish the perpetrators. She really found this hard to believe. This kind of reality denial became quite common in the years to come – it seemed that many Americans are so deeply wedded to the notion that we are – by definition – "the good guys" that they find it almost impossible to believe that we would engage in the kind of sadistic depravity that took place in that prison.

Abu Ghraib was especially troubling for me, because just months earlier, I had very sincerely and publicly defended the way in which U.S. soldiers were treating prisoners. As part of the Embassy's "public diplomacy" program (the new Ambassador had apparently been told by the White House to "do something" about the Bush administrations shockingly low poll numbers in the UK) I'd been sent out to talk to a group of adult university students. One nice English lady had asked about reports of prisoner abuse by U.S. forces in Afghanistan. I very confidently dismissed these reports, assuring the woman that U.S. military forces were highly disciplined, had clear rules on how to treat prisoners, and that this kind of abuse simply couldn't happen. In fact, I said, prisoners held by us were probably living very comfortable lives. I thought about that little speech as I read the reports on Abu Ghraib.

Then it got worse. The State Department had been sending officers to Baghdad to help staff the new occupation government – the "Coalition Provisional Authority." Shortly after the Abu Ghraib story broke, one of them returned to London on leave. He came in to the Embassy and gave us a briefing on what was going on in Baghdad. The tone reflected the arrogant cockiness of the Bush administration and their CPA minions in Baghdad. ("If you don't like what we're doing there, well, we have extra helmets and flak jackets – critics are free to volunteer to come on down!") When I asked about Abu Ghraib, the briefing turned very disturbing: this guy actually defended the sexual humiliation that the American soldiers had engaged in, claiming that this kind of thing was necessary in order to deter attacks on American personnel.

I was the only one in the room who voiced objections to these comments. I noted that American soldiers had been dealing with prisoners for a long-time, and that what we'd seen at Abu Ghraib was very definitely wrong, very clearly criminal behavior. (During the 1980s I had worked with prisoners of war in Central America so I had a good sense of how completely beyond the pale the Abu Ghraib incident was.) The briefer wouldn't budge. He again justified what had happened as being necessary to "protect American lives." I didn't realize it at the time, but this little briefing was probably my first encounter with what would become – for me – one of the most despicable elements of the Bush administration's conduct of the war in Iraq: The apparent belief that American lives are somehow inherently more valuable than the lives of people from other countries. Over the next few years I saw many examples of this. You'd see it in the way casualties were counted (Americans were counted with great precision, but they didn't even bother to count Iraqi dead), in the response to the killing of Iraqi civilians (our military guys usually used the very hypothetical word "regrettable"), in the sudden abandonment of our generations-old opposition to torture. The word seemed to be out: Anything goes if you can claim that it helps protect American lives.

This approach did not go down well with the Brits. I'd discovered earlier in my tour in London that our special relationship with our British cousins will only get you so far, and will often bring more grief than support. You see, the British know us very well. In other countries, in a situation like this the language barrier often works to our advantage: sometimes it seems that the foreigners don't quite understand what's going on. They can't really listen in on our internal debate. They don't have the background to completely digest it all. Not so with the Brits. They understand every syllable, every bit of nuance. They know. They can't be fooled. "Oh come off it!" is one of their favorite phrases, and they particularly enjoy using it on Americans. One of my bosses was shocked when, soon after his arrival in London, a very distinguished upper-class Brit abruptly cut him off in mid-sentence as he tried to defend U.S policy. "No," said the Brit, "you people have gone completely off the rails." We got a lot of that. During 2004, UK newspapers reported that British officers in Iraq were very upset about the way our troops treated Iraqis – one memorable report quoted a UK officer saying that we treated them as (using the Nazi phrase) "unter-menschen." Sub-humans.

Very early on, I started to hear critical comments about U.S. military behavior even from the diplomatic representatives of the new Iraqi government. At a diplomatic reception, I spoke with Iraq's first post-Saddam Ambassador to Britain. I was surprised to find him openly critical of the U.S. military forces that had so recently liberated his country from the tyrant. He spoke of the "cultural insensitivity" of the U.S. soldiers. I fired back and defended our troops, pointing out that they are soldiers, not diplomats, and that they were – as we spoke – risking their lives in a shooting war. The Ambassador seemed unmoved by my comments. Back in the Embassy, colleagues with experience in the Middle East dismissed the Ambassador's remarks. "Oh the Iraqis are just chronic complainers," they claimed.

The negative feedback wasn't coming only from our official contacts. Central London has a large Iraqi population centered in the Bayswater neighborhood, very close to the U.S. Embassy, and not far from where we lived. There were Iraqi kids in school with our kids. Elisa got to know little Mohammed's mom, and one cold winter afternoon early in 2005 asked her about her family. As she spoke about Baghdad, the woman started to cry. Not knowing that Elisa was married to a U.S. diplomat, she candidly described the terror of life under U.S. occupation, the fear of the checkpoints, the fear that results from having tens of thousands of heavily armed foreign teenagers in your home town.

After Abu Ghraib, each day seemed to bring news that deepened my conviction that this war was a disastrous mistake. On a shelf behind my desk at the Embassy I started to collect articles that documented the ongoing catastrophe; the pile of articles grew very quickly.

On Memorial Day, 2006, I got a very poignant reminder of the toll that this war was taking on American families. A large Congressional delegation led by Speaker of the House Dennis Hastert came to the UK to conduct a memorial service at the American military cemetery near Cambridge. I was the Embassy representative on the visit. The cemetery looks a lot like Arlington national cemetery – thousands of neatly lined-up tombstones, each representing a fallen U.S. serviceman. Several of the Congressmen were veterans of WWII. The U.S. Air Force sent fighter jets from RAF Lakenheath to fly a "missing man" formation over the cemetery. At precisely the right moment, the jets roared overhead, with one of them arcing upward, representing those who'd been lost. At about this time a cell phone rang, and a U.S. Air Force Colonel who was accompanying the delegation stepped away to take the call. Thinking that there might be some logistical problem with the plane that was to carry the group to their next stop, I asked him about the call. It wasn't about the airplane. The Colonel told me that the call was from Walter Reed Army Hospital. He told me that his son, an Army officer, had been wounded in Iraq – the call was an update on his boy's condition. Surprised, I asked if his son was going to be all right. With sorrow, the Colonel told me that the wounds were very serious. He'd survive, but it was obvious that they were dealing with devastating, life-changing injuries. Suddenly, the cost of war was no longer represented only by those tombstones from battles 60 years in the past.

This was, of course, a multifaceted tragedy – there were many things to be upset about. As a former army officer, of course I was appalled by the toll this war was taking on our soldiers. But perhaps because of my professional and family background, I was also very concerned about what used to be called the "hearts and minds" aspects of the situation: how our actions in Iraq were causing us to lose the support of the people we had supposedly gone out to liberate.

The core principal that guided our work on insurgency and counter-insurgency in Central America was the notion that the key to success was winning and sustaining the support of the people of the region. One of my army superiors had said, "The only important territory in Central America is the area between the ears of the ordinary Central American citizen."

Reading reports on prisoner abuse, and "regrettable" collateral damage to civilians, it was obvious to me that we weren't going to be winning any hearts and minds in Iraq. From my perch at the Embassy at Grosvenor Square I could see that we couldn't even maintain the support of the British people.

But more than my professional background, I think my personal, family background was what made the stories out of Iraq so disturbing. War is the ultimate manifestation of nationalism, of the "us and them" mentality. When we go to war, we've essentially decided that our differences with THEM are so severe that we can actually KILL THEM. It's bad enough when soldiers are being killed, but it gets even more horrifying when the killing sanction is extended to civilians. And that's what all those articles in the pile behind my London desk said was happening. Sadly, the Brits seemed to be right – we did sometimes seem to be treating Iraqis as "untermenschen."

In 2006 we went back to the Dominican Republic to visit my wife's family. Whenever we go back there is a steady stream of friends and relatives coming to see us. We had CNN beaming in by satellite, so I could keep up with the latest news, which at that point was dominated by depressing reports of continued carnage in Iraq. A few of the stories focused on the plight of ordinary Iraqi families caught up in the mayhem. As I turned from the TV and returned to the family gathering around my father-in-law's dining room table, I was struck by how much the scene in our Dominican home looked like the televised scenes from those Iraqi homes. There was the same kind of multi-generational mix, a similar spectrum of skin colors. Even the construction of the houses seemed somewhat similar. Of course, I knew that we were dealing with two vastly different cultures, but it occurred to me that the hyper-nationalist military mentality that rationalized the killing of tens of thousands of Iraqi civilians could easily be applied to MY relatives in that Dominican living room. After all, like the Iraqis, they too were not citizens of the United States. They too were not us. Their collateral damage deaths would, I suppose, be termed "regrettable."

Back in London, the mess in Iraq was having an impact on our personal interactions with people. Being a U.S. diplomat started to feel – as the Brits would put it – "a bit dodgy." Long accustomed to being the good guys, it wasn't a lot of fun to now be wearing the black hats. Even among the Americans in London, you got the sense that by working in the Embassy you were seen as doing something of questionable morality. And this attitude was coming not from a bunch of fuzzy headed liberals – we were getting this from bankers working in the City of London.

Things got even worse when Israel invaded Lebanon. Suddenly, Lebanese civilians were being added to the pile of regrettable collateral casualties. For me, the Lebanon war was a particularly striking example of the inequities and absurdities that arise from the "us-versus-them" nationalistic mindset. As an army almost completely subsidized by the United States rolled north into Lebanon killing people with weaponry made in the U.S., we mounted a hurried diplomatic effort not to stop carnage – but to evacuate from the area any American citizens who might be in harm's way.

Leaving aside the rationales and justifications for the war, at a personal level, looking at it from London's hyper-cosmopolitan "international zone" it all just seemed so absurd, so unfair. We were all living in an area in which there was an unspoken understanding that "nationality doesn't really matter" yet we were watching on TV kids being killed largely because of their nationality, while our government scrambled to get "our" people out of the way.

For a lot of Brits, Lebanon seemed like the last straw. I got angry e-mails from friends who'd lived largely apolitical lives. It was even too much for Elisa. Outraged by the images of suffering streaming out of Lebanon, Elisa and the kids organized a little sidewalk violin concert in front of our house. Following the example of London's street musicians, the violin cases were left open to collect the coins of passers-by. A sign announced that the money would go to the children of Lebanon. I'm ashamed to say that I had mixed feelings about that little concert. On the one hand, what could be wrong with raising money for wounded children? But on the other hand I knew that this could be seen as a rebuke of U.S. policy, and I was in London to support U.S. policy. Briefly, the war in Lebanon seemed to work its way into our kitchen – Elisa and I had an argument about the concert. Of course, she was right. In retrospect, the fact that this noble effort made me worry about a possible conflict with U.S. policy... well, that's a clear indication that there was something wrong not with the concert, but with the policy. My angst notwithstanding, the concert was a big success. At one point a professional violinist from across the street heard the music and joined in, at first playing from his apartment window, then later coming down to the street to join in. Even though the kids at that point knew only two or three tunes, they collected several hundred pounds sterling; they later delivered the money to the Red Cross.

****

There is a stuffy little meeting room in the basement of the U.S. Embassy in London. It is kind of wedged between the cafeteria and the Embassy's in-house pub ("The Regal Eagle" – get it?). Some time ago some ambitious embassy management officer must have seen some promotion potential in the idea of naming various rooms for famous American statesmen. Poor Ben Franklin somehow got the basement room. They acquired a nice portrait of Mr. Franklin in profile with one of his best loved quotes inscribed below:

"They that can give up essential liberty to purchase a little temporary safety, deserve neither liberty nor safety."

We didn't get down to that meeting room too often, one day, during the darkest period of the Bush administration, during the time of

91

waterboarding, enemy combatants, extraordinary rendition and all the other assaults on civil liberties, we gathered in the Franklin Room to discuss some mundane Embassy matter (probably the visit of a Congressman). As we waited for the meeting to begin, several of us looked at Franklin and his quote. Somebody asked – only half sarcastically I think – whether we should take that quote down: "Is that really still consistent with Administration policy?" It was really sad. But I guess it served as a useful reminder of the synthetic and ephemeral nature of claims to national distinctiveness, ours included. And of course, once you throw the Bill of Rights under the bus, with it you discard any claims of American exceptionalism.

When I went to school I was taught that the essence of the American national identity was the core set of political principles embodied in our Constitution. We were different from other countries – our sense of "us" was based not on the kind of old ethnic or racial identities that defined the nations of the old world. We were a nation of immigrants, open to all, bound together by principles, principles that we would adhere to, no matter what. We'd let the nut case neo-Nazis march, even in poor old Skokie, Illinois, because civil liberties were important, and we were absolutist in our commitment to them. So when after 9-11 our commitment to these principles started to waiver – when people began to accept the idea that we had to somehow "balance" freedom and security – this raised questions about our national identity. If we are no longer the people with an absolute commitment to the principles spelled out in our Bill of Rights, well, who are we? This was an especially vexing question for someone stationed in Britain, a country that, in spite of the terrorist threat, seemed far less cavalier than we were about abandoning core-value civil liberties.

We sometimes got reminders of the fact that many of the folks back home were still strongly supportive of the war, and of the us-versus-them mentality that supported it. During the summer of 2004 we went back to the U.S. on home leave. We went to the beach with my siblings and their families. We really tried not to talk about politics, but some of them kind of forced us to do so. I think they expected us to be enthusiastic about the Iraq operation, and disappointed when they found out what we really thought about it.

A bit later we were visited in London by American friends. They are evangelical Christians, and they definitely share in the conservative political views that often seem to come with fundamentalist religious beliefs. (Elisa and I had decided to overlook the fact that they were associated with an evangelical university at which we would have been prohibited from dating each other.) Trying to be nice hosts, and knowing

92

that prayers at dinner time would be part of their routine at home, we asked them to say grace at our table. We soon found that even dinner prayers had become politicized and militarized: Each night, our visitors would pray for the American soldiers in Iraq.

Of course, we had no objection to that – in my house, as I was growing up, evening prayers always included "a prayer for our boys in Vietnam." But we found the tone and content of these Iraq war prayers troublesome. They almost seemed to be assuming that God was on our team, that God should share in our special concern for people of our nationality, that God was American.

After a couple nights of this, I asked our visitors if they would include in the evening prayer a few words on behalf of the innocent Iraqi civilians who were being killed and maimed in the war. They seemed really surprised by this request. They eventually complied – sort of – but their prayers for Iraqis definitely lacked the zeal used in the prayers for U.S. troops.

Around this time, a movie came out that seemed to capture British sentiments about everything that was going on, and about us. "Love Actually" starred Hugh Grant (who happened to live in our neighborhood). Grant plays a somewhat flustered and uncertain British Prime Minister who, of course, falls in love. It is mostly a love story, but the tension in the movie is provided by the Americans. The British officials were portrayed as reasonable, rather docile chaps. The Americans seem to barge into every meeting armed to the teeth with power-point slides, exuding arrogance and confidence, and prepared to give the hapless Brits their marching orders. I have to say, there was an element of truth to this – very often our approach seemed to be summed up by the phrase "our way or the highway!"

In the movie, the visiting U.S. President was almost reptilian, sort of an amalgam of the worst personal features of LBJ, Nixon, Clinton, and W. The tension comes to a head when the President makes a pass at the girl who the Prime Minister is falling in love with. This results in what became known in the (real) British political vernacular as "The Love Actually Moment." Hugh Grant's character calls a press conference, takes to the podium, asserts British independence and publicly breaks with U.S. policy. At the corner cinema on Fulham Road near our house, this "love actually moment" caused the normally phlegmatic Brits to burst into cheers and applause.

****

Our tour in London also provided some glimpses into the military industrial complex that President Eisenhower had warned us about, and that depends so much on nationalism: During a visit to the UK of NASA Administrator Mike Griffin, a visit to the Farnboro Air Show was on the agenda. As a lifelong fan of airplanes and rocket ships, I opted to go along on that trip.

With memories of the airshow in Rhinebeck N.Y that my dad had taken me to as a kid, I guess I was expecting the show to be focused on the joy of flight, and scientific advances, and cool new airplanes. Instead I found a trade show of the death and destruction industry. Spread out around an English military airport, the marketing machines of the world's major arms manufacturers had set up the facilities to hawk their wares. It was like one of those itinerant carnival amusement parks – lots of make-shift cabling, lots of temporary vans haphazardly parked on stomped down grass. But instead of Ferris wheels and merry-go-rounds there were "pavilions" presenting the latest products of Northrup-Grumman, and Lockheed Martin, and BAE Systems.

The atmosphere inside the pavilions was like that of an auto show for very high-end cars. Professionally cheery young women (the so-called "booth-babes") greeted us at each pavilion (Griffin had a budget of 17 billion dollars, so he was greeted with great enthusiasm.) But instead of cars, these people were presenting the latest bombs, bombers and missiles. There seemed to be a very deliberate effort to sugar-coat and sanitize the products, to gloss over what it is that they really do. One carefully crafted wall display, for example, extolled the virtues of a new missile that was "capable of engaging the full spectrum of targets." A picture in the background showed people and buildings and tanks and ships. I guess that was the "spectrum." Perhaps the marketing guys figured that something like "Rips apart everything from infants to aircraft carriers!" would be a bit too strong.

It was a very hot day, made even hotter and more unpleasant by the huge generator-powered cooling systems attached to each of the sales pavilions. As we wound our way under the hot sun to our awaiting van, we struggled through hot exhausts from the air conditioners, then through the deafening roar and nauseating fumes of the generators. That little walk to the car seemed to sum it all up: Death and destruction were the products; noise, pollution and global warming the side effects. It was like a visit to the military-industrial circle of Dante's Inferno. I was glad to get out of there. The whole thing made me want to take a shower.

There is a statue of General Eisenhower in front of our Embassy in London. I walked past it on my way back from Farnboro. Of course I can't be sure, but I suspect he might have had a similar reaction to that air show:

Every gun that is made, every warship launched, every rocket fired signifies in the final sense, a theft from those who hunger and are not fed, those who are cold and are not clothed. This world in arms is not spending money alone. It is spending the sweat of its laborers, the genius of its scientists, the hopes of its children. This is not a way of life at all in any true sense. Under the clouds of war, it is humanity hanging on a cross of iron. ~Dwight D. Eisenhower, speech, American Society of Newspaper Editors, 16 April 1953

****

By the time we got to Rome, we were completely fed up with the mindset and thinking that had led to the war in Iraq. Looking ahead to the national elections of 2008, obviously we were not going to vote for the party that had led us into this madness. Sometime in 2007 Elisa came across a book by a fellow named Barack Obama. She really liked it. I was skeptical – I just didn't think was possible for a black man to be elected president in our country. But Elisa brought me around. She was very enthused. She got in touch with the Rome "Democrats Abroad" group and volunteered to help make sure that the many U.S. citizens in Rome were registered to vote and had access to absentee ballots.

Every election year, the State Department would send out to Embassies a cable outlining the election do's and don'ts for U.S. government employees. The guidance for Embassy personnel was essentially the same as that for federal employees back home. It was all very reasonable and common sense: Essentially you could participate in the democratic process as long as you kept it separate from your work. We were careful about staying within the guidance. (Sadly, the State Department later changed their guidance; Embassy personnel and their spouses are now prohibited from doing the kinds of things that Elisa did.)

Elisa really got into it. She visited the schools at which Americans were studying and distributed pro-Obama material to Americans at tourist sites. She even made a speech (in English, for a gathering of Americans) at Rome's famous Piazza Venezia. It was all a wonderful experience for her, and we were very pleased that the kids were getting chance to see American democracy in action. All of this seemed to serve almost as an anti-venom for the years of Bush-era Iraq war poison.

Tension built up all during 2008. Like many people, we became obsessed with the polls and addicted to Real Clear Politics. Jon Stewart, Steven Colbert and the Saturday Night Live crew provided comic relief and Will-I-Am played on our car stereo.

Election night was time shifted for us. We tried to stay up for the results, but we were too tired. I tossed and turned and finally got up around 4 am Rome time. When I turned on the TV, the first words I heard were "and there is a celebration in Arizona tonight!" Oh no! I thought. Could we have lost? It took me a few tense minutes to figure out that things were in fact looking good in Ohio and Pennsylvania.

Elisa came out to the living room just as the polls were closing in California. She was still wiping the sleep from her eyes, when Wolf Blitzer announced that Obama had won. Elisa thought Blitzer was calling a single state, not the whole thing. I explained and she went nuts. There was a lot of jumping up and down and yelling and phone calling.

The next morning Billy and I went down to Alberto's grocery store. Everyone there knew we were Americans, and they all knew what had happened. But Italians are very private about their politics and especially about how they vote – they do not wear their political hearts on their sleeves. So even though we knew that Obama would have taken 95% of the Trastevere vote, the grocery store crowd was, that morning, kind of restrained. But there were a lot of coy smiles and you could almost feel a desire to yell, and jump, and high-five.

When I got to the cash register, Alberto smiled and said to us, "Ha vinto!" ("He won!") A woman behind us in the line added some emphasis: "Ha *stra*vinto!" ("He won BIG!") Everyone smile. It was a good day to be an American in Trastevere. For us, that marked the beginning of the end of the Iraq insanity.

****

Obviously our contact with the bases and our observations on the Iraq war had contributed to the shift in worldview that we experienced during our decade abroad. But there was something else going on in our lives that I think had a more profound effect. Amidst all this military madness, we were raising a son, someone who, if he followed in the family's military traditions could easily find himself in a few short years in the big green patriotic machine. When I was growing up, my father had encouraged my brother and me to serve in the military (we both did). Indeed, my involvement in Special Forces may have been the result of my dad taking the family to see John Wayne's movie "The Green Beret." I remember it well – we went to a drive-in in the family station wagon.   My father's worldview was based on WWII patriotism.   His only experience outside North America was the South Pacific in 1945 and '46.   People of his generation never questioned the patriotic assumptions that cause people to see military service as a necessary and virtuous experience.   But I had had a very different set of experiences, and when I talked to my young son, I found myself hoping that he wouldn't follow in those boot steps, that he would never have to learn how to use white phosphorus and Claymore mines.

HOSPITALS AND DOCTORS

"So little fellow, where are you from?" asked the nurse during a home leave medical exam. My 9 year-old son furrowed his brow, thought for a few seconds, and replied (quite sincerely), "I don't know."

"The only real nation is humanity." Paul Farmer M.D.

I came very close to being arrested in the emergency room of the Spiritu Santo Hospital in Ponta Delgada. It was near the end of our time on the island. Elisa had had a bad reaction to some dental anesthetic, and for several weeks she'd been in very bad shape, often hovering on the verge of passing out. We'd been in frequent phone contact with the nurse at the American Embassy in Lisbon, and finally it reached the point where I needed to take my wife to the emergency room.

We'd been on the island for almost three years. We knew a lot of people, and felt like we knew our way around. I'd been in and out of that emergency room several times over the years, usually looking in on American citizens who – usually through bizarre circumstances – had found themselves in need of emergency care in the middle of the Atlantic Ocean: One lady had been thrown off her cruise ship when she developed symptoms of heart trouble. There had been a nineteen year-old American sailor who'd taken a bad fall on the aircraft carrier George Washington, and had been flown to us for emergency surgery. In each case, "O Consul Americano" (me) had been given access to the emergency room. But on that day that I brought Elisa in, the staff suddenly decided to get very rigid about the rules.

We spoke to the triage nurse. She didn't seem very concerned. She seemed to assign Elisa a low priority, and said that she'd have to stand-by in the waiting room. OK, no problem, but I said I wanted to wait with her. I explained that she was woozy, that she'd had allergic reactions that had almost closed her airway, and that her Portuguese wasn't that strong. Could I please wait with her?

At this point, the Portuguese medical bureaucracy started to rigidly enforce the waiting room rules. A young doctor was called. No, he insisted, Elisa would have to wait alone. I tried to reason with him, emphasizing that Elisa might not be able to clearly explain her symptoms to them, and that she might just pass out (and pass away) unnoticed in the waiting room. He wouldn't budge. Who knows? Maybe he didn't like Americans. Maybe he just enjoyed exerting a little power over a family

98

seen as being prominent. Whatever the reason for this silliness, I just couldn't leave Elisa there alone, so I had to insist. I refused to leave. It got kind of ugly. The doctor threatened to call the police. I called the Consulate and asked them to brief the police chief (a good contact of ours) on my possibly imminent arrest.

The standoff continued for too long. Elisa was getting more upset. Finally, I told the doctor that perhaps he should start acting less like a lawyer and more like a physician. He shot back that if we were unhappy with him, we should ask for another doctor, which I promptly did. His replacement was more interested in medicine than rules and regulations. Soon Elisa was being cared for and admitted. And I didn't have to go to jail.

There is a hackneyed old phrase about the best way to gain insights on a foreign culture. According to this old line, you should visit the whore houses and the cemeteries. I don't know about that – I don't have ANY experience with the former, and only a few visits to the latter. But instead of whorehouses and cemeteries, I'd suggest that schools and the hospitals are the best places to get insights about foreign societies. Our two kids have been very healthy, but they had the normal share of sniffles, fevers, scraped knees, and bumped heads. My wife had some medical problems also, and I ended our decade abroad with the rather spectacular rupture of my Achilles tendon mentioned at the beginning of this book. So we got a good look at the hospitals and medical systems of all three countries, and I think we did gain some insights. And of course we learned a few things about our own medical culture.

In the summer of 2000, we departed from the U.S. as very satisfied users of the U.S. medical system. Elisa had had a difficult first pregnancy. There was pre-term labor, Billy arrived about 6 weeks early, and Elisa's blood pressure rose to dangerous levels right after she gave birth. Billy had an apnea episode, so for his first few months he was on a heart and breathing monitor. The second pregnancy was a bit easier, but by the time we left the Washington area, my Blue Cross/Blue shield card practically had the numbers worn off of it.

One of our first priorities in the Azores was finding a pediatrician. We'd heard there was a Spanish-speaking doctor on the island, so we went to him first. Unfortunately he'd been in the Azores for so long that his Spanish had kind of merged with his Portuguese, severely limiting any communication advantage that working with him might afford. And somehow he and Elisa just didn't click, so we went to see another pediatrician. I'll call him Dr. Montes. In his office we found excellent care, but we also experienced a medical culture clash, and took a 50 year trip back in time in the area of doctor-patient relations.

The physical setting of Azorean medical offices was very different. Gone was the air of cool efficiency that marked our doctors' offices back in Virginia. After a time in the waiting room (that part was just like home) we went in to see the doctor. The office was very small, and very warm. The Azoreans are not big on air conditioning, or even fresh air. (During one early meeting with the Consulate's local staff, a sneeze from me caused one local employee to make a semi-panicked dive for nearby open window. You'd have thought he was a security agent trying to protect me from an incoming bullet. Azoreans believe that fresh air causes disease.) The windows in Dr. Montes's office appeared to be painted shut. Sweat was running down my back as we discussed the children's medical care. Well "discuss" is not really the right verb. What really happened was that Dr. Montes gave us a brief overview of how things would work: he would make all the decisions, and we would follow his instructions. Welcome to 1950!

Dr. Montes produced the Portuguese list of necessary childhood vaccinations. We immediately noticed that on the list was a tuberculosis vaccine. We told the doctor that the U.S. Embassy had recommended that our kids NOT get the TB vaccine. We explained that this vaccine is not given to American kids, and that if our kids received it, when they got back to the U.S. they would test positive for TB and might be placed in some sort of quarantine at the beginning of every school year. Dr. Montes reacted unhappily to our effort to get involved in medical decisions, and seemed totally undeterred by our TB-shot argument. He insisted that the kids would get the shot. Politely, we insisted they would not. He grew somewhat exasperated. In an effort to convince us, he said with some emotion: "Look, if Maria gets TB, will those people in the U.S. Embassy who you are quoting be taking care of her?" I think he expected us to relent, but the argument kind of ended when we quietly told him that, yes, in the event of a serious illness the State Department doctors would take charge, and would send us back to the USA.

We can't be too hard on Dr. Montes. He is a great pediatrician and took wonderful care of our kids. And on the vaccination issue we later experienced the U.S. flip-side of this kind of medical cultural problem: We were back in Northern Virginia on home leave. Elisa wanted to take the kids in for check-ups with their American pediatricians. The American doctor looked through the kids' files, and briefly focused on the vaccination records. She saw something that bothered her. At first I worried that we might have missed some important shot. But no. The problem was cultural: "Look at the way this Portuguese doctor has written the dates in the shot record," she said, holding the familiar yellow multilingual World Health Organization card. "He wrote ALL the dates incorrectly. He put the day first, then the month! They are ALL wrong!" I thought she must have been kidding. Surely she must have known that this is the way Europeans write dates. "Come on doctor, 300 million Europeans can't all be wrong!" I joked. She didn't laugh. "No, he has written the dates incorrectly. When you get back to Portugal please tell him how the dates should be written and ask him to write them correctly in the future." She was dead serious.

****

By the time we got to the Azores, Elisa had been through an enormous amount of change in a very short period: In less than four years she had married, moved from her home country to the United States, learned English, had two children, and, while still nursing a baby and with a toddler in tow, had moved to an island in the North Atlantic where, at the age of 28 she was given the title "Consulesa" and thrust into the island's elderly-dominated Portuguese-speaking social elite. That's a lot of change.

In the Foreign Service we get instruction and reminders about the difficulties of culture shock and adaptation to new places, so when Elisa had a hard time adjusting to the Azores, I at first attributed it to culture shock. But it deepened and continued. She couldn't sleep and she lost a lot of weight. She didn't like me playing the role of Consul. "Who is this Consul guy?" she'd ask, "I want my Bill back!" She hated being the Consulesa – early on, she found herself being approached by people who seemed to want to be her friends, but who really just wanted to be seen with the wife of the Consul. She wasn't herself. She seemed lost and sad. She was deeply hurt when, after throwing a baby shower for a friend, she overheard one of the local guests saying that the new Consul's wife had to learn a thing or two about how to properly entertain in Azorean high society – petty comments like that would send her into a downward spiral for weeks.

After a couple months of this, I called the medical office of our Embassy in Lisbon and asked to speak to the psychiatrist. I arranged for him to speak to Elisa on the phone. That seemed to help a bit, but not enough. I started to think that we would have to leave the Azores, that we would have to end our tour early. On a visit to Lisbon, I talked to my boss (the Deputy Chief of Mission) and warned her that we might have to curtail our assignment. There was a big risk in leaving early – it would take months for us to get out, and I feared that if I pulled the trigger and got orders to depart, by the time we'd be packing up, Elisa would have pulled out of culture shock and we'd all want to stay. There was also the matter of where we'd go, and where we'd live. I worried that the chaos and uprooting of another move would pile additional stress on Elisa. We decided to hang in there. I'm still not sure that was the right decision.

Neither of us knew much about depression. We were both wary of medication, in part because Elisa was still nursing Maria (Maria nursed until she was four years-old). With our lofty social position in the fish-bowl of Azorean society in mind we were foolishly reluctant to seek the help of a local doctor. I suppose we also had doubts about whether we could find qualified help out there on the island. (Later, we discovered that we shouldn't have been concerned about this – the Azoreans, it turned out, are remarkably open about seeking help for depression, and there were many doctors there who could have helped.)

Somehow, Elisa pulled through. Charity work at the hospital helped – there she met kids and families with problems much worse than hers. And it was there that she met Rocio, a young female pediatrician from Spain who had taken a job on our remote island and who was also struggling with the Portuguese-Spanish language transition. Rocio introduced Elisa to a wonderful group of expat Spaniards who couldn't have cared less about my job or our social position. This really helped Elisa. But it wasn't really a cure. The cure would come later, in London...

****

In the UK our plan was to find a pediatrician, and then make use of our stateside medical insurance to pay for the care (essentially what we'd done in Portugal). Very quickly, however, we discovered that the vast majority of doctors were part of the National Health Service (NHS) and most of them were general practitioners. Appointments with non-NHS pediatricians were hard to come-by, but there was an NHS clinic right around the corner. When we enrolled at this clinic (called The Radcliffe Surgery), we tried to set things up so that our care would be billed to our U.S. insurance company. But the clinic personnel just shook their heads and explained that they couldn't do this even if they wanted to – there was no billing office, no one to process the insurance paperwork. We found out that we were, in fact, eligible for NHS enrollment because Elisa was working at the kids' school and paying British taxes. Oh well, we thought, welcome to socialized medicine! Welcome to the NHS!

Shocking as this may seem, we kind of liked it. To be fair, we were living in a very posh section of London – the NHS we experienced was probably quite a bit better than that of other areas. But we got the feeling that we were in a system that really was designed to do its best – within resource constraints – to take care of us. Blue Cross/Blue Shield never gave us that feeling – with them, it always seemed like their priority was finding excuses that would allow them to not take care of us.

Compared to the U.S. system, the NHS is a bit "no fills" and there is a whiff of big brother about it – you don't get to pick your doctor. Even among the group of doctors at your local clinic, you don't get to pick and choose – when you sign in at the front desk, you will be seen by the next available GP. You don't get to go directly to a specialist – not even a pediatrician. It is the GP at your local clinic who will decide if you need a specialist. But on the other hand, if you called in and said you were too sick to come to the clinic, they'd offer to send someone to the house.

The British "stiff upper lip" and "musn't grumble" attitudes were sometimes noticeable in our interaction with the NHS. The Brits (doctors and patients) seem a bit less pain-averse than their American counterparts. And – no doubt with cost constraints in mind – the doctors were reluctant to order up the kinds of expensive tests that U.S. doctors often ask for.

We also made occasional use of the local NHS hospital (Chelsea Westminster). We'd bring the kids to the emergency room for the normal cuts, bruises and fevers. They had a special, separate emergency room for children – this was great because it kept the kids away from the injured drunks in the main emergency room.

The NHS staff's inability to take payment from us extended to visiting family members, but that did not prevent them from getting care. My mother-in-law was with us for most of our last year in London, helping out while Elisa studied. The contrast between the way she was treated by the U.S. and the UK systems was striking: The U.S. system refused to have anything to do with her. I could not use my family Blue Cross/Blue Shield policy to have her treated. And even the American Embassy medical clinic refused to do anything for her. Once, when we were worried that she'd been exposed to the flu, I told a doctor at the Embassy medical clinic about my concerns. He quickly wrote a prescription for an anti-viral medication, but before I could use it he called me – very concerned – and asked me to destroy the piece of paper – he wasn't authorized to treat the parents or in-laws of Embassy personnel, even if they were (as Yuya was) officially part of an Embassy family. I had to rip up the prescription and pay a private physician 50 pounds to write the same thing.

Contrast all this with the NHS approach. When Yuya developed a bad cough, we took her in to Chelsea Westminster Hospital. No questions asked, she was quickly seen by an excellent doctor, and handed her the medication she needed. Again, we offered to pay, but they wouldn't hear of it. The Brits were far more human, far more humane in their treatment of my wife's mother. When she walked into that hospital, they saw an older woman who was not feeling well, not an alien without the correct insurance card in her pocket.

****

In London, the cure for Elisa's depression came to us via Billy's poor handwriting. Mothers of pre-mature babies often have a sense of guilt; even though there is nothing they could have done, they worry they should have done more to carry the baby to full term. Billy's early arrival also left Elisa hyper-sensitive to any signs that Billy might have some sort of medical or developmental problem. So when Billy's first grade teacher began to complain that his handwriting was a bit sloppy, Elisa was very concerned. Things got worse when, instead of just helping him to improve his handwriting, the teacher offered what sounded like a medical diagnosis. Billy, she said gravely, was suffering from "dysgraphia." You know, kind of like dyslexia, but for handwriting.

I was skeptical. Elisa was very concerned. She started spending a lot of time in the dysgraphia blogosphere. The school recommended a course of "occupational therapy." Elisa immediately signed Billy up, and soon every Thursday evening he and I would head off in the London subway to his therapy session.

My skepticism deepened as I watched what they were doing. There seemed to be quite a lot of stretching exercises, followed by long sessions in which Billy and a well-endowed young woman from South Africa would play catch with a medicine ball. (When I asked Billy what he thought of the whole thing, he said, "Well, I don't really know why, but I really like playing catch with that girl!" Indeed.) I had real doubts about their usefulness, but Billy and I had a lot of fun going to and from these sessions. Billy was only six at this point, and, like most little boys, he very often needed to take a pee. I had learned that the time interval between his first warning ("I think I might have to pee!") and the declaration of a full blown urinary emergency was quite short. This would usually happen as we were walking through the London night from the South Kensington tube station to our house. Billy and I came up with a special, semi-concealed place (on posh Cranley Gardens) where he could relieve himself. I'd stand guard and try to distract any passers-by. Billy was always mortified about having to pee in the bushes, but once the operation had successfully concluded, we'd laugh and take pride in our success at covert urination.

This was all great fun, but we wondered if the therapy was doing any good. More importantly, we wondered if it was really necessary. Did Billy really have a problem? I decided to consult with Embassy London's medical section. I'd heard that the psychiatrist there, Dr. Fred Summers, was a quite good on child development issues. We told him about Billy and, obviously with the intent of putting Elisa's mind at ease, Fred set up a full day of tests for Billy with a child psychologist. (As expected, the tests showed no problems of any kind; sadly for Billy, this put an end to the medicine ball sessions.)

Fred is a very perceptive doctor, and, while talking about Billy, he saw something in Elisa that caused him concern. He wanted to talk about how *she* was doing. She told him about the suffering she had endured in the Azores, and admitted that the symptoms weren't completely gone. Sometimes she had trouble sleeping. Sometimes she worried too much...

Dr. Summers concluded that Elisa was in fact still suffering from mild depression. He talked to her about treatment and prescribed medication. Elisa immediately felt much better. This was really life-changing treatment. Because of Dr. Summers' care, Elisa's enthusiasm and energy returned and she very quickly got strong enough to go back to school, to the Inchbald School of Design.

****

Because the U.S. Embassy in Rome had an excellent in-house medical clinic that took care of almost all our needs, our interaction with the Italian health care system was relatively infrequent. But when we did make use of it – mama mia! – it was always a real cultural experience.

There was a public hospital right on our piazza in Trastevere – Piazza di San Cosimato. Early in our time in Rome, Elisa developed a painful problem right at the start of a long weekend. The Embassy clinic was closed, but the duty nurse advised us to go to the hospital emergency room. We were amazed. The waiting room was nearly empty. The staff was efficient and courteous. Our foreign nationality didn't bother them a bit – they explained that because we weren't in their system, we'd have to pay a small fee – the equivalent of about $15 – after we were taken care of. Elisa's problem was quickly diagnosed, medicine was prescribed and the doctor even gave us his personal cell phone number in case we needed to follow-up. Wow, we thought, the Italians have their act together! If this is socialized medicine, color us red!

On our way out, the receptionist gave us our bill and explained that we could pay in person at the administrative office around the corner. Off we went. The service had been so good that we actually looked forward to paying for it.

But then we got there. Opening the door (yes, it creaked!) we peered in on what looked like a scene from the medical-admin circle of Dante's inferno. The room was dimly lit. Far too many people were stuffed in there, all of them in a hodgepodge of what at times looked like waiting lines but that frequently seemed to collapse into rugby scrums. A good portion of the people seemed to have hacking, tubercular-sounding coughs. If you weren't sick when you went in there, you would be when you came out. We didn't go in. Without even thinking about it, we both decided that this was no place for diplomats, and informally invoked our diplomatic immunity. I think I still owe them 15 bucks.

In Italy, as in many European countries, pharmacists have a somewhat larger role in the medical system than they do in the U.S. People will often turn to their local pharmacists for advice and even for simple diagnoses. In Italy, it was always "over-the-counter" advice and diagnosis, almost always within earshot of neighbors waiting in line for their turn. Just as the layout of Italy's apartment buildings allow people to hear all about their neighbors' marital problems, Italy's pharmacies seem designed for similar transparency on the medical front, and serve up daily reminders that there is no word in Italian for "privacy." They'll often have a pathetically inadequate "privacy line" painted on the floor, but it is usually only a foot or so from the counter. And no one seems self-conscious enough to whisper. So days in Italian pharmacies are filled with a steady stream of almost public discussion of insomnia, pregnancy tests, incontinence, impotence, hot flashes, and birth control options. It is quite a show. Like they say, in Italy, life is a stage.

Over time, Elisa and I got fairly proficient at Italian but still, because of the baroque complexity of all things Italian, we seemed to need help when it came time to navigate the Italian medical system. That help came from Dr. Rosa Tavano and her staff at Embassy Rome's excellent medical unit. For example, one afternoon during our first full summer in Rome, eight year-old Maria was playing in our living room. She bumped her elbow's "funny bone" and ran to Elisa complaining of the pain. Then suddenly she turned pale, her eyes rolled upwards and she passed out. She was completely unconscious for around a minute before Elisa could get her to come around.

This, of course, scared the hell out of us. In a flash, Elisa was on the phone to the Embassy. Maria quickly regained consciousness, but clearly some tests were required, tests that would have to be done in Italian hospitals. Dr. Rosa and her staff made the appointments for us, and then served as kind of cell-phone guardian angels, monitoring from the Embassy each step of our progress. "Are you at the emergency room yet? Who are you talking to? Where are they sending you next? What test do they want to do? Let me talk to the doctor…" Dr. Rosa was amazingly supportive. She is completely bilingual, and completely bi-cultural. With us she was an American, but with the Italians she was an Italian (and as the U.S. Embassy's doctor, an Italian with prestige and clout). Dr. Rosa could make things happen fast in a country not known for speed.

Sometimes this took a little finagling, the application of a bit of Italian *furbizia*. As we took Maria from test to test (at one point they were concerned about possible epilepsy), they decided that what was needed was a special electroencephalogram for children. This machine was not available at the hospital where Maria was being tested. If we tried to schedule the test at another hospital it might take weeks. But if the request for the test were to come from the other hospital's emergency room, the test would be done immediately. We were getting ready to leave on a long vacation trip and wanted this resolved before we went. At this point about 24 hours had passed since Maria's fainting spell. The advice on how to deal with this problem came via cell phone, almost in a whisper (I won't say from whom). "Take her over to the Bambino Gesu Hospital emergency room and tell them she fainted this morning."

Now, we don't like to lie, especially in front of the kids. But sometimes, well, when in Rome… Pulling off this little scam was complicated by the presence of one of Billy's school pals, the son of a Norwegian diplomat, who was at our house that afternoon. Elisa had to take all the kids to the hospital with her. So the Norwegian kid had to be briefed on our little Italo-Dominican-American finagle – he seemed perplexed by the whole thing. But he kept his mouth shut and the tests were done immediately. We were relieved to learn that it wasn't epilepsy. Maria just has a bit of low blood pressure. To be on the safe side, the staff of this public hospital insisted that Maria be admitted and that she spend at least one night under observation. I understand that that kind of thing is fairly unheard of in the U.S these days – the insurance companies usually won't permit it.

****

107

The Achilles tendon injury that I mentioned in the opening chapter provided another example of the kind of differences in medical culture that you have to deal with while overseas: When they were getting ready to discharge me from the hospital after sewing my tendon back together, the surgeon's assistant gave us instructions on the medications I'd have to take. I'd need some anti-coagulants, he explained, and he told me to take one injection every day. We knew that the Italians – like many other nationalities – were big on injections. In some countries patients don't feel that they've gotten their medical money's worth unless they are jabbed with something. We'd also heard that Italian medical culture includes a lot of self-injection instructions from the doctors, but we'd never actually faced the prospect of doing this ourselves.

When he told us about the injections, my first reaction was to tell the doctor that as an American, I just couldn't possibly do this myself. "We don't do that!" I argued pathetically. He didn't accept this. I then asked if we could get the injections done at the local pharmacy. The assistant clearly saw this as crazy talk. It was, for him, as if I'd suggested that I get the pharmacist to help me swallow a pill. No, he said, I should do it myself. He gave us a little 30 second class and handed us the prescription.

I couldn't do it! But Elisa saved the day and agreed to administer the shots, jabbing me in the abdomen once each morning. Even though I had wimped out, this little in-house injection incident somehow made us feel a bit closer to Italian culture.

The clash between the U.S. approach to medicine and the Italian/European approach was sometimes brought home to us during our visits to the American bases. We'd often use the temporary housing facilities on these bases, and – perhaps because we had small kids – we'd sometimes find the need to use the medical clinics on these bases (there is an agreement between the State Department and the Defense Department that makes this possible).

Entering those clinics marked a return to U.S. medicine, with all its strengths and weaknesses. The first order of business was always money. Before we could talk to any medical people, we had to deal with administrative folks intent on confirming our eligibility, insurance coverage, etc. (this was quite a contrast with what happened in British and Italian hospitals).

One of our last trips in Italy was to Tuscany. There we stayed at a small Army Base near Pisa called Camp Darby. Elisa developed a headache early in the trip, and – wanting to avoid seven days of on-the-road suffering, we decided to go in to see the doctors at the base clinic. We thought it was a sinus infection and were hoping for some antibiotics.

After the usual administrative and insurance hassles, we went in to see the doctors. They checked Elisa out and seemed to conclude that there was nothing much wrong with her. But when she complained that her pain was severe (she is very sensitive to pain), the doctors seemed to shift into their very American "let's order up some tests" mode. Let's get a CT scan!

Of course, we were going to follow their advice, but we were dismayed to learn that the nearest CT scan machine was down in the Italian public hospital in Pisa – about 30 minutes from the base, and – because it was already after-hours, we'd have to start out in the emergency room. That gave us pause, but, with fond memories of our experience in the Trastevere emergency room in mind, we decided to give it a try.

Right away, we knew we were in a very different place. Pisa is in Northern Italy, and is supposed to be more modern and efficient than the central and southern parts of the country, but apparently the Pisa Hospital emergency room hadn't gotten the word on this. It was jam-packed with hurting people. A good portion seemed to be homeless. There was also a large contingent of very old people, several of whom seemed to be on their final visit to the hospital. In the finest traditions of the Italian civil service, the hospital staff seemed to maintain an aloof distance from all of them.

As soon as we checked in, I began to doubt that we'd ever get a CT scan. The triage nurse seemed to be deliberately unimpressed by our being from the U.S. Embassy in Rome. Our referral from the medical clinic at the base seemed to deepen her antipathy. "They sent you here for a CT scan?" she asked. "For a headache? Mama mia! Signora you need a couple of aspirin, not a CT scan! We don't order up CT scans for every woman with a headache!" (She was probably right.) She then told us that if we wanted to continue to push for the scan, we'd have to wait to talk to the doctor, warning that we'd be seen based on the priority that she had assigned to our case. From the look on her face, we realized that it would be a very long night. We opted to return to the base and to try a couple of aspirin.

****

We came away from our exposure to the medical systems of Portugal, Britain, and Italy with the realization that there is nothing inherently superior about the American system of medicine, or indeed about American systems in general. We received wonderful care (albeit with some interesting cultural twists) from the doctors and nurses of all three countries. And it was nice to be in the hands of systems more focused on medicine than on profit, more concerned about the medical needs of their patients than about their nationalities or their immigration status or their health insurance coverage.

More importantly, we came away with a reinforced sense of our common humanity. After you (or your family members) have been sick or injured overseas, after you've been cared for by "foreign" doctors and nurses, well, it just serves as a reminder of what should be obvious – we're all human, we all have the same physical frailties, the same needs for care and treatment. Differences based on nationality are far less significant than the human frailties that we all share. Patriotism and nationalism often makes it difficult for us to see this common humanity.

When I was in the army, we'd sometimes go deep into the Honduran countryside. There we would find life-threatening poverty and severely malnourished children. The young American soldiers who were with me were often from tough inner-city backgrounds, but they had never seen poverty like this. Some of them were Spanish-speakers. In one village a young mother with two very sick little kids came running up to us seeking medical help. She thought we were doctors. We couldn't help her. The soldiers seemed to want me to dial 911 and call for an ambulance. They were angry and frustrated when I told them that what they were seeing was normal for southern Honduras, that this would not be seen by the Honduran authorities as an emergency. But I was heartened by their reactions: they saw a human being in distress and wanted to help. They didn't put on nationalist blinders, declare the victims to be foreigners and wash their hands of the whole problem.

During my first overseas tour in the Foreign Service, I was working with the Nicaraguan Contras along the Honduran border with Nicaragua. We had funding from the U.S. Congress to provide medical care to Nicaraguans who came across the border, but we weren't supposed to treat Hondurans. One day our doctors were brought a tiny, almost skeletal infant. The little girl was in very bad shape, in danger of dying from dehydration. And she was Honduran. The doctors decided to break the rules. They decided to treat her. They put her on our helicopter and flew her to the Honduran capital. That little girl lived because those doctors were willing to overlook nationality, because those doctors were more focused on our common humanity.

In his book "Mountains Beyond Mountains" author Tracy Kidder described the long, arduous hikes that Dr. Paul Farmer makes to treat desperately poor Haitians in isolated villages: "He's still going to make these hikes, he'll insist, because if you say that seven hours is too long to walk for two families of patients, you're saying that their lives matter less than some others', and the idea that some lives matter less is the root of all that's wrong with the world."

110

PLAYGROUNDS, PARKS, VACATIONS, PARTIES (AND GOOD DEEDS)

"The world is my country, all mankind are my brethren, and to do good is my religion." Thomas Paine

Playgrounds had been a very important parts of our life in Northern Virginia, and having been told that Ponta Delgada was a "family friendly post" we assumed that this would continue on our new island home. Bad assumption. We very quickly found out that the nice shiny, bright, safe kid parks that dot the Northern Virginia landscape simply did not exist in the Azores. The Azoreans claimed that they had playgrounds, and we very actively looked for them during our first weeks on the island. It always took us a suspiciously long time to find them, and when we did get there it was always a disappointing experience: Instead of bright paint, rust. Instead of grass or shock absorbent ground covers, broken beer bottles and hints that hypodermics and condoms were among the rubble. Instead of the happy laughter of playing kids, the disheartening whistle of North Atlantic wind under slate-gray skies.

There were, we soon discovered, no birthday parties either. Or at least none that our kids were invited to. This was a cultural and social class thing: Azoreans apparently celebrated birthdays within the family. And even if they were inclined to invite outsiders, some might have been hesitant to invite kids from a family perceived to be above their social ranking. We were the maximum outsiders and, unfortunately, my job and the over-the-top house that came with it made us appear in the eyes of the Azoreans to be up there with the unapproachable rich and famous. Oh how we would have preferred to be normal! In a heartbeat Elisa would have traded that big house for a few birthday party invitations for Billy and Maria.

Billy and Maria in their Azorean backyard.

But we did have a big backyard... It was huge and covered with the kind of soft grass that little kids can safely fall down on. In the far corner there was an area with trees and plants that we called "the jungle." We took the wood from some of the shipping crates and had Luis the gardener turn it into the frame for a sandbox (with black, volcanic sand). Soon a swing set arrived from the States and the backyard started to look like a playground.

There was, however, one thing that REALLY didn't fit in with our new playground theme: the statue. Very prominent in the yard was a sculpture of the torso of a woman. It was an anatomically correct sculpture, and, to make matters worse, we later learned that it had been modeled by an actual Azorean woman. (A number of male guests at official social functions pulled me aside and – with Rodney Dangerfield-like gestures – alluded to having *known* the model.) Obviously the sculpture had to go. I tried to get it moved to storage, but our local employee in charge of these kinds of things somehow convinced me that this was physically impossible – he sort of claimed that the base of the statue was connected directly to the bedrock of Sao Miguel Island. My fallback position was to make the lady decent. In a move that shocked the sensibilities of Ponta Delgada's artsy crowd and forever branded us as

112

complete philistines, I ordered a skirt to be made. Somehow Mr. Silva got this job. It turned out to be more of a toga than a skirt, but it got the job done.

All that was missing now were kids to play with. Maria was too small to really care about this – she was totally content with the attention of Margarida ("'gida!") and Ana Paula. But Billy need some pals. Once again, Ana Paula came to the rescue. Her son Ivo was just a little older than Billy – soon Ivo was out in the backyard just about every day after school. Out in the jungle, he taught Billy how to climb trees and how to find the most interesting Azorean bugs and critters. "Jimmy-Jimmies" (wood lice) were a favorite (they would curl up in their shells when you caught them). Snails were everywhere (an Azorean delicacy). There were gecko lizards; we built a trap and caught one – live. The kids named him "John the Lizard." There were little bugs that could maintain a very steady position (we called them "helicopter bugs"). During the day you could see hawks circling high overhead. In the evening small bats would take to the sky. In short, it was a great place for a little boy.

Elisa eventually found ways to overcome the social barriers and get other kids into the backyard. I think it all started with a Halloween party soon after 9/11. We'd been on the island for over a year at that point. We'd had several big official social events. Now it was time to put our party-organizing apparatus to use for purely recreational purposes. The house was big enough so that the kids could go trick-or-treating indoors. Elisa set up a spooky, scary tunnel that the kids had to crawl through. There were games in the backyard.

There was something about the party that the kids didn't even notice but that was very important to us: This was a very egalitarian, very American Halloween party. Kids (and parents) from all social classes were invited. The richest man on the island (Luis Bensaude) was there with his kids, as were the families of drivers, and housekeepers and Portuguese army sergeants. That kind of mix would never ordinarily happen in the Azores, but it worked well in the residence of the American Consul, and it seemed very appropriate there. The kids had a great time, and none of the high-class parents fainted at the sight of working-class guests.

Speaking of Halloween, in the Azores we were probably the first diplomats there to participate in an important Foreign Service tradition: Trick-or-Treating inside the Embassy (in our case the Consulate). In most countries there is no Trick-or-Treating. In some places, even if this American tradition has taken hold, the streets are just too dangerous for American diplomatic kids. So in most Embassies they organize an in-house trick-or-treat, with the U.S. Embassy playing the role of the U.S.

Halloween at Embassy London

neighborhood. In Embassy London the kids would go from office-to-office knocking on doors (often high-security doors) screaming "trick or treat!" The London Embassy was big enough to nicely simulate a large American neighborhood – the kids would be worn out by the time they got to the upper floors. In Rome, Embassy families would decorate their cars and minivans, and the kids would go from car-to-car in the parking lot. The U.S. Marine Corps detachment at Embassy Rome always turned the cafeteria into a *really scary* haunted house. In Ponta Delgada our Consulate was tiny, but so were our kids – they didn't notice that the Portuguese employees were scurrying from office to office and disguising their voices in an effort to give Billy and Maria more opportunities to knock on doors and shout "Trick or Treat!"

We had lots of other parties. Elisa would sometimes invite all of Billy or Maria's classmates over to the house after school. For the kids it was like a class trip. It was happy bedlam all afternoon. This was all for fun, but these events proved to be diplomatically useful – one day a high-ranking visitor was coming through the Azores and I was contacted by Washington and asked to get a message to him. But his plane was just re-fueling and the passengers weren't even going to disembark. I needed to get on the plane. I explained the situation to the Portuguese police official in charge of airport security. He quietly told me, "My daughter was at your house last week. Come on, I'll take you onto the plane."

During our last year in the Azores we started to make more use of the front yard. Elisa planted beautiful flowers that grew along the fence. We'd all go out to the front yard when she tended to the flowers. It was fun to watch the people walking by; there was more life there than in the more isolated backyard. In that final year, Billy got the idea of having some "sells": setting up some little stands to sell things. First there was the juice sell, then the pretty rock sell, then the flower sell. We'd let him set up his stand at the top of the stairs, then Mr. Silva and I would pre-screen potential customers (and sometimes provide them with money) so they could then go inside the gate and up the stairs to make their purchases. This was a lot of fun.

And of course there were the official diplomatic events. That was, after all, why they gave us the big house. The official "national day reception" (on the Fourth of July) was the big one for us. We'd invite around 300 people. It was sort of like setting up a wedding. It was a lot of work, especially for Elisa (and Uncle Sam wasn't even paying her) and a lot of stress. The day before the big event, Elisa, Margarida and Mr. Silva would head out into the countryside in the Consulate's armored Crown Victoria, in search of flowers. (We had our doubts about the legality of this, but fortunately we never had to invoke diplomatic immunity.) The Azoreans were very punctual – precisely at six they'd show up, almost en masse, at the front door. We'd have a receiving line and greet everyone (one year

115

my mom was with us and she stood in the line too). The guests would munch on finger food and drink for an hour or so, then I'd make my speech. Typically I'd read from the Declaration of independence and talk about the long history of friendly U.S. - Azorean relations. Precisely at eight the Azoreans would head for the door. We'd say goodbye to everyone, then collapse from social exhaustion.

Newspaper coverage of our July 4th event. The flag is being held up by our swing set.

Maria, Billy, and classmate Antonio salute on July 4 (and thumbs up from Maria)

Each May, the Azoreans would hold their religious festival. This was known as "Santo Cristo." It revolves around their veneration for a statue representing Christ. It is known as Santo Cristo dos Milagres (Holy Christ of the Miracles). Over the years Azoreans have donated millions of dollars in gold and jewelry to this statue. Once a year, they take it out for a LONG procession around town. Azoreans fly in from all over the world to participate. Everyone participates. As Consul, I marched in three of these processions. Santo Cristo was a big deal for the Azoreans.

Preparations would be underway for weeks. On the day of the procession, floral displays would be set up on the cobble stone streets. At around 4 pm, Mr. Silva would take me down to the church at the Campo de San Francisco. Usually I'd be accompanied by the American Commander from Lajes Field. At the church there would be several hours of milling about. Then the procession would begin. Then there would be several more hours of milling about as we waited for it to be our time to walk out of the church and into the streets.

In the Santo Cristo procession

The procession was very slow, and very solemn. Congressman Barney Frank had a lot of Azoreans in his district and so was a frequent participant in Santo Cristo. He gave me pointers on the proper way to march: Two or three steps, followed by a two or three minute wait. Then repeat the procedure. No smiling. No waving to friends in the crowd. Solemn.

117

Serious. This would go on for nearly four hours. Santo Cristo wasn't a lot of laughs.

Although it was a bit painful, Santo Cristo was in many ways a nice event. It was important to the Azoreans, and it was an opportunity for us to show respect for their customs. People would put on their Sunday best, and stand solemnly in the street to watch the procession go by. This was a chance to see the good people of the Azores. For weeks after the procession, Azoreans would come up to me and say with a smile, "I saw you in the Santo Cristo." For me, the highlight of the procession was whenever I'd pass Elisa and the kids. My friend Jose Antonio Mota Amaral arranged for the family to view the event from the balcony of a government building. I'd look up and see my own cheering section giving me discrete and solemn encouragement.

****

Ponta Delgada was hard on Elisa. I was kept busy with work at the Consulate, and didn't really have to confront the day-to-day difficulties of the place. Elisa had no such diversion or protection, and was feeling very depressed during our first months on the island. Thinking that helping others would be the best therapy, she began to seek out opportunities for volunteer work.

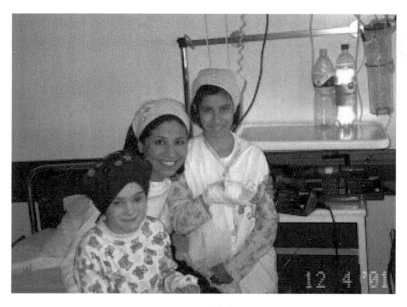

118

First she went to the Espirito Santo Hospital to work in the pediatric ward. Even the act of volunteering proved difficult – Elisa came up against naysayers who tried to make things difficult for her. But she persevered and soon was part of the team at the pediatric ward. One of the kids had to wear a head scarf – in solidarity, Elisa wore one too.

Doing charity work in Ponta Delgada was much more difficult than it should have been. It is not easy for an outsider to do good deeds in a very traditional society. We found that the Europeans were, in general, much more change averse than Americans. This is illustrated by the apocryphal story of the back and forth in Britain between a megaphone-bearing protest leader and the crowd he is attempting to rally:

"What do we want?"
"Gradual Change!!!!"
"When do we want it?
"In due course!!!"

Good works become even more difficult when the person who is trying help is young, and the group she is working with is old. That is undoubtedly one of the factors that made things difficult for Elisa.

Early in our tour Lile Braz of the Ponta Delgada Rotary Club approached Elisa and Veronica seeking help on a fundraising dinner. Lile (who would later become Maria's godmother) wanted to use a little diplomatic cachet to attract diners. Unable to directly use the cachet of the U.S. Consulate, the three came up with a good idea: They would organize an "Association of Consular Spouses" to support charity works.

Elisa immediately moved to bring into the organization the other Consular spouses. All were married to "Honorary Consuls," usually local luminaries who – on a part time, pro-bono basis – represented the interests of foreign governments. Meetings of the new association were held at our house, and the group decided to support a number of charity activities. All seemed to be going well.

Then one day Elisa got a call from one of the spouses inviting her to a previously unscheduled meeting. Surprisingly, it was being held at a new location. Elisa was very pleased, seeing the meeting as evidence that the locals were taking charge, evidence that the organization might last beyond our time on the islands. Elisa happily got all dressed up for the meeting, which would be held in a Ponta Delgada hotel.

I knew it had gone horribly wrong when, late in the afternoon, I got a teary phone call from Elisa. She'd left the hotel and was calling from the

119

dark, dank streets of downtown Ponta Delgada. The meeting had been an ambush. The old witches had set the whole thing up with the express purpose of dressing Elisa down (in rapid-fire Micalense), lecturing her on the supposed "inappropriateness" of the Association.

That meeting put an end (for a while) to several friendships (but time heals all wounds). It turned me against many of the Honorary Consuls. In retaliation, I took many of them off the invitation list for the July 4th reception. That may seem petty, but that's a harsh move in a town where July 4th is a major event on the social calendar. There was simply no way I was going to invite these people into our house after the way they had treated my wife.

But many good things came out of this. In spite of the small-minded stinginess of these pompous old biddies, the key initiatives of the Association continued. Outings for handicapped kids were organized. Money was raised for worthy causes. And, most important, the kids at the Mae de Deus orphanage started having their birthdays celebrated.

Mae de Deus (Mother of God) was located just blocks from both our house and a similar distance from the home of Jay and Veronica Barry (Jay was the American Vice Consul). Both Elisa and Veronica soon fell in love with the kids there. They were shocked to discover that these poor kids didn't get birthday parties. Many of the kids there had never had anyone celebrate their birthday. Elisa and Veronica decided to change that.

Elisa used her connections and diplomatic skills to convince local merchants to contribute toys and food for monthly parties. These events were a lot of work. Almost the entire burden was carried by Elisa, Veronica, and Lile Braz. I would make a cameo appearance on my way home from work. The kids were really thrilled to have someone take note of their birthday. The adolescent girls at the orphanage would all be dancing to the Shakira CD that Elisa always brought along. It was a lot of fun. Once a month that orphanage would be filled with cakes and soda and toys. We celebrated the arrival of each kid whose birthday fell in that month. This tradition – launched by Elisa and her friends – continues today.

Through her volunteer work Elisa came to know of other kids in need. There were several "shelter homes" in Ponta Delgada where kids from problematic families were housed. On a visit to one of these homes Elisa met Paulo. He was ten years old, a tall, good-looking kid with a big smile. In this particular home, each kid had a chart on a clipboard on the door of his room. With unintentional cruelty, the social workers used these papers to chart the number of family visits that each child had. The kids quickly understood the significance of the charts, and began comparing the number of visits. Paulo hung his head when he told Elisa that there were no marks on his chart because no one had ever visited him. This broke her heart. Soon Paulo and his friend Nuno were coming to our house for ice cream parties.

Just days before we were to leave Ponta Delgada, Elisa called to inquire about Paulo and his sister Paula. They had recently been moved to the Mae de Deus orphanage. Elisa was horrified to learn that Paulo was about to be forced out. The orphanage cared for adolescent girls, but not boys (the mix would have been too volatile). Paulo was getting to the age where the nuns feared trouble. So they were looking for a new home for him, probably 900 miles away in continental Portugal. Paulo and his sister would almost certainly be split up. The poor kids were about to lose the only element of family stability in their lives.

Unwilling to leave Ponta Delgada with the fate of these kids up in the air, Elisa started looking around for a temporary home for them. Amidst the chaos of the preparations for our move, and all the going-away events, she was trying to find a home for two defenseless orphans. She had almost run out of hope when she decided to call her friend Isabel. She and her husband Jose were devout Mormons. They had four young kids of their own, and were barely getting by on Jose's Army Sergeant's salary. Elisa called and explained the situation to Isabel. She was stunned by the response. Without even meeting the kids, Isabel said she thought she and Jose would be willing to adopt them.

This was like a dream come true. Meetings were arranged, and authorities were consulted. Soon it became clear that the miraculous adoption was going to take place.

I think this adoption was the most important outcome of our three years in the Azores. For us, it was more important and significant than all the big politico-military events involving the use of Lajes Field or the visit of the President of the United States. Because of the love that Elisa had in her heart, two children were saved from empty lives in Portuguese institutions, and were given a new chance in the care of a really wonderful family. It was a wonderful way to end our tour.

****

Parks and parties were a bit different in London. One of the first things we found in our new neighborhood was a beautiful little park with a swing set and grass and flowers right around the corner from our house. It was on the grounds of St. Mary of the Boltons Anglican Church. This was a big discovery – with our concrete-covered micro-yard, the kids really needed a place to play. But in what became one of our first encounters with the British class system, we quickly discovered that this playground (and many others like it) was not open to the public. If you wanted to use it, you had to apply for access and you had to pay a fee (around 400 dollars for the year). For us that wasn't a lot of money, but it seemed like a lot to pay for something that came for free in Virginia. And it somehow seemed to us that playgrounds should be free.

We paid the fee and got our key, and in that park we soon came in contact with some other unusual features of London life. Back in Virginia, the playgrounds had been a place to meet other parents. We had hoped that the neighborhood park would play a similar role in London. So we started trying to strike up conversations with the other parents. It didn't go very well because we quickly discovered that most of the other adults in the park were not the kids' parents. They were nannies. Even on the weekends, the kids were being taken to the park not by their moms and dads, but by their nannies. It was quite sad, and not only for the kids. We'd soon learn that third world poverty had forced many of these women to leave their own children with relatives in the Philippines or other countries. So here they were, missing their own children, taking care of kids who were missing their own parents. This was another early reminder that even though we were in an English speaking country, we were in a place very different from what we'd been used to in the States.

Fortunately not all the parks were "members only." About a half mile from our house, just off Chelsea's famed Kings Road was St. Luke's Anglican Church. It had a big playground right next to it, and this one was open to the public. In this one, we came into contact with the other end of the London social spectrum. Even though it was in the heart of Chelsea, this park was right across the street from a large block of rent-subsidized low income housing known in England as "council flats." The accents and the clothes were very different, and the playground behavior was a bit rougher. I guess it was a bit more like the neighborhood in New York City that I'd lived in as a kid. St. Mary of the Boltons was posh. St. Luke's was, well, not posh.

A bit further away from our house we had some of the great parks of London: Hyde Park, Kensington Gardens, and, (across the Thames) Battersea Park. Hyde Park was a big part of my life in London because I walked through it each day on the way home from work. I'd often have lunch in the park, often on the benches around the Serpentine Lake.

Early in our time in London we didn't get up to Hyde Park and Kensington Gardens very often – they were out of range of Maria's stroller, and driving our minivan up there was difficult. But in our last years there we were up in those parks more and more often. Both Billy and Maria learned to ride their bikes on the shores of the Serpentine. Elisa took roller skating lessons there. We'd feed the ducks and take long walks. In Hyde Park we could usually leave the van near the Serpentine (for an exorbitant fee). Down near Kensington Gardens parking was harder to come by, but we soon discovered the magic of the diplomatic parking spot. Wherever there was an Embassy, the Metropolitan Police would set aside a few parking spots for cars with diplomatic license plates. They were obviously supposed to be for the diplomats working in that particular Embassy, but, well, how much work could really be going on in the Mongolian Embassy on a Sunday afternoon? We used a bit of diplomatic license (plate!) on these occasions – we became self-declared honorary, temporary Mongolian diplomats.

Kensington Gardens was beautiful – well worth risking diplomatic problems with The Republic of Mongolia. Up in the north-east corner there was a wonderful playground that had apparently been set up by Princess Diana. There was a pirate ship, and an Indian village and swings. It was great.

Kensington Gardens and Hyde Park were north of us, uphill, away from the Thames. In the opposite direction, just across the river from our

123

neighborhood, was Battersea Park. Battersea was quite a bit less posh. Walking through Kensington Gardens we'd frequently cross paths with London's rich and famous, or at least with the Queen's Horse Guards. In Battersea you'd see young fellows in gang-wear walking pit-bulls. But it too was a lovely park. We'd go there to watch the bonfires on Guy Fawkes Night, and Billy and I went there to fly model airplanes.

The kids learned to swim in a pool operated by the city council of Chelsea. Even though it was in one of the richest neighborhoods in London, it had a distinctly socialist, utilitarian, council flat kind of feel to it. And there was also a very noticeable nanny-state influence. All kinds of seemingly safe practices were strictly forbidden. I seem to recall the backstroke having been prohibited – you could hit your head on the wall! (Hyde Park had these wonderful paved pathways: NO BIKE RIDING! We'd also find trees that were perfect for the kids to climb up on: NO TREE CLIMBING! Sometimes it seemed that Britain had decided to prevent kids from having any form of fun.) I once tried to take a picture of Billy and Maria at the pool. We wanted to send it to the grandparents. One of the lifeguards came running over to stop me. "No photographs of the children!" he said sternly. "But these are MY children," I replied. "Doesn't matter," he said, "pedophiles you know!" To use a phrase invented by the Brits, it was all a bit "shambolic" – the lifeguards who were suddenly so diligent about the no pictures rule performed their lifeguard duties fully dressed in street clothes, and seemed to spend most of their "on-duty" time staring off into space (not at the kids!) or "chatting up" girls.

But even with all the nanny state shambolism, we found the old council pool to be in many ways preferable to the posh and expensive pool in the private gym near our house. There we often bumped up against the intolerance and impatience of London's upwardly mobile twenty-somethings. We found British society to be relatively child un-friendly, certainly compared to Portugal, and even more-so when compared to Italy. Some Brits seemed to view children (even their own) as an inconvenience. That may explain their fondness for boarding schools. We often thought that dogs get better treatment than kids in the UK The managers of the private gym seemed to grudgingly recognize that some of their customers had offspring – they set aside a few short time slots as "family time" (i.e. kids can go into the pool). One day Elisa and the kids arrived about fifteen minutes early. They found the pool empty except for one young woman swimming far away at the other end. The kids jumped in, and the woman immediately complained to the authorities, who ordered our kids out of the pool. As the Brits would say, "typical!"

124

There was no shortage of birthday parties in London, in fact managing the social calendars (and gift requirements) of Billy and Maria became a major chore for Elisa. And what parties they were! Soon the parents seemed to be in competition, and we feared that one day the kids would do what some of their parents did and invite all their friends to a beach party in Jamaica. We fell right into the competitive mode. We didn't sponsor any Caribbean fly-aways, but for one of Billy's parties we did a sleep-over *in* the Science Museum. For one of Maria's parties we took the whole gang to the basement of the Natural History Museum where the staff very kindly showed them all kinds of interesting things. The museums were very child friendly.

****

Because we had reverted to "small fish in big pond" status, we didn't have to participate in many official diplomatic social events in London. We'd occasionally find ourselves sipping ginger ale at a reception up at Winfield House (the U.S. Ambassador's residence), but usually we were free of this kind of duty, which was fine with us. But there were some events that caught our attention. One afternoon near the end of our time in London I got an e-mail from the Embassy's protocol office. It seems that Her Majesty the Queen was putting together an event at Buckingham Palace for Americans resident in London. The Embassy had been asked to submit suggestions for the guest list. They wanted people who in some way represented a segment of modern American society. Elisa had missed out on an earlier opportunity to attend a Buckingham Palace event, so I'd been on the lookout for an opportunity to get her into the palace to meet the Queen. Here was my chance. "Juana Elisa del las Mercedes Ruiz de Meara – Garden Designer" went on the list. I noted that Elisa would be an excellent representative of our Hispanic population, and our recent immigrants. A week or so later, a very nice and very formal invitation was delivered by the Royal Mail. Wow! Elisa was really going to meet the Queen. An enthusiastic round of dress selection, hair styling, manicuring and pedicuring began.

At this point Elisa was deeply involved in a year-long garden design program at London's Inchbald School of Design. The course had provided good opportunities to build friendships with young Brits. Happily, we'd found that, as often happens with foreigners, Elisa seemed to be considered exempt from the class tension that marks British social interaction. She seemed to be considered "out of the game" and none of her classmates seemed to be focusing their class radars at her. But one innocent mention of the upcoming event at Her Majesty's place changed all that.

Some of Elisa's classmates seemed genuinely shocked and dismayed that she was going to Buckingham Palace. Being on that invitation list seemed to confer on Elisa upper class status, and plunged her into the class war. Some of her classmates now seemed to be looking for proof that she was somehow unworthy of this invitation. They started questioning Elisa about the protocol aspects of the event. The curtsey issue became a bone of contention: Did Elisa plan on curtseying when she met the Queen? Left unsaid was the real questions: Did she even know HOW to curtsey? Was she WORTHY of meeting the Queen?

Elisa's inquisitors rolled their eyes when she told them that she didn't know if she'd be doing the curtsey thing. The mere suggestion that she might NOT was, they claimed, insulting to their Queen. It really got quite unpleasant, and was for us a reminder that class tensions are very real in the UK.

We did some research and consulted with the Embassy protocol people and learned that curtsying was entirely optional. Because the curtsey (or the male equivalent head bow) is a gesture of respect given by subjects to their Kings and Queens, it seemed a bit silly for an American woman to be doing this. We also learned that many Brits (especially those not in favor of the monarchy) had stopped bowing and curtsying. Prime Minister Blair's wife Cherie was in this category.

Elisa spent the afternoon getting ready for the big event. Because I was not representative of any interesting elements of American society, I had not been invited. I put Elisa in a Black Taxi, aimed it at Buckingham Palace and went home to spend the night with the kids.

The event did have a harrowing moment, but it had nothing to do with the curtsey. As the cab pulled up to Buckingham Palace, security officers asked to see Elisa's invitation. She reached into her purse... and discovered that she had forgotten it! Oh no! Social disaster loomed. Elisa's pulse rate soared. Fortunately, on this kind of thing our British cousins are much more sensibly flexible than we are. They just checked Elisa's ID, saw her name on the list, and she was in.

The Queen and Prince Philip were wonderful. Elisa was honored to have met them – this was, of course, one of the highlights of her time in London. They were very gracious and put Elisa right at ease. And they didn't seem at all bothered by the fact that when Elisa met them, there wasn't even a hint of a curtsey.

****

We'd read that life in Italy is centered on the piazza, but we really hadn't understood the extent to which this included the lives of children. There were some nice parks fairly close to our apartment, but they were kind of difficult to get to, and soon the kids saw Piazza di San Cosimato as their go-to playground. At first glance, from a parent's perspective, it didn't look like much of a play area. It is more like an outdoor communal multi-purpose room for the neighborhood. It is wedge-shaped with the wide part of the wedge to the North. Every morning (except Sunday) this top part of the wedge hosts an amazing open-air market. Until around 2004, the rest of the piazza had – like many other Roman piazzas – degenerated into a de-facto parking lot for the neighborhood. Facing very vocal (and no-doubt gesticulating!) opposition from parts of the community the local council had succeeded in turning the bottom part of the wedge into a playground for kids. They imposed a "no motor vehicles" rule for the piazza – it seemed to be about 80% effective; in Italy, that's good enough. They put up a kind of jungle gym with benches around it for the parents and grandparents. The very bottom of the wedge (immediately adjacent to the jungle gym) seemed to be reserved for drunks and drug addicts from Eastern Europe. Like I said, it didn't look like much, but the kids loved it. And we came to love it too.

Bravi! A football spirals over the Piazza!

127

Piazza di San Cosimato soon became the preferred destination for Billy and Maria. It trumped the Coliseum, the Pantheon, Circus Maximus... For them, no place was more fun than the Piazza. The jungle gym was, of course, a big attraction, but there was a lot of other activity: Billy and I would play catch with an American-style Nerf football. For several reasons this attracted a lot of attention: American heads would turn when they saw our football spiraling through the Roman sky – they were obviously pleased to see something from home. Italian adults seemed to admire the beauty of a well-launched spiral and would reward us with a "Bravi!" or a "Bellisimo!" Italian children were intrigued and confused. They had been so thoroughly programmed for soccer (calcio) that they really didn't understand the game of "catch" as we practiced it. Very often some little Italian kid would stand there watching us. We'd toss him the ball and ask him to join in. He'd usually drop the ball to the ground and try to kick it.

Maria was into gymnastics, and for her the piazza was a stage (as it was for all the Italians). We'd wait for the right moment (maximum audience!) and then I'd ask Maria to give them a cartwheel. "Brava! Bravissima! Che bella!" Indeed, in Italy life is a stage. And it was fun to perform there.

The piazza was also the place for bike riding and skateboarding, but the chaos of the area made these activities a bit more hazardous than normal. The kids would have to weave their way between pedestrians, garbage trucks, motorinos (motorized scooters), and the ever-present winos and drug addicts. But somehow it worked and – thank God – no one got hurt during our three years on Piazza di San Cosimato.

Near the piazza there were retail opportunities for the entire family. There were cafes and pizzerias and kiosks and toy stores, and ice cream stands. The kids especially liked the tobacco shops. It's not that they had become early smokers – tobacco shops are a key part of Italian life. There you can buy candy, postage stamps, and (if a pyrotechnics-linked holiday is approaching) fireworks. You can buy minutes for your cell phone and tickets for the bus. Italian tobacco shops reminded me a bit of the traditional New York City candy stores. We had a favorite ice cream place that was run by Sicilians. There as a nice little flower shop on the piazza. We always got a laugh from the fact that in Italy, it seemed that the only businesses that were in the 24/7 mode were the flower shops – the Italians clearly had frequent need for flowers, even at 2 am.

The piazza was especially fun during holidays. Carnival brought kids in costume, water balloon fights and hours of fun with little spray cans that sent streams of multi-colored foam out over the jungle gym and into the trees. New Year's Eve was all about fireworks, and huge thunderous explosions would rock the piazza. We even got to see it under snow – the first accumulation in 26 years. It was beautiful.

Our kids became very proficient in the use of Trastevere's ancient drinking fountains. They are about the size and shape of an American fire hydrant. Water flows continuously from a downward curving pipe. The pipe explains the nick name of the fountains – Nassone (big nose). There is one correct way to drink from a Nassone, but most outsiders don't know how to do it. Each summer we'd witness many German tourists risking back and neck injury as they tried to position their mouths in the flow of water from the big nose. They failed to see the very small hole that had been drilled in the top of the pipe near the curve. If you blocked the main flow with your hand, a very convenient stream of icy cold water would shoot up, practically jumping into your mouth. Billy and Maria took great delight in introducing visitors to this marvel of Italian hydraulics.

Occasionally Billy and I would climb steps up onto the Janiculum to use a small piazza directly in front of a famous church called San Pietro in Montorio. For many years this was believed to be the site on which St. Peter was crucified (upside down). (They later found out that this crucifixion had taken place elsewhere.) There were fewer people here than in St. Cosimato, and there were great views of Rome. We'd kick around the soccer ball, doing our best not to hit the tourists. A beautiful park ran along the top of the Janiculum hill, with amazing views of Rome off one side and of Vatican City off the other. There was a little arcade. The central piazza of the park had a statue of Garibaldi, for it was here that he fought one of his most important battles. Every day at exactly noon, soldiers of the Italian Army fired off a 105 mm canon – the boom would reverberate through Rome. (The first time he heard it, a colleague who had been in Baghdad during the war thought the boom was from a car-bomb. I guess it takes time to downshift from Baghdad to Rome.) Nearby there was a statue of Garibaldi's courageous and fiery Brazilian wife, Anita. The statue shows her charging into battle on horseback, firing a pistol and holding the reigns with one hand while holding her baby to her breast with the other. We took our Brazilian friends up to see Anita. They were proud of her.

****

We probably should have traveled around Europe more while we were there, but in the early part of the decade the kids were small and travel wasn't easy. Getting away from the Azores was expensive. Uncle Sam paid for one or two R&R trips and we used these to go to the U.S. and to the Dominican Republic to see our families.

Also during our time in the Azores we went to the South of France where we met up with friends from Virginia who were living in Germany. We stayed in a big resort designed for families. At a time folks back in the States were raging at the French for their refusal to be bullied into the Iraq War – people were spilling French wine into the sewers and in the Congress they changed the name of French Fries, calling them Freedom Fries instead. But there we were in Provence, defying the call for nationalistic indignation, with the French and with families from all over Europe, everyone peacefully enjoying some days in the sun with their kids.

From London, France was very easy to get to and we went there quite often. You could even take a day trip – you'd drive down to the entrance to the Channel Tunnel, and just drive your car right onto the train. Thirty minutes later you'd be in the relatively wide-open spaces of northern France – we'd go to the beach, have a French lunch, and have the kids back in London and in bed by 10 pm. We made several trips to Paris (taking my mother along on one). I speak no French. For some reason, whenever I ran into language barriers in France, I'd start speaking to people in...Portuguese. Elisa would howl with laughter when this happened. The French seemed amused by it also.

We became regular visitors to a number of places on the periphery of London. The Palace at Hampton Court was one of our favorites – Elisa loved the gardens and there was plenty of room for the kids to run around. They became quite familiar with the history of the palace and the story of its most famous occupant, Henry VIII. (Maria reacted quite strongly when she learned of his cruelty to his wives: In her bedtime prayers she took to

130

asking god to "protect everyone in the whole wide world... except Henry the eighth.") We liked Windsor quite a bit, especially its "crooked tea house" on Britain's smallest street. We found a little town called Bray, near Maidenhead. We'd take boat rides on the Thames and have lunch at our favorite pub: The Crown in Bray. (The Crown had real British food, with exotic British names. We had a good laugh when we saw the reaction of Elisa's urologist brother when the waitress asked him if he'd like to try the Spotted Dick.)

We flew to Geneva and drove from there up to a friend's ski chalet in the Alps (the snow, the cold, and the ski-centered lifestyle was a bit of a shock for a girl from the Caribbean).

More to Elisa's liking was the island of Ponza. Just 20 miles from Rome, out in the Med, we went to Ponza in a group that included Serbian/French friends from London, and Italian friends who I'd met years before in the Basque country. The waiters at the Ponza restaurants were obviously used to dealing with foreigners, but I think even they were surprised by the multi-lingual nature of our group – at our table we were yacking away in Serbian, French, Spanish, Italian, and English.

We also went to Italy's bigger islands: Sardinia and Sicily. We travelled by ferry, opting for the overnight trip. It was wonderful – departing from either Rome's Civitavecchia port, or from Naples, we'd drive our car right onto the ship late in the afternoon. We'd all grab our overnight "boat bags" and head to our two bunk-bed cabin. We'd have dinner on-board, then head out on-deck to watch the Italian peninsula disappear into the eastern dusk. We'd look at the Milky Way from the Tyrrhenian Sea before heading to the bunk beds. Dawn would find us arriving at Cagliari or Palermo. We'd hop in the car and drive off to a new adventure. It is a really great way to travel.

We seemed to really connect with Sicily, perhaps because one of Elisa's grandfathers had come from that island (throughout our tour in Italy, I embarrassed our kids by telling Sicilian ice-cream merchants – jokingly – that our kids were part Sicilian, and should therefore get a discount.) Elisa loved the color and the light. The food was great, even in the context of Italy's fabulous cuisine. The people seemed even kinder and friendlier than the Romans (and that's saying something – the Romans are very nice). As noted earlier, we stayed at U.S. Naval Air Station Sigonella, on the eastern side of the island, near Mount Etna and the city of Catania. From there, we'd set out to explore. We went west to the Greek ruins at Agrigento, south to Syracuse, up north to Messina. Palermo was beautiful, but it had a somewhat menacing feel to it.

Our kids were old enough to know that we were visiting an island known for organized crime. Most visitors will see no evidence of the mafia's presence, but Billy and Maria were already shrewd observers, and they were on the lookout for signs of the mafia. In Monreale, near Palermo, Maria thought she found some: In Rome, the letters SPQR are everywhere: Senatus Populusque Romanus – The Senate and People of Rome. You'll find it on public buildings, mailboxes, sewer caps, T-shirts. In Monreale's piazza, Maria saw SPQM. "Look! SPQ MAFIA!" Later in this trip, as we headed back to our quarters on the base, Maria, obviously thinking about the organized crime problem, came up with a distressingly American approach to the problem: "Daddy, why don't we just send the American soldiers out there and tell them to take care of the mafia?"

Speaking of the Mafia, our favorite find was the town of Savoca. Near the eastern resort town of Taormina, this is where Francis Ford Coppola shot most of the Sicilian portions of his film "The Godfather." The real town of Corleone is in western Sicily, but the real Mafia is stronger there. That, and proximity to the nice beach hotels of Taormina probably led Coppola east, to Savoca. The residents of this beautiful little town have been capitalizing ever since on their Hollywood connection: Bar Vitelli, where Michael Corleone and his bodyguards met Apollonia's father, and the church in which the wedding scene was shot, have all been kept as they were in the early 1970s when the film crews arrived. Indeed, during one visit we discovered an apparently thriving business in Godfather-themed weddings. (Italian friends back in Rome didn't know what to make of this, and worried that they might actually be Mafia-themed weddings.) We had great fun sitting where Michael Corleone and his gunmen had say, re-enacting conversations from the movie. Back at the base, we'd rent the DVD and look back to 1971.

Italy is so beautiful and interesting that soon after we got there, we lost the incentive to travel beyond its borders. The highways are good (except for in the South) and it we found road travel there easier than car trips in the UK. We'd load our old minivan onto overnight ferries and sail off to Sardinia or to Sicily. It was wonderful. And then, in our last year, we rented that apartment in Ponticelli and opted to spend a lot of our free time there.

****

I always feel a special fondness for the places where my kids played when they were small, and for the places that we took them on vacations. It doesn't matter to me if the playground is in New York or Virginia or London or Rome – when we drive past it, I remember Billy and Maria playing there and I get that same warm feeling. It doesn't matter at all that some of these playgrounds are in foreign territory. For me this is another reminder that on the really important stuff, human emotions just don't recognize national borders.

Death Cheese and Cars that Can't Read
Linguistic Adventures in the Old World

I came across a sit-com that we'd watched back in the States and was surprised to see they were showing it in English. I called out to Elisa: "Hey honey, they are showing 'Friends' in English!" I guess my joy at this discovery was a little too evident, because four year-old Billy looked up from his toys, looked me straight in the eye and said, very seriously, "Portuguese is good too daddy."

We were in St. Peter's Square in Vatican City on Christmas Day. Pope Benedict was in the window, giving his traditional multi-lingual-to-the-max Christmas greeting. Swahili! Spanish! Tagalog! Ethno-linguistic groups in the huge crowd would cheer when they heard the Pope speak in their various mother tongues. Billy was eleven years old at this point, and wondered about the real limits of the Pope's linguistic range. He looked up at me, raised an eyebrow and asked, "Klingon?" (No).

Prior to the Azores, I had only worked in Spanish-speaking countries. Language proficiency was very important to me. I always felt that American officials should be fluent in the language of the host country.

We are Spanish speakers. Spanish is Elisa's first language, and I started studying Spanish at age thirteen. My dad was a New York City cop assigned to a neighborhood that had become very Dominican. I had to pick a foreign language in high school and asked for his advice. Probably as a result of the language barriers that he struggled with every day, he instantly told me that Spanish was the way to go.

I love Spanish. This was the first foreign language I'd mastered. This was the language that had carried me to adventure and intrigue in Central America, and, in the Dominican Republic, to the girl who would become my wife. When we met, Elisa didn't speak English. So we spent our first four years together completely in the Spanish language. Then we moved to the States. When my son was born, my mother-in-law held him in her arms and implored me to "make sure that this boy learns English too!" She just assumed that her grandchildren would be primarily Spanish speakers.

But it didn't work out that way. Elisa joked that they must give the little guys some sort of injection at birth that turns them into little gringos, because despite all our efforts, and in spite of the fact that their mother's "mother tongue" is Spanish, both our kids showed strong preferences for English from time that they started speaking.

Perhaps this would have been different if we had gone to a Spanish-speaking country when they were small. We tried. But we ended up getting assigned to the Azores. My mother-in-law was with us when we got our travel orders. She was a bit concerned about the language issue, so I decided to comfort her by letting her hear how very similar Portuguese is to Spanish. On the computer, I summoned up a web site that played the news programs from the Azores. Bad mistake. She probably would have been comforted by Brazilian Portuguese – it sounds a lot like Spanish. But I had selected Continental (European) Portuguese. To my mother-in-law it sounded a lot like Bulgarian.

Before we left for the Azores, I was put through about three months of language training at the Foreign Service Institute in Arlington, Virginia. Each morning I would head off on my bike for six hours of linguistic torture. My tormentor was from Luso-phone Africa. This was fine – the Africans speak Continental Portuguese (not the Brazilian variety). But I soon found that there were political and personal problems in that language class: The instructor was from a Communist family. Note that I use a capital C here. I am not being figurative. I mean card-carrying. Let's put it this way: In her country's civil war, her family was not on the side that we were sending weapons to. So there was, from the beginning, a definite political undercurrent. To make matters worse, she had married an American. An American diplomat. And, wouldn't you know, the divorce proceedings were going into high gear just around the time that I – another American diplomat – walked into her classroom. I don't want to give her name, but to my ear her first name sounded (appropriately) like an amalgam of Anguish and Agony. I'll call her Angonisha.

Working with her was not easy. They needed me out in the Azores as soon as possible, so I was only given three months to achieve the level of proficiency that students normally attain after six months of study. Everyone knew that Spanish fluency would be a big help – the two languages share about 85 percent of their vocabularies, and the grammar is quite similar. In fact, at one point the Foreign Service Institute had offered a special "conversion course" in which Spanish speakers could, well, convert, but I got the sense that the Portuguese instructors found this concept offensive. Angonisha certainly wouldn't have liked it – she treated the Spanish language as a linguistic infection. Each time that I'd slip and say something in a slightly Spanish way, she would pounce. One day about half-way through my course I finally reached the point where I was starting to feel competent about putting real Portuguese sentences together. Angonisha hadn't been pouncing quite so much. This is a big moment in language training, and, as I was gathering my stuff in preparation for the

136

bike ride home, I said to my instructor, "Wow, I think I had a really good day – I felt quite fluent!"

"Yes," snapped Angonisha, "but that's because you've been speaking SPANISH all day!"

For Spanish speakers one of the tough things about Portuguese is the fact that this language is more phonetically complex than Spanish. It simply uses more sounds. There are lots of nasal sounds and diphthongs that we don't have in Spanish. (This explains why Portuguese speakers can almost always understand spoken Spanish, while Spanish speakers are baffled by Portuguese.) These new sounds would really crack Elisa up. She would hear me practicing pronunciation at home, with all these weird noises coming out of my nose... She found this very amusing.

There were four students in Angonisha's class. The others were scheduled for the full six months, so they didn't share my sense of urgency. One of the students was the husband of a woman being assigned to Mozambique. This poor fellow had never before studied a foreign language, and he was struggling. One of the tricky parts of the Romance languages is the verbs – they all change depending on who is doing the action, and when they are doing it. The conjugations are quite complex compared to English. The struggling student wasn't getting this, and Angonisha's very limited supply of patience had already been exhausted. So she turned to me: "Bill, could you explain to Bob how we conjugate a verb?"

I went to the board and took Bob through all the different persons of a few tenses of a simple Portuguese verb. Soon the blackboard was filled with the complex matrix typical of a Romance language verb conjugation.

"Wait a minute," said Bob, "you mean to tell me that each one of these verbs change each time you talk about a different person or group of people AND they also change depending on WHEN the action takes place?"

"Yes!" cried Angonisha, thinking that a breakthrough had been achieved. But before I could enjoy my brilliant pedagogical success, Bob threw up his hands:

"Well how the HELL are we supposed to remember all that!?"

****

When a Foreign Service officer goes through language training, his or her spouse can also go through the course. But that would have been impossible for Elisa – Maria had been born just about the time I was starting the program, Billy was two years old. And we were getting ready to move to an island in the middle of the Atlantic Ocean. Elisa had no time for language school. She would have the total immersion, in-country experience.

We jumped right into the language as soon as we arrived in the Azores. For some strange reason involving diplomatic protocol and the scheduling of late summer vacations, it had been determined that within an hour or so of our arrival I would have to present myself to the Portuguese central government's representative in the island. So as soon as we got to the house, I wiped the baby drool off my suit and headed off with Mr. Silva to the office of the Portuguese Civil Governor. We had a very nice chat, at the end of which he very kindly complemented me on my Portuguese. As he walked me to the door, he asked, "How long have you been speaking our language?" I couldn't resist. I looked at my watch and replied. "Oh, about 45 minutes."

We had decided that in Portugal we'd speak Spanish at home. We wanted the kids to become fluent in the language of half their family. Unfortunately this didn't work out. Having Margarida and Paula in the house all day meant that we had the Portuguese language in the house all day. Spanish and Portuguese are so close that it is very difficult to be constantly switching back and forth between the two languages. (I once asked a Portuguese official what language they use when meeting with counterparts from Spain. He thought about it for a second then smiled and replied, "English!") If you try to switch between the two you end up speaking a horrible mish-mash: "Porta-nol." So we quickly kind of gave up on Spanish and decided to speak either English or Portuguese at home.

The kids picked up Portuguese very quickly. They learned it mostly from Margarida and Paula, which meant they had picked up the heavy accent of the island: they learned "Micalense." Other than Mommy and Daddy, Maria's first real word was in Portuguese. Margarida and Paula would answer the phone with "'ta?" (a contraction of Esta? – are you there?") Soon little Maria was sitting in her high chair, pretending to answer the phone in the same way, with a perfect Portuguese nasal sound. When she wanted to be picked up she call to Margarida" " 'Gida! colo!" Maria became a huge fan of a Portuguese breakfast cereal called cerelaca: "Paula! Cerelaca!"

Billy's Portuguese became quite good, and he too picked up the distinctive Azorean accent. One afternoon, I secretly listened in as he talked to Paula about wildlife (he was on the toilet – poor Paula was keeping him company): "Na Ameeeerica, temos animais muito graaaaaa." He sounded very Azorean.

Billy and Maria ALWAYS spoke to Margarida and Paula in Portuguese. They'd be speaking to each other in English, then automatically switch to Portuguese to talk to Paula and Margarida.

Early in our tour, probably during the summer of 2001, Billy and I decided to go fishing. We bought some gear and bait from a guy who ran a maritime supply store down the street from the house. When he sold us the rod, he gave us a quick briefing on the fish we were likely to catch. In rapid-fire Micalense, he warned of the red fish – they had poisonous barbs near their gills. As we headed away from his shop on our way to the water, little Billy (not yet four years-old) wanted to make sure I completely understood what the man had said. "Watch out for the RED fish Daddy, the RED ones are very dangerous! Poisonous!" he warned. (He obviously had more confidence in his Portuguese ability than he had in mine.) Sure enough, the second fish we hooked was one of the dreaded red ones. I was careful about removing the hook.

In his book "Iberia" the author James Michener wrote that among people who have learned to speak both Spanish and Portuguese, there is a usually a strong preference for one or the other, and the preference is almost always for the one that was learned first. That was certainly the case with me. I became quite proficient at Portuguese, but I never really came to like it. When I'd hear Spanish spoken, it would sound crystal clear – in comparison, Portuguese was always relatively murky, garbled, harder to follow. I think Elisa disliked it at first, but came to like it more than I did. Elisa had a wonderful Portuguese teacher, Ana, who came to give her one-on-one classes twice a week. Ana became Elisa's friend, and I think they both looked forward to what soon became a combination of language classes and tea parties.

****

After Portuguese, our next language challenge was the English of England. Not a foreign language for us (well, for Elisa it was) it nevertheless presented some interesting linguistic challenges. Soon after we arrived we hopped in a cab and headed up to Oxford Street to buy poor Billy a small TV set so that he could watch his beloved cartoons. The cab driver was Cockney from London's East End, and he liked to talk. I was getting most of it, but Elisa was really shocked. "What language is he speaking?" she whispered to me.

139

We never became really proficient at Cockney rhyming slang, but we quickly got fairly proficient with English slang and usage. We found some of their ways of expressing things very useful. "Sorted" was one of my favorites. They use it for "all arranged" or "all taken care of." "Rubbish" is a very useful English word it sounds best when applied to nonsensical talk and not to actual garbage. "You are, of course, talking rubbish Nigel!" "Lovely" is a word used very often by the English – by both men and women. I don't think I would use the word in the Bronx, but in South Kensington it seemed quite acceptable and raised no questions about my masculinity. It was lovely. "Gobsmacked" is a wonderful word that made its way into our vocabulary. Imagine the shock you would experience if you were suddenly slapped in the face with a large cold fish. You'd be gobsmacked. Indeed you would. We also became aware of the linguistic pitfalls: "pants" means underpants, not trousers – that one causes a lot of trouble. Many newly arrived Americans immediately start saying "Cheers!" but we never liked that. Somehow it seemed like they were trying to pretend to be Brits. So no "cheers" for us. And definitely no "Cherrio" or "Cheers and Beers." "Posh" is a very important English word, used to describe rich folks, upper-class people, and the facilities and accouterments that surround them. We started using this word quite early, perhaps because we were living in the neighborhood considered to be the epicenter of posh-ness. But it took us a while to get familiar with the words and – more important – the accents that delineate the all-important British class system.

At first we were kind of oblivious to the whole thing. Perhaps with the exception of the really out-there Cockneys, they all sounded like Brits to us. But fairly soon, we started to notice the class differences in speech and accent and vocabulary. We also learned that this is a very touchy subject in the UK. Talking about accents and social class there is kind of like talking about race in the U.S. It's a touchy subject. In the U.S. you could ask a new acquaintance "Hey Bob, is that Boston that I'm hearing in your voice?" But you would never ask a Brit, "Hey Ian, lemme guess – lower middle class, aspiring to middle-middle, right?" No, definitely not.

One of the odd things about getting to know the accents is that as we grew more knowledgeable and proficient, we began to kind of internalize some of the English class attitudes. The working class accents grew painful to listen to, and we began (unfairly) to associate them with folks who wear sweat suits all the time and are inclined towards Pit-Bulls and Rottweilers. Perhaps because we were living in the Royal Borough of Kensington and Chelsea, the upper class accents came to sound very nice to us.

We loved our time in England, but I missed the challenge and fun of working in a foreign language. Largely because of our common language, England felt almost too familiar. Often we'd joke that next time we'd try to be assigned to a *foreign* country.

Our linguistic wish came true. While of course it has a lot in common with the other romance languages, Italian is much further away from Spanish than Portuguese is, and was therefore much more of challenge for us. I knew that I wouldn't have time for full-time language study before getting to Rome – we couldn't leave London early because Elisa was finishing up her garden design studies. And we needed to be in Rome in time for the kids to start school in the fall. So I was pretty much going to have to come up with a way to learn Italian without the full-time training that normally precedes a foreign assignment. As soon as I got the assignment I scrambled to find ways to learn. I got a copy of the Rosetta Stone language learning program (the one that is advertised in the backs of airline magazines) and soon my office in Embassy London was filled with repetitive bursts of Italian words and phrases. I signed up for weekly afternoon language classes at the Italian Cultural Center in London's Belgravia section. I found London's Italian book store and stocked up on dictionaries and grammars and learning aids. I filled my I-pod with podcasts from the Italian public TV and Radio system RAI – I'd be walking through Hyde Park trying to figure out what Federico Rampini was saying in Italian about the history of ancient China.

Italian really is quite different from Spanish and Portuguese. This was good news and bad news. Good because we wouldn't be dealing with quite so many romance language interference issues. Bad because there would be a lot more new vocabulary and grammar to cram into our heads.

We found many of the differences quite surprising. If you want to say "I was surprised," in Spanish it comes out: "Me sorprendio" In Portuguese you get "Fiquei surpreso"
But the Italians can say it this way: "Sono rimasto stupito." To us, it sounded like they were saying "I remained stupid." In Italian "car rental" is "auto noleggio." It seemed like we were saying that the cars can't read.

Some very commonly used words that were very familiar from both Spanish and Portuguese have completely different meanings in Italian. The verb salir, for example. In Spanish it means "to go out." In Italian it means to go up, as in up the stairs. And in Spanish the verb "subir" means to go up. In Italian the same word means "to suffer."

And there are words in Italian that Spanish speakers find quite shocking. The word for "soft," for example. In Spanish: suave. In Italian: morbido.

Morbido? Really? It sounds like death! Death cheese! Morbid bread! Sono rimasto stupito!

Soon after we arrived in Rome, Elisa and I signed up for language lessons at the Embassy's in-house language school. When I met my instructor, I immediately started to get Portuguese flash-backs.

My teacher was an older woman. She must have been approaching 80. She had unusual interests – she was deeply interested in psychological yoga (the kind you do completely in your head) and wanted to talk about this – a lot. She reminded me a bit of Angonisha, but in an odd political juxtaposition, this lady was from the opposite end of the political spectrum. I mean completely the opposite end. She was so far to the right that – I swear – she even *looked* a bit like Mussolini. As with my Portuguese teacher, I will not use her real name. Let's call her Martella (roughly "The Hammer").

Political differences notwithstanding, Martella shared something with Angonisha: a deep hatred for the Spanish language. Martella also treated it as if it were an unfortunate infection, something to be eradicated as quickly as possible. She took particular delight in stopping me every time I used an even remotely Spanish-sounding pronunciation. The Italian word for "and" was especially useful to her in this linguistic sadism. In Italian, "and" is spelled "e" and it is pronounced like "eh". In Spanish, "and" is spelled "y" and it is pronounced "eeee". I found that in all languages, one uses the word "and" quite frequently. Far more frequently than you might think! But if your Italian teacher is Martella, and if, as you struggle with new vocabulary and the weird Italian way of handling the past tense, you momentarily forget about the pronunciation of that little one-letter word, the HAMMER will come down on you. "NO! Eh! No Spanish!" She made no effort to hide her delight in making these corrections. Entering her classroom was like walking into a Spanish-Italo linguistic minefield.

Angonisha's political commentary had come from the far left, Martella's came from the far right. We quickly learned that almost ALL of Italy's problems had one cause: foreigners, specifically immigrants. She seemed to forget that all her students were, well, foreigners, and that many of us were married to, well, immigrants. But even if she were to remember this, I don't think Martella would have been deterred. If Italy had a Rush Limbaugh, Martella would have been tuned in 24/7 (shouting "mega ditto"– however you say that in Italian).

I don't want to be too harsh on Angonisha and Martella. I learned a lot from both of them, and while they might have benefited from a bit more balance and a bit less harshness, they were both – in their own special ways – nice people.

The balance and harshness problem disappeared when, during my second year in Italy, I was assigned to the tiny classroom of Emanuella Borsari. There is no need for a pseudonym here, because it would be quite impossible for me to write anything unfavorable about Emanuella. She was a poised and elegant Italian lady in her fifties. She is from the north, from Emiglia-Romagna. For two hours each week it was my privilege to come under the tutelage of Emanuella. I probably learned more about Italy from her than from anyone else. At this point, the two or three students in my group constituted the advanced class. We were beyond verb drills and basic grammar and spent a lot of our two hours per week discussing (in Italian of course) articles from the local newspapers. This was very beneficial for several reasons: Our Italian was getting better – Emanuella wouldn't pounce on our errors, but she would gently let us know when we were mangling Dante's language. We usually selected articles that had to do with issues we were following or working on in our Embassy jobs. And finally – and I think this is the most important benefit – going through these articles with Emanuella allowed us to gain insight into how these issues looked to an Italian. Things that seemed shocking or absurd to us sometimes seemed normal and understandable to Emanuella. And vice versa. And sometimes, problems that were a bit abstract and theoretical for us were made very real through our discussions with her. For example, in my office (the Embassy's economic section) we were often reporting on how Italy's low economic growth rate was causing high unemployment among the country's young people. We all knew there was a lot of suffering behind those statistics, but the suffering was made real when Emanuella would describe (sometimes through tears) the job-search plights of her own children.

****

Language barriers make the divisions between nations – the divisions between us and them – seem very substantial, very real. But we learned that once you pierce the language barrier, your new skills give you the key to open doors to other cultures. Once you open these doors, you quickly learn that what we have in common with the speakers of that previously incomprehensible tongue far outweighs any differences that might exist between us and them.

SCIENCE AND TECHNOLOGY

"It almost never feels like prejudice. Instead it seems fitting and just – the idea that, because of an accident of birth, our group (whichever one it is) should have a central position in the social universe. Among Phaeronic prince-lings and Plantagenet pretenders, children of robber barons and Central Committee bureaucrats, street gangs and conquerors of nations, members of confident majorities, obscure sects, and reviled minorities, this self-serving attitude seems as natural as breathing. It draws sustenance from the same psychic wellsprings as sexisim, racism, nationalism and the other deadly chauvinisms that plague our species. Uncommon strength of character is needed to resist the blandishments of those who assure us that we have an obvious, even God-given superiority over our fellows. The more precarious our self-esteem, the greater our vulnerability to such appeals." Carl Sagan

"Heroism on command, senseless violence, and all the loathsome nonsense that goes by the name of patriotism - how passionately I hate them!" Albert Einstein

"Nationalism is an infantile disease. It is the measles of mankind." Albert Einstein

As Christmas 2005 approached I began my annual search for a gift for my wife. Suddenly, it came to me via the internet. It was perfect: National Geographic had launched a new project: National *Geno*graphic. You send them 100 bucks and they send you a little DNA sampling kit along with some booklets and a DVD. You scrape a little material off the inside of your cheek and send it to them in a bar-coded vial. Using a code that comes with the kit, you monitor a web site that updates you on the progress of your DNA analysis. After about six weeks, the web site tells you that your analysis is complete, and that a map showing the migrations of YOUR ancestors is ready. It was very exciting. The site seemed to say "Click here to find out where YOU came from!"

Well, it is not so much where you come from as it is how you got there. We know that we ALL come from the Rift Valley in Africa. What the National Genographic project shows you is the path taken by your ancestors in their migratory path out of East Africa.

For Elisa, information about this path was important. She had long been curious about her ancestry. Most people in the Dominican Republic can trace their origins to three parts of the world: Europe (from the Spanish colonizers), Africa (from the slaves brought to the island by the Europeans), or from the island of Hispaniola itself (from the indigenous people who were there when Columbus arrived). It is, in the words of the Dominican musician Juan Luis Guerra "Una raza encendida: blanca, negra y Taina!" ("A fiery race: white, black, and Taina!" Taina refers to the tribe that was living on the island when Colombus arrived.)

Of course, after 500 years most Dominicans have elements from all three groups in their personal backgrounds. The National Genographic project does not determine your personal ethnic mix. Instead this project looks at the geographic path taken by the chain of individual human beings that stretches from you back to our origins in East Africa. For women, the project uses mitochondrial DNA and looks at the maternal chain: mother, grandmother, great-grandmother... all the way back. Scientists know that certain changes in human DNA occurred in certain specific places during certain time periods. If your DNA has these changes in it, then your ancestors were in that place at that time. Using these DNA markers, National Genographic draws the map of the path taken by YOUR ancestors.

Elisa really liked the gift. We took the sample on Christmas morning and had it in the mail as soon as the post offices opened. Soon we started checking that web site every day. When it seemed to be taking too long, some of Elisa's Dominican skepticism kicked in and she wondered aloud if my gift might be part of some elaborate scam. Finally, the site reported that the results were in, and that Elisa's map was ready.

YOUR MAP

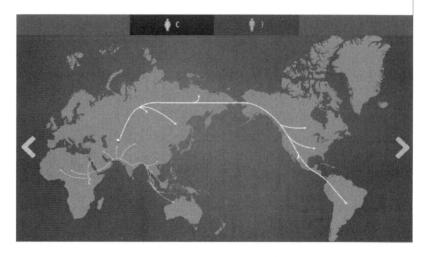

It was beautiful, and it was just what she'd hoped for. The line on the map stretched north from Kenya's Rift Valley through the Middle East, Central Asia, and Asiatic Russia. Then it was across the land bridge into present day Alaska, down the West Coast of North America and into Latin America. That is the path that Elisa's female ancestors had taken from the Rift Valley to Island of Hispaniola. This was proof that Elisa is a true daughter of Hispaniola, a descendant of the original inhabitants of that beautiful island, of the happy people that Columbus encountered when he arrived in 1492. The results made Elisa feel strong – she is the descendant of the strong women who made that long journey across mountains, deserts, glaciers and tundra.

Elisa's Dominican skepticism about the results was allayed by the fact that we had included no identifying information about her in the package we'd sent to National Genographic. The only information they had about us was my very Irish surname and our Embassy military address. The only way they could have known that this was someone from the Caribbean was from the DNA. This was the real thing. This was the map of the long 50,000 year journey taken by the several thousand female relatives that stand between Elisa and the origins of the human race.

The results made Elisa feel more truly Dominican, but they also reminded all of us of our deeper, human roots. Sure, we told the kids, "your mommy comes from the Dominican Republic," but the map shows that her relatives also came from what we today call Mexico, and California, and

Alaska, and Russia, and Arabia, and ultimately, from East Africa. All of us have in our DNA a map with a line stretching back to East Africa. How silly it is for people to base their identities on the last few steps of that journey, ignoring the rest of the trip, ignoring their connections to the rest of humanity.

****

Like most little boys Billy went through a period of intense interest in dinosaurs. We were in London at this point, and South Kensington, home of the Natural History Museum, was just about the best place in the world for a dinosaur obsessed little boy. We made many visits to that magnificent museum. And we even made our own little paleontological discovery.

Soon after our arrival in London, I took the kids to the park at St. Mary of the Boltons. The little pathways there were filled with pebbles. To keep Billy busy while I read my book, and to encourage his scientific inclinations, I suggested that he search the rocks for fossils. We had in the house a fossil that I'd found as a boy – it had somehow survived 350 million years in the dirt and a few decades moving around with me – so Billy knew what to look for. I barely had time to open my book when he came running back to me yelling "Look Daddy! I found one!" Sure enough, there, embedded in the little pebble, were the imprints of ancient sea-creatures.

Billy's discovery in the park was the first in a series of fossil-related events for our family: We took a trip down to the Isle of Wight on England's south coast. This was dino country – those white cliffs are filled with old bones, and each passing storm brings more of them to the surface. On home leave in New Jersey Billy found another fossil. Maria found one too. Eventually we took our little collection to the experts at the Natural History Museum. Billy and I sat down with a real paleontologist who identified for us all of our treasures. Later, during a vacation back in the States, we all went on a dinosaur dig out in desert of Western Colorado.

We also got interested in ancient Roman coins. This started with a little kit given to us by my mother. It contained a handful of ancient coins (there are a lot of them out there) along with instructions on how to clean and identify them. It was great fun to figure out which Emperor was depicted on our little coins. Billy and I added to our collection with purchases from the Trastevere flea market. Like our adventure with Elisa's DNA, I think our amateur paleontology and Roman coin collecting caused our family to have a time horizon a bit longer than most.

Then there was the astronomy. Having grown up during the race to the moon, I have always been very interested in the space program and

147

my.   In Santo Domingo I had bought a small telescope from a
ng diplomat.   Soon I was out in my front yard before dawn
exploring the heavens.   The depth of my fascination for this stuff is, I
think, proven by the fact that I convinced my bride that we should include
in our honeymoon itinerary a trip to the Kennedy Space Center in Florida.

My little telescope had gone with us to the Azores.   There – on those
rare occasions when the Azorean skies were not obscured by low-gray
clouds – I sometimes set it up in the backyard and let dinner guests take a
look at Jupiter or Saturn or the Andromeda galaxy.   We had a bit of an
awkward moment when I told evangelical friends that the light they were
seeing had been traveling to us for more than 2 million years.   This of
course clashed with their bible-based calculations of a 4,000 year old
universe.   Billy later noted that my 350 million year-old fossil also posed
a serious challenge to the 4,000 year theory.

While in London Elisa got me a better telescope for Christmas.   We
would sometimes set it up on the sidewalk in front of our house and show
Saturn's rings to passersby. (Some of the more cynical Brits refused to
believe that what they were seeing was actually Saturn – one guy asserted
confidently that I'd put some sort of transparency in the telescope tube.)

There was a Wall Street Journal "Pepper and Salt" cartoon that captures
astronomy's effect on our thinking: It shows a fellow looking through a
telescope at what appears to be the Andromeda galaxy. He comments that
it is hard to worry about the national debt when contemplating objects like
Andromeda. Indeed, the cosmic perspective provided by astronomy made
all the national problems and conflicts that we were working on seem petty
and trivial. I'm a big fan of Carl Sagan – when I was sent into Haiti just
prior to the 1994 U.S. military incursion into that country, I carried with
me his book "Cosmos." His "big picture" observations provided welcome
relief from the very local problems we were dealing with.

In his book "The Pale Blue Dot" Sagan perfectly captures the way an
awareness of the cosmos makes our bloody terrestrial rivalries seem so
absurd. Sagan had arranged for the Voyager 1 spacecraft to turn its camera
back toward earth from beyond the orbit of Pluto. Here is what we saw:

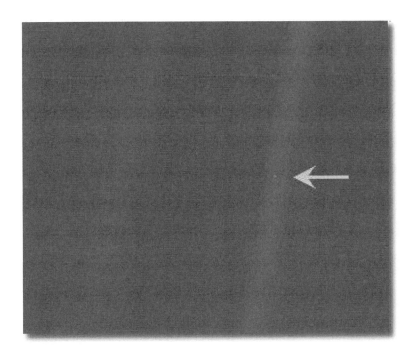

"Consider again that dot. That's here. That's home. That's us. On it everyone you love, everyone you know, everyone you ever heard of, every human being who ever was, lived out their lives... The Earth is a very small stage in a vast cosmic arena. Think of the rivers of blood spilled by all those generals and emperors so that in glory and triumph they could become the momentary masters of a fraction of a dot. Think of the endless cruelties visited by the inhabitants of one corner of this pixel on the scarcely distinguishable inhabitants of some other corner. How frequent their misunderstandings, how eager they are to kill one another, how fervent their hatreds. Our posturings, our imagined self-importance, the delusion that we have some privileged position in the universe, are challenged by this point of pale light... It has been said that astronomy is a humbling and character-building experience. There is perhaps no better demonstration of the folly of human conceits than this distant image of our tiny world. To me, it underscores our responsibility to deal more kindly with one another and to preserve and cherish the pale blue dot, the only home we've ever known."

I learned early on that it really wasn't a good idea to talk about astronomy with colleagues from work. Any mention of my pre-dawn efforts to observe the planets or distant galaxies usually resulted in awkward silences or ignorant wisecracks. And I knew that if they found astronomy to be weird, well, ham radio would be considered completely beyond the pale.

My interest in radio electronics began at around age 12. One thing lead to another and soon I was – at age 14 – a full-blown FCC-licensed amateur radio operator. I was a ham. In the bedroom that I shared with my long-suffering brother, I built a rather monstrous shortwave radio station with which I could communicate with like-minded fiends from around the word.

Ham radio was one of the things that led me into the Foreign Service. In the short autobiography that we all had to write during the State Department's hiring process, I cited ham radio as one of the things that got me interested in the world beyond US borders (in spite of this admission, they offered me the job). As a kid I would often run up stairs from my basement "ham shack" to report to my parents that my signals had spanned the oceans and that I had been talking to someone in New Zealand, or in Russia...

Ironically, the hobby that led me into the Foreign Service later contributed to my questioning of some of the nationalist assumptions than many see as underpinnings of the career. Long before the internet put us all in touch with a global community, amateur radio had us talking – at times incessantly – to people with similar interests from other countries. Electromagnetic waves respect no borders. In our radio conversations we discovered that all around the world, guys like us had gone through eerily similar journeys to electronic geek status: it usually started around the age of twelve, often with an inexplicable urge to disassemble the family radio or television set. There was often a lull in radio-activity once an interest in girls developed, but the interest in electronics lingered, usually to resurface later, often after life stabilized after college and marriage.

The cross-border friendships facilitated by this inherently international hobby has probably caused more than a few radio amateurs to wonder – as I did – about the real importance of the national divisions that separate us. But I became especially vulnerable to this kind of introspection when I started to pursue my hobby while living overseas. Now the foreigners were more than just friendly voices coming through my headphones. Now I was there with them, struggling to resolve technical problems, scrounging for parts, building absurdly large antennas. One of my closest friends in the Azores was an old fellow named Messias Moniz. We met at the local amateur radio club. Messias was a retired telegraph operator for the Marconi Company. He and and I would talk on the radio in the evening. He'd always close by asking me to pass his best regards to Elisa and the "Cristalinhos" – the little crystals. That's Portuguese radio slang for the kids. Messias and I got into several radio adventures. At one point we were bouncing signals off the international space station (this was written up in the radio magazine QST). Before I left, I built for Messias a special "homebrew" radio transmitter. Radio – the technology that had allowed me to contact people who were far away – had later allowed me to grow close to people when they were close-at-hand.

And of course there was the internet. We were enthusiastic early adopters of the new technology: I'd sent my first e-mail while in the Dominican Republic in 1993. There were no internet service providers in the country at that time – it seems incredible now, but I had to place long-distance phone calls to Miami so that I could connect to the Compuserve node there. This was way too expensive. But Dominicans love new communication technology and soon internet service became available. Elisa would come to my house and get on the World Wide Web and Internet Relay Chat.

During our decade in Europe, the internet was a lifeline to friends and family. I don't know if Elisa would have made it through the Azores tour without it. And as the years went by we seemed to be adding layers upon layers of internet connections. Facebook was, of course, a big hit with Elisa – she'd marvel at her ability to reconnect with childhood friends and classmates. The kids logged onto Club Penguin. I soon had hobby-related web sites and blogs in operation.

The internet soon became an important part of our lives. And it was another reminder for us of the global, cross-border nature of our lives. The people we kept in touch with were spread out all around the world. In this new medium borders and nationality had become almost meaningless. As had happened with ham radio, this technology made us more conscious of our global citizenship.

****

I spent my last year in London as the Embassy's Science and Technology Officer. I took this job in part because I knew that it would give me the chance to meet some of the top people in British science. It did, but sometimes I found the results to be a bit awkward and disappointing.

My introductory call on Dr. Martin Reese (Lord Reese), President of the Royal Society, was a good example. I had been reading Reese's books for many years. He is one of the world's top cosmologists and at the time of our meeting was also "The Astronomer Royal." He was holding posts held by Isaac Newton.

I was a big fan, but he really didn't seem to know what to make of me. The Royal Society's head of international relations had set up the meeting and ushered me into Reese's London office. I tried to break the ice with what I hoped to be an endearing story: I told him that we were both astronomers, but at completely opposite ends of the spectrum. "You, Lord Reese, are The Astronomer Royal, while I just have a small telescope that I use with my kids to look at the moon and the planets from our front yard!" He didn't laugh. He didn't even smile. Clearly, he wasn't amused. "Well I don't actually look through telescopes, you know." I had known that. I was just trying to be nice.

We got through the meeting, but I had the distinct impression that he was, in a way, looking down on me. This is an unusual situation for an American diplomat. People are generally delighted to talk to us. They are usually pleased that representatives of the U.S. government are interested in them, and are almost always intrigued by our work. Lord Reese seemed neither pleased nor intrigued. Instead, he seemed to be wondering why he was wasting time with me.

I think I can understand his perspective. His life's work is focused on figuring out the origin and the fate of the universe, while my job was protecting the interests of one of planet earth's political jurisdictions. I guess it didn't help that I was at the time serving under a government (the Bush administration) that seemed contemptuous of science.

Lord Reese's attitude may have just come with the territory: Being above nationalistic issues has a long history at the Royal Society.   In "Seeing Further – The Story of Science, Discovery & The Genius of the Royal Society" author Bill Bryson wrote:

"In an age when sabers hardly ever ceased rattling, the Society became the least nationalistic of national institutions. The name itself is telling. Royal Society of London describes a location, not an allegiance. Had it been the Royal Society of Great Britain it would have been a very different organization whether it wished it or not. So throughout its history it has been the most admirably neutral and cosmopolitan of entities. When Benjamin Franklin was the voice of revolution against Great Britain, he was still an esteemed and welcome member of the society... the Society refused to expel fellows from enemy nations during either of the world wars, and was one of the first bodies to re-establish links after them."

****

I first met Astronaut Mark Kelly in Winston Churchill's wartime bunker. It was November 2006, and NASA Administrator Mike Griffin and the crew of Space Shuttle mission STS-121 had come to London on an official visit; the crew had carried into space the Royal Society's Copley Medal, which would soon be presented to Stephen Hawking. Churchill's bunker was part of the cultural exchange. Mark introduced me to his fiancé Gabby Giffords. Wow, I thought, this guy is an astronaut, and his fiancé has just been elected to the U.S. House of Representatives. I was impressed, but wary – would these folks turn out to be an obnoxious power-couple? Happily I soon found out this was not the case – they were very nice, very down-to-earth.

After the tour of the bunker, we all went to the Library of the Royal Society. Stephen Hawking and Martin Reese were there. Astronauts are usually the most interesting and accomplished people in the room, but not in that room. Not only did we have Hawking and Reese, but Isaac Newton himself seemed to be present. The Royal Society folks had – with what had to have been a forced non-chalance – placed on the table the original manuscript of Newton's Principia Matematica. It was just lying there on the table, open to a random page, with Newton's penmanship exposed for all to see. Next to it was a small reflector telescope, one of two that Newton had built himself. The American visitors were suitably and genuinely gobsmacked.

This was all great stuff, but for me the most memorable part of the astronauts' visit came on the last night. The NASA delegation was kind enough to invite Elisa and me for an informal "pizza and beer" evening at the house they were using. For someone who had grown up with the Apollo program and who, as a kid, had wanted to be an astronaut, this was a clearly an event not to be missed. It was all very friendly and informal. The topics of conversation were very unusual. What is blast-off like? What were your first impressions of zero-gravity? Elisa asked Mark Kelly if his mother worries when he goes into space – Gabby Giffords laughed and said Mark's mom has two reasons to worry: Mark's identical twin brother is also an astronaut.

Most of the talk was about the nuts and bolts of spaceflight, but then we heard one of the astronauts say something that was more political, more connected to the diplomatic world that we lived in. It was about looking back at the earth and realizing that the national borders that mean so much to us, that we kill and die for, aren't very real. A quick web search reveals that this kind of one-world sentiment is quite strong among the ostensibly ultra-patriotic astronaut corps:

"When you're finally up on the moon, looking back at the earth, all these differences and nationalistic traits are pretty well going to blend and you're going to get a concept that maybe this is really one world and why the hell can't we learn to live together like decent people?" – Colonel Frank Borman, Apollo 8 astronaut

"From our orbital vantage point, we observe an earth without borders, full of peace, beauty and magnificence, and we pray that humanity as a whole can imagine a borderless world as we see it and strive to live as one in peace." – Commander William McCool speaking three days before he was killed when Shuttle Columbia broke up during re-entry. He had John Lennon's "imagine" playing in the background as he spoke.

"I really believe that if the political leaders of the world could see their planet from a distance of 100,000 miles their outlook could be fundamentally changed. That all-important border would be invisible, that noisy argument silenced. The tiny globe would continue to turn, serenely ignoring its subdivisions, presenting a unified façade that would cry out for unified understanding, for homogeneous treatment. The earth must become as it appears: blue and white, not capitalist or Communist; blue and white, not rich or poor; blue and white, not envious or envied." – Michael Collins, Gemini 10 and Apollo 11 astronaut

"We went to the Moon as technicians; we returned as humanitarians... You develop an instant global consciousness, a people orientation, an intense dissatisfaction with the state of the world, and a compulsion to do something about it. From out there on the moon, international politics look so petty. You want to grab a politician by the scruff of the neck and drag him a quarter of a million miles out and say, 'Look at that, you son of a bitch.'" – Edgar Mitchell, Apollo 14 astronaut.

This shift in attitude from nationalism to a more global, cosmopolitan worldview is so widespread among astronauts that it has been given a name: The Overview Effect. As I myself moved ever further from a nationalistic view of the world, I found it reassuring that many of the astronauts had gone through a similar shift: I wasn't the only former military officer who, after taking a look at the really big picture, had a change of heart about the way the world is organized. The fact that many of these quotes came from American patriotic icons who had been my boyhood heroes made them even more significant for me. The astronauts'

154

epiphanies seemed to hit them quickly, the result of looking back at earth from orbit or from the moon. My epiphany came at much closer range, and over a longer period of time. But the conclusions were much the same.

THEM
FOREIGN FRIENDS

"Patriotism is an attitude of favoritism toward 'my country' and 'my people.' If egotism or pridefulness toward oneself is a vice, then patriotism or pridefulness toward one's particular country is likewise deplorable."
The Quaker Tony White, writing in "The Friends Journal"

"So, does he have any *foreign* friends?"
Over the years I'd grown accustomed to the questions of the security clearance investigators. These poor fellows would show up in the office from time to time, working on the periodic updates of the clearances of someone in the office. We all came up for updates every five years. A colleague's time had come.

"Well, he's been in the Foreign Service for 28 years, so I certainly *hope* he has some foreign friends!"

I really expected my response to elicit at least a little chuckle from the inquisitor. When it didn't, I got kind of worried.

"No, no,.. I'm not talking about professional contacts. I mean, you know, real personal *friends*."

Realizing that this was not the time to get into a long discussion of the useful role of personal friendship in American foreign relations, I decided to go minimalist. I quickly determined that at that moment I couldn't remember my colleague ever specifically telling me that any of his friends were not American citizens.

"Not as far as I know."

Seemingly satisfied, the investigator jotted this all down in his notebook, and we moved on to the other questions that fill the days and notebooks of security clearance investigators.

Later, in our office we all had a kind of snooty laugh about the "foreign friends" question of the gum-shoe security guy. Oh how unsophisticated he was! Apparently he didn't realize that all of us live our lives surrounded by fascinating foreigners, many of whom, do in fact become our friends. *Foreign* friends.

While this guy may have missed an important memo ("Cold War Ends") and probably was a being a bit overzealous, when you think about it, he may have been onto something with his "foreign friends" questions. If you start out with the assumption that national loyalty is supremely important,

156

well, any personal loyalties that cross the national lines should be viewed with some suspicion, right?

We have a lot of foreign friends. This was brought home to us when it came time for me to fill out the forms for my own security clearance update. Apparently as a result of 9/11, the U.S. government had adopted some new security clearance forms. The idea was to have one standardized form for the employees of all government agencies. I guess someone working in Iowa for the Department of Agriculture would have no trouble with the part of the form that asks for a detailed listing of all "foreign friends," but for us, this part of the form was really daunting. We looked carefully at the form and tried to parse the instructions, hoping to find some loopholes that would spare us from having to come up with the names (including middle names – I'm not completely certain about the middle names of my siblings) and the government ID card numbers of hundreds of people around the world. But there was no denying the reality – we had been consorting with foreigners. A lot. I'd been overseas 19 years. Elisa, well, she was outside the United States from birth to age 25, and then from age 29 to 39. We knew that we'd never be able to put down on that list all the friends we'd made in more than 50 years of life beyond America's shores. But Uncle Sam wanted the information, and, being good soldiers, we decided to do the best we could. We decided to focus on the people who are closest to us, and on the people who – in the eyes of that security inspector – would register as being REALLY foreign. In other words, we wouldn't really worry too much if we missed a Canadian or two or the odd Brit. But we'd be very careful about not missing any Iranian friends.

Filling out that form was like a trip down memory lane. Here are some highlights of a few of the names that came up as we struggled with that security form:

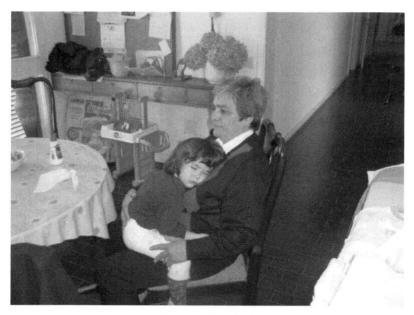

Maria and Margarida

"Well, we obviously have to list Margarida." There was no argument there. It is difficult to imagine someone outside the family being closer to us than Margarida. The housekeeper at the Consul's official residence in the Azores, Margarida quickly became a surrogate grandma for Billy and Maria. She helped us deal with three years of Cerelaca spills and skinned knees, of bee stings and lost toys. Margarida is a deeply good person and in spite of having a life that wasn't easy, she was always happy, always spreading joy and laughter in that big house. And there is an element of stability, solidity, and resilience to her character – she is like the grandmother who tells you that everything will be all right, and makes you believe it. This was very important to Elisa when she was struggling with depression in the Azores. Margarida was her rock, the person who helped her through tough times. We grew so close to Margarida that as the time approached for us to leave, we really just couldn't bear the thought of taking Maria and Billy out of her arms and saying good bye to her. So we cooked up a scheme to at least postpone the heartache: We arranged for her to come to London with us. We knew she couldn't stay permanently –

she had a job, and a family of her own – but she obviously shared our desire to postpone the goodbyes and agreed to stay with us in London for a few weeks to help us get settled.

Margarida, Elisa, Maria, Paula

"Ana Paula has to be on the list!"   She was the cook at the residence in the Azores, but was much more than that to us. She was the one who brought us into The Enchanted Castle. She brought her son Ivo to the house to play during those early days when Billy was lonely and bored. She taught Billy about all the bugs and other natural wonders of the backyard. One day she smacked Billy on the back and cleared his throat when he started to choke on a hard candy. We would have tried to take Ana Paula with us too, but that would have been completely impossible – she had Ivo and a new baby to care for. So we had to say goodbye to Ana Paula in Ponta Delgada. That was tough.

Mr. Silva

"Mr. Silva! Definitely Mr. Silva!" No argument there. Francisco Silva was always *Mister* Silva to us. He was the only one of the Consulate employees to be referred to in this formal way. It was not that he ever insisted on it, and it was not because he was in any way aloof. It seemed to me that we all got into the habit of calling him *Mister* Silva in recognition of his kind, gentle, dignified manner. Mister Silva is, you see, a real gentleman, and for this reason, it just seemed right to treat him with a bit of extra courtesy. Mr. Silva did many things for the Consulate and for our family. He was the driver, so he carried me to and from the Consulate twice each day (I went home for lunch). En route, we'd give Billy and Maria rides to and from school. Mr. Silva LOVED the big armored Crown Victoria that the State Department sent us. When it first arrived, he'd pop the trunk and marvel at the enormity of the engine. It was by far the biggest sedan on the island – Mr. Silva had to be careful not to park or drive too close to the car of the Azorean President (we didn't want to invite invidious comparisons). I used to joke with Mr. Silva that he could make some extra money by giving tours of the car (and the engine compartment). He handled all the mail deliveries for the Consulate. When Washington got hit with an anthrax attack, we had to put Mr. Silva on special antibiotics:

he had been handling diplomatic pouches that had come through the postal facility that had been exposed to the deadly powder. Whenever Elisa had to do something official, he'd take her to the event. Even before I appointed him Consulate security officer, Mr. Silva was very protective of all of us – he was a natural choice for the security job. Mr. Silva is the kind of guy you'd want watching your back. I always thought that being driven around by Mr. Silva was one of the major perks of being the American Consul in the Azores.

"Hey honey, what about Elias? He was our friend, but I don't think we ever got his last name." We weren't really close, but Elias was memorable. We met him on the sidewalks of South Kensington in London. He was struggling with six dogs, yelling at them in Portuguese as they made their way to Battersea Park. Our house in London was too small for a dog, and Elisa was looking for opportunities to give our kids some canine companionship. Portuguese language skills provided the opening. She learned that Elias was from Brazil, and was working as dog walker for London's rich and famous. He quickly agreed to let us tag along from time-to-time on the dog walks.

"You know, sometimes I think my life is some sort of miracle," he told us. He explained that he had come to London as a kind of handy-man for a rich Brazilian banker. Walking the banker's dog was part of his job. Soon neighbors asked if their dogs could go with him. His boss agreed, but advised him to charge (a lot!) for the service. The fee was soon set at 25 pounds sterling per walk, 40 pounds on weekends. Soon Elias had twelve clients. The dogs would have to go out twice per day. Every day. Do the math! That's at least $400,000 per year. "For walking in the park!" Elias exclaimed as we walked the dogs. "This is my office! This is a miracle!"

"What about Jasmine and Tom?"
"Well, we'll have to list her, but not him – he's American."
"Yea, but didn't they all just get UK citizenship also?"
Jasmine and Tom met at grad school at Yale. She is from Singapore; he's from the U.S. Our kids were in the same school in London. We met them at Billy's birthday party where Tom proved to be very adept at breaking open the Mexican piñata. Like many of our friends in London, Tom works in finance in the City of London. After many years of residence there, their family became eligible for UK (and European) citizenship.

"Lile Braz has to go on the list."

"Of course. We're so close to her – they'd put me in JAIL if we didn't list her."

Lile is Maria's Godmother. That put her beyond "friend" status and put her closer to the "family" category. She and Elisa met in the Azores through the charitable works of the Rotary Club. Lile's husband is the Honorary Consul of Belgium in the Azores – for three consecutive years, he and I marched solemnly together in the seven hour-long Santo Cristo procession. That kind of made us the Azorean equivalent of blood brothers.

Mari-Angeles, Rocio, Elisa, Monica

"What about the Españolas? Rocio, Monica and Mari-Angles?" "Yes, for sure!" Rocio was a pediatrician from Spain – Elisa met her at the Ponta Delgada hospital while doing volunteer work. Like us, Rocio was struggling with island life and the Portuguese language. Rocio introduced us to a small community of young-ish Spaniards who, for one reason or another, had come to live 900 miles off the coast of Portugal. Monica was a social worker at the school just across the street from our house (we later travelled to Extremadura Spain for her wedding). Mari-Angeles was in the Azores with her geneticist husband who was doing research. Mari Angeles had a little boy, Antonio, who joined Billy and Maria in forming the international contingent at the Enchanted Castle School.

"Katja?" Yes, definitely. She's still a German citizen." Katja and Elisa met in the new moms' playgroup in Falls Church, Virginia when Billy was a baby. Katja's daughter Emily is Billy's age (when they were babies, Katja and Elisa talked about how nice it would be if they would someday marry). Katja and her American husband, Tyler, are Mormons, and during our time in Virginia brought us so deeply into their circle of young Mormon friends that we sometimes felt like honorary member of the Church of Latter Day Saints. After we moved to the Azores, they moved to Germany. One summer we all met up for a vacation in the South of France.

Croquet with Sir Jeremy and his son

"Sir Jeremy?"
"Definitely – definitely a friend, and the Knighthood is a dead give-away that he's a foreigner!" I had found it difficult to make friends with Brits. This came as a surprise – we had expected to be greeted with open arms by our British cousins, but we soon found that there were some cultural factors that stood in the way of friendship. Drinking and the culture of the pub was part of it – for many British men "friend" is defined as someone who regularly accompanies you on drunken pub crawls. I don't drink, so for me

the barrier to entry was quite high. But there were also people like Sir Jeremy Morse and his wife Belinda who didn't let our abstemiousness stand in the way of friendship. Our tiny concrete garden was adjacent to Jeremy's garden, separated from their space by a flimsy fence. At first, when Elisa would be out in the garden puttering around, Jeremy or Belinda would appear on their side of the fence. Elisa expected to say hello to the neighbors, but they would kind of avert their gaze and pretend not to see her. How strange, we thought. It took us a while to see that this was a cultural thing: far from being unfriendly, they were just being very English – they were trying to respect our privacy.

Jeremy and Belinda also provided us with an introduction to another important English cultural factor: the belief that it is extremely rude to brag about yourself, to toot your own horn. It was only through Google that I learned of Sir Jeremy's illustrious carrier in British banking, of his service to the Bank of England, of his status as one of England's best chess players, or of the fact that he sometimes designed the crossword puzzle for the Times of London. He never mentioned any of that.

Belinda was also very accomplished, and equally reluctant to tell us about her accomplishments. One afternoon we were out at their country house for lunch. After a round of croquet we sat in their beautiful garden. I commented that it would be a great place for a writer or an artist. "Well," she said very quietly, "I have done a bit of writing here." It was difficult, but using her statement as an opening I got Belinda to tell me more about this "bit of writing." It turned out that she'd published four books! She was in the process of finishing another one, the biography of an English woman who had provided heroic leadership during an uprising in India.

Living next door to Jeremy and Belinda was for us one of the best things about our tour in London.

"Don't forget the Princesses!"

They were in Italy. One day as I walked through the Piazza di San Cosimato on the way home from work, I was greeted by Maria and one of her school friends.

"Daddy, daddy! This is my friend Livia! She's a Princess daddy! A *real* princess." The little girl cringed and kind of covered her eyes in embarrassment. She'd obviously been through this before. She is a real Italian Principessa. Her family has a castle. (Tom Cruise got married there.) The first time Livia came to our house, as she was walking with Maria through the courtyard of the apartment complex (about 200 units!) she looked around and, obviously thinking that it was all ours, told Maria that we had a nice place!

"Joao and Cris?"

For sure. We met in London. They are Brazilians – Joao works for a major multinational company. At first we spoke to them in Portuguese – we were fresh from the Azores and pleased to have a chance to show off our skills. Their kids went to Southbank School – Victoria is Billy's age,

165

Julia was with Maria. Victoria arrived speaking very little English – within a year or so you'd have thought she grew up in New York. Julia and Maria were very close. For a while, it looked as if they might follow us to Trastevere, but the Italian visa bureaucracy somehow couldn't cope with the notion of a Brazilian, working for an Anglo-Dutch company, resident in London who wanted to move to Rome. So Italy missed out. Years later, we all had a laugh when Maria got a very "international kid" text message from Julia: "BAD NEWS! WE'RE MOVING BACK TO BRAZIL!"

"Should we put Teresa on the list? I'm worried that she's illegal..."
Teresa is from Bolivia. She's a dear friend of ours. She cleans houses and works as a nanny in London. Her life is not easy. Like tens of thousands of women in London, she lives thousands of miles from her loved ones, working in cold, dark, rainy Britain in an effort to support her family back home. As is often the case, the family that she works for is border-line abusive, perhaps taking advantage of the possibility that Teresa's papers are not completely in order, and of the fact that she has developed emotional ties to their kids. She is not in the best of health. She struggles. One of her daughters died in Bolivia while she was in London. Perhaps for immigration reasons, she couldn't even go back for the funeral. Teresa is a reminder that for many, the international life is filled with hardship and heartache.

"What about Colleen and Alfred?" (These are not their real names.)
"She's Irish and he's Australian, so they're a long way from "axis of evil" territory, but they are friends and they are foreign, so they should go on the list." I'm not sure about the statute of limitations in Australia, so here I'll obscure their identities. Colleen was still in her teens when she de-camped from cold dark Ireland for the sunshine of Australia. She got a job in a bar and it was there that she met Alfred. He was apparently one of the regulars. One day she was lamenting the fact that the Australian immigration authorities were getting ready to send her back to the bogs. Only marriage to an Australian would allow her to stay. Even though they barely knew each other, Alfred, uh, offered to help. What started out as immigration fraud soon turned into true-love. Twenty years later they were our friends in London. Billy and Maria went to school with their daughter. (Maria was a huge fan of the Australian animal expert Steve Irwin. When we learned that Irwin had been killed, we tried to shield Maria from the bad news. It was to no avail. The next morning, as soon as we arrived at the bus stop, in her a strong Australian accent Colleen's daughter dramatically

announced Irwin's death: "Maria! Did ya eer? Steve Irwin was KILT! By a STING RAIY! Got 'im right in the 'art! THUNK!")

"How about Alexis and Laura?"
"I think so. They both have jobs that they security people would want to know about." He is a French journalist and she is a Portuguese official of the United Nations. Maria went to school in Rome with their daughter Chloe. They live in Panama now. Or is it Havana? I used to run into Alexis from time to time in the street outside Palazzo Chigi, the offices of the Italian Prime Minister. Alexis would be out there with a camera man and France 24 microphone whenever Berlusconi had done something especially wacky or egregiously lecherous; I'd stop and cautiously share some snide comments about the Prime Minister. Sometimes, if Laura was away on U.N. business on a night that Alexis had to report, I'd find Chloe at our house – Alexis would have asked to Elisa to take care of her until the end of the French news program.

With Natasha and Alessandra on the way to Ponza

"Natasha?"
"Yes, of course. She's the former ping-pong champion of Yugoslavia right? Plus she has a very Russian-sounding name and a very Russian-sounding accent. They would want us to put her on the list." Natasha is

Serbian (and perhaps now a Brit) who went to college on a ping-pong (OK, table-tennis) scholarship and represented Yugoslavia in that sport in international competitions. We met when Maria and Natasha's daughter Alessandra were in pre-school at the Bousefield School in London. Perhaps because they were both somewhat exotic foreigners, Elisa and Natasha became friends very quickly – on the day they met, Elisa came running into the house to tell me about this amazing person named Natasha. We went with Natasha to her ski place in the Swiss Alps. Later she and her kids traveled with us (by hydrofoil!) to the island of Ponza, out in the Med near Rome.

"Eddie?"

"Of course he's definitely a friend." Eddie drove our kids to and from school in London for four years. I would often hitch a ride on his bus. Eddie would carry me a few blocks in the direction of the South Ken Tube station. One morning, Eddie said something that really surprised me.

"I remember in the war when they had unexploded bombs still sticking out of the sidewalk, and all they did was to put a little rope around it. Now they rope off pear trees because of the danger of falling pears! Heck, trains went in and out of Victoria Station with the bombs falling!"

I didn't realize that he was speaking of personal experiences. I'd guessed his age to be around 65 max, too young to remember the war. But listening to him I began to suspect that Eddie was older. I mentioned that

I'd heard that our neighborhood had been hit pretty badly. He kind of scoffed at the notion that this wealthy part of London had suffered during the war: "This area only suffered when the flying bombs started. Then they started to get a taste of what the East End had had... I remember seeing a flying bomb come in. I was standing on the south side of the river, and all of a sudden, there it was, flying over." Obviously he was reminiscing about a Nazi V-1 buzz bomb.

"How old were you Eddie?" I asked.

"Thirteen," he replied. Then, saving me from doing the math,

"I'm seventy-six years old."

The next day I told him that Elisa and I had both been surprised by his age. I jokingly told him Elisa wanted to know his secret.

"Oh, don't you know?" he asked. "It's because we didn't have enough to eat during the war... But of course, I probably had even less to eat before the war."

Eddie explained that he had grown up in a care home – an orphanage. His parents had split up during the great depression. At the age of four, he had been sent to an orphanage in Cheshire. He and his brother had made the trip, by train, by themselves. His brother was seven. They had checked themselves into the orphanage.

Eddie told me that he had lived there with a bunch of other boys under the care of two women. He said they were not affectionate to the kids. "Like school teachers they were," said Eddie. He and his brother remained in the home until the war started. At that point it was turned into a center for refugees from the continent. Eddie and his brother were moved down to a home in Kent. "That was nicer," said Eddie.

He stayed in the Kent home until the age of thirteen, when he and his brother went back to London to live with their mother. In London, their house faced the railroad tracks. Anti-aircraft guns had been mounted on rail cars. Often at night these gun trains would stop right in front of the house, and would open fire on the Germans flying overhead.

Eddie was a lot of fun, especially for the kids. His wartime childhood had left him inured to Britain's health and safety obsession – during our first year in London we were surprised (and somewhat concerned) when Billy reported that Eddie had stopped the bus during a rare London snowstorm and had allowed the kids to engage in a snow-ball fight near busy Kensington High Street. Years later the kids told us that Eddie let them help him change gears on the bus, and would (at their insistence) go a bit faster over the speed bumps (so the boys on the back seat could get a little taste of zero-g). I guess if you grew up with V-1 Buzz Bombs, it would be hard to consider traffic and little snow to be dangerous. Even though

Eddie was the product of a very rough childhood, and was very "East End," he had a soft side too: When Maria had been frightened by a scary movie, she told Eddie that she was scared. He let her sit right behind the driver's seat and (between gear shifts) held her little hand.

"Maymoona!"
Yes. Maymoona lived around the corner from us in London, and her kids went to the Bousfield School. She is Muslim, of Pakistani descent. Her husband always struck me as the stereotypical Englishman – tall, thin, phlegmatic. We'd often see him weaving his way through London traffic on a bicycle, with one or two kids hanging onto him or the handlebars for dear life. He and Maymoona had been together for many years, but had not yet formally tied the knot. Then they decided to have a traditional Pakistani wedding in London and we were invited. It was the best wedding I had ever gone to. They had it at the London Physic Garden in Chelsea, a really beautiful and historic center of botanical science that was right in our neighborhood. Maymoona and all her female relatives were dressed in the beautiful gold-colored bedazzled dresses of the sub-continent. A Muslim Imam presided. For the reception, they brought in a team of Bollywood dance instructors – we all learned how to dance and chant as they do in the Indian movies. It was all great fun.

"Gosh, Ermano. Shouldn't we put poor old Ermano on the list? After all, we have lots of little things that he gave us." I would have gladly put Ermano on the list, but I'm sorry to say that we didn't have his last name. He was in his seventies and lived near our piazza in Trastevere. We'd see him every day as we had our coffee. He'd always say hello, and if the kids were with us, he'd always have little gifts for them – small plastic toys, little flashlights... He gave out these gifts (he gave them to lots of people) purely out of the goodness of his heart. I wish I had his last name so I could put him on the list.

"Jose Antonio Mota Amaral?"

"Definitely. A great friend. And there is the family political connection."
In the Azores, I used to take an afternoon walk along the waterfront. Every
day, I used to joke to the Consulate staff that I was going out for a security
inspection, or to check for hostile submarines. On these walks, I would
always cross paths with a friendly guy a bit older than me. We started out
just nodding greetings to each other. Then we'd talk a bit. Then, after a
while, we'd do our walks together. Soon it was a daily routine.

The political connection never really came up. Jose Antonio's brother –
Joao Bosco Mota Amaral – was the former President of the Azores, and
during my time in the islands was President of the Portuguese Congress.
In my preparations for the Azores Consul job, I had read about him, and
this ended up helping me on my final exam in the Portuguese language
course – the instructors presented me with an article about a person who
I'm sure they considered a relatively obscure politician. The article focused
on his connections to the secretive Catholic religious order Opus Dei.
Having been reading about the Azores, I knew all about Joao Bosco Mota
Amaral and about Opus Dei, so I was able to ramble on at length (and get
an "A"). When we first got to the Azores, we crossed paths with Joao
Bosco himself while walking with the kids on that same waterfront avenue.
I introduced myself, and introduced Maria, who was in her baby carriage.
Charmed, the grand old man of Azorean politics burst into song ("Maria! I
just met a girl named Maria!" from West Side Story). But Jose Antonio
wasn't involved in politics so he and I always talked about other things.

Later, that waterfront avenue was re-named for his prominent brother: Avenida Joao Bosco Mota Amaral.   But for me it will always be Avenida *Jose Antonio* Mota Amaral.

"What about Xabier and Noelle?"
"Definitely. They are very close friends. He's Basque and his name begins with an X. And she's very French! The investigators would want to know about them!" Xabier and Noelle lived around the corner from me when I was stationed in the Basque country. This was during those dark and lonely days before I met Elisa. Xabier and Noelle sort of adopted me – I was brought into their family and became a regular visitor to their conversations in front of the chimney. They stayed with my parents during a trip to New York. I was at their daughter's wedding. We sailed along the North Coast of Spain on their sailboat (Xabier is an accomplished sailor – he crossed the Atlantic in that boat. But I discovered that I was not made for the sea.)

"Guna! Definitely Guna!"
"He's a great friend and he's as exotic as you can get!"
Guna is from Sri Lanka and we met him underground. I mean literally underground. He works as the night attendant at the parking garage in our apartment complex in Rome. As I've mentioned, the Italian doormen treated us with disdain – it may have been because we were seen as renters, perhaps because we are Americans, maybe just because we were transients in a place where the average stay is 50 years. But Guna and his extended Sri Lankan family made up for all of this nastiness. He was unfailingly kind and helpful. Like Teresa, he was living his life far from home in an effort to support his family. He was in Italy legally, and had permission to work, but he suffered from anti-immigrant discrimination – when it came time for the complex to select a new doorman (this would have been a considerable step up), Guna was passed over. The residents preferred an Italian doorman (even if the Italian was as dumb as an oyster). Back home, he was a teacher of physics and math, but he could make more money parking cars underground in Rome, so that's what he did. What a shame.

172

"Walter, Renata, and Ira ?"

Definitely. I met Walter and his wife Renata in 1989 in a bar called the
Club Nautico Catamaran in Algorta, Vizcaya, Spain. I don't drink, but
Spain's intense social life is built around bars, so the Catamaran Nautical
Club became my local bar, and I became one of the regulars. Walter and
Renata are Italian – he was in Spain running a chain of clothing stores for
Luciano Benetton. Through that bar we all got very close to the local
community, but I think our common status as foreigners in a somewhat
insular place forged a special bond between the three of us. About a year
after I left the Basque country, just before I went to the Dominican
Republic, in a fit of nostalgia for that beautiful place by the sea I took a
month of leave and returned to Spain. But, proving that you can never go
home again, I found myself feeling out of place. Lots of friends (including

Walter and Renata) had moved. Things just weren't the same. Luckily, Walter was in town checking some of his stores. Sensing my distress, came up with the solution: "Come back with me to Italy!" Soon we were off on a most excellent European adventure, stopping in France, Monaco and several places in Northern Italy before meeting up with Renata at their house near Venice. Walter saved the day! We've stayed close over all these years. They came to visit Elisa and me in the Dominican Republic. We took the kids to see them in Italy. Their daughter Ira spent a summer with us in London. We're very close.

Friendship is one of the key bulwarks of nationalism. For most people, their circle of friends lies entirely within their national borders, and this inevitably reinforces the "us – them" feelings that underlie nationalism and patriotism. But when you live outside those national borders as we have, the friendships you develop "out there" have the opposite effect. One by one, these friendships seem to chip away at the notion that we have some special bond with people who happen to have been born in the same place that we were born, or who have a passport issued by the same government that issued ours. We even found the phrase "foreign friends" kind of distasteful – it seemed to imply a kind of differentiation or compartmentalization that was alien to the way we lived. We didn't put our friends in little national boxes. We had friends, not [FILL IN THE NATIONALITY] friends. We had learned earlier how hurtful this kind of differentiation can be: During her first year in Virginia, Elisa's feelings were hurt when a woman who she considered a friend referred to her as "one of my Latina friends." Friendship should have no compartments.

Sometimes when people talk about patriotism and "love of country" they seem to imply that we should have some sort of some special, preferential fondness for our countrymen, that our human sympathies should somehow respect national borders. If that's the case, well, large numbers of foreign friends *should* be seen as being subversive. So maybe the security guy was right to be concerned about "foreign friends." But look at it this way: Should we really like our foreign friends less than we like those who are from the U.S.? When I rode the bus to work every morning in Rome, as I looked around at my fellow passengers, should I really have felt some sort of special fondness for the one or two of them who were from the United States? Should I have automatically liked them more than the Italians? Sorry, but that makes no sense to me.

There are, however, people who do think this way, who do put national boundaries on human sympathy. One day during language class in Rome, we were discussing a newspaper article about a police attempt to confiscate

174

the goods that an African street merchant had been trying to sell in Trastevere. The poor man went into a panic. He started crying and screaming. He pleaded with the cops – he told them in broken Italian that the merchandise they were trying to confiscate represented his life savings, and that his family back in Senegal would go hungry if he lost it. Italian passersby were shocked to hear this, and, to their credit, intervened – they asked the police to let the fellow go. I expressed sympathy for the street vendors, and for the poor people in Africa. But one of my classmates (a senior officer in the Embassy) seemed annoyed by my expression of sympathy: "Why should we feel concerned about these people from Africa? They are not our problem. They are not American citizens."

One final note on security clearances and foreign friends: After some deliberation and renewed scrutiny of the security form, we came up with our official list of declarable foreign friends. For a variety of reasons some of the people mentioned here didn't have to be listed. And there are people who we were close to who – for a number of reasons related to the instructions on the form – didn't have to be on the list. But finally I got the form completed. The sensation was similar to what you feel when your tax return is finally done. I brought the form in to the Embassy and, proud of our diligence, presented it to one of the security officers. She looked through it, and, arriving at the Foreign Friends section, rolled her eyes and groaned.

"What the matter?" I asked.

"This might cause you trouble," she said.

"Why?" I asked.

"Too many foreign friends."

OTHER PEOPLES' PATRIOTISMS

"Nationalism – of whatever stripe – is something that brutalizes people. German nationalism stupefied and drove crazy the most cultured race in Europe. In the same way Spanish nationalism was another of the abominations of the General (Franco). In the same way the Basque nationalism that we have with us today is another abomination."
Basque historian and anthropologist Julio Caro Baroja in a 1990 interview in the Spanish magazine Cambio 16

It didn't happen often (in fact it only happened once). We were having an informal lunch with the Ambassador of the United States of America in Italy. It hadn't been planned or scheduled. A colleague and I had gone – as we usually did – to the little snack-bar cafeteria on the Embassy compound on Rome's beautiful Via Veneto. The Ambassador (with whom we met with each weekday at 9:15) had shown up unexpectedly and had seemed a bit out of place among his subordinates. We waved to him and he headed our way, tray-in-hand.

He seemed surprised that I was brown-bagging it with a peanut-butter and jelly sandwich. I gently fired back at his plenipotentiary teasing by telling him that my sandwich made me the envy of the lunch room, because I was probably the only one in the room with a home-made lunch prepared by a loving spouse.

Of course, we talked about Italy. As I munched on the PB&J, we talked about the many things holding back the economy. We spent a lot of that lunchtime conversation complaining about Italian absurdities. In these kinds of conversations I always tried to find at least one positive thing to say about Italy. It is after all, in spite of all its problems, one of the world's most interesting and beautiful countries. My opportunity came when the Ambassador commented on the Italians' lack of patriotism. It is well known that the loyalty of most Italians is primarily focused on the family, and rarely extends beyond the range of the church bells of their home town.

"Well, Mr. Ambassador, I have to tell you, I see that as a positive thing."

I went on to explain that because the Italians don't have intense feelings of national identity, it would, I thought, be very difficult for some demagogue to convince the Italians that they should head down the road to slaughter Frenchmen, or Tunisians, or Austrians... or Iraqis. The Italians just wouldn't go for it. Certainly not the way we recently had in Iraq. So maybe what the Ambassador considered a vice was in fact a virtue.

He seemed torn by my comments. On the one hand, as an Italian-American he seemed to like the idea of converting an Italian shortcoming into something positive. On the other hand, well, he was now the representative in Italy of the demagogue who – using the tools of nationalism and patriotism – had led us down that road to slaughter (in Iraq). So I guess he must have found it hard to accept my argument. Like I said, that was our last lunchroom conversation.

But I understood what the Ambassador was saying, for I had a lot of patriotism and nationalism in my own background. As a boy, one of my favorite books was "Johnny Tremaine," a tale of adolescent derring-do in the Revolutionary War. As a high school senior, one of my English class projects was analyzing the lyrics of the John Lennon's song "Imagine." I harshly criticized the song, especially the bit about "imagine there's no country... nothing to kill or die for." I was a flag-waving, patriotic kid. Patriotism and dedication to national defense, were, of course, the prime motivators when I was in the army. And later, when I became one of a handful of U.S. Embassy liaison officers to the Nicaraguan Contras, nationalism became and especially serious thing – deadly serious. In my book "Contra Cross" I wrote, "In all of my dealings with the Contras, I always had it in the back of my mind that if somebody had to fight and die in Nicaragua, it was far better for the United States if Nicaraguans were doing the fighting and dying." And that's what we had done – we had worked to keep them fighting. So I knew what the Ambassador was talking about, but the truth was that I had a lot more experience than he did with the real-world implications and consequences of nationalism and patriotism.

On one of my last days in their country, I got a little reminder of why the Italians have so little enthusiasm for nationalism. The moving company had arrived at our little apartment and the crew was finishing up the process of putting all of our worldly possessions in big cardboard boxes. We were all taking a break and I was sitting on the floor eating an apple. In front of me was a cardboard box from The Franzosini Brothers shipping company. It proudly proclaimed: "Fratelli Franzosini – Trasloci Nazionale e Internazionale" ("Franzosini Brothers – National and International Moves.")

The Nazi in the Italian word Nazionale kind of catches your eye, doesn't it? It should. For me it was a reminder that the Italians have a lot of bitter experience with nationalism and patriotism. Italy was the birthplace of 20th century Fascism, and signs of the Mussolini era are still easy to find: In Rome, many buildings (including the U.S. Embassy) bear inscriptions such as "Ano V." Like many dictators, Mussolini re-started the calendar –

Ano V meant that the building went up in the fifth year of his regime. During our first months in Italy we found a little town (Antrodoco) that had a strange inscription carved out of the trees on a side of a mountain: DVC. At first we thought it might be for the local soccer team. An old lady in the town sheepishly clued us in: "Il Duce!"

Hitler had found inspiration in Italian fascism, but during the last years of the war, with Mussolini gone, Italy's German friends turned on her and the country found itself under the Nazi jackboot. Looking up from the cardboard box, right out our bedroom window I could see the Ghetto, Rome's traditional Jewish quarter. That's where, on October 16, 1943, the Germans rounded up 1,007 Jews and sent them to the concentration camps. Only 15 survived. So the Italians know a few things about where that word nazionale can lead you.

I had had some previous run-ins with that N word and the cruel absurdities that come with it. In Central America we had been completely focused on the global Cold War struggle against the local allies of the Soviet Union. But as we worked with the Salvadorans and the Hondurans, we got very frequent reminders of the nationalist tensions that existed between them. These two tiny neighboring countries had actually gone to war with each other in 1969. They shared a common language, a common history, a common religion, a common culture... Yet they had convinced themselves that they were so profoundly different that – after tensions peaked during a soccer game – they should go out and kill each other. It was ridiculous. But later I would come to conclude that it was only marginally more ridiculous than the nationalism that sometimes drives U.S. citizens to the battlefields.

For my second tour in the Foreign Service, during those dark days before marriage and children, I had been sent to Spain. This was compensation for my first tour having been in Tegucigalpa, Honduras. I'd been assigned to Madrid, but shortly before it was time for me to go, the State Department called and said they had something for me that might be "even better": they asked if I'd be interested in going to Bilbao instead of Madrid. The phone line was very scratchy, and I guess I suspected that some well-connected Washingtonian was trying to steal my Spain slot, so instead of hearing Bilbao, I heard Malabo. Malabo is the only Spanish-speaking post in Africa. And it is just about the worst place in the world. It is in Equatorial Guinea. Think Cannibalism. Cannibalism within the government. A colleague was in my office when this call came. I put my hand over the phone and told him, "These jerks are trying to send me Malabo, and they are trying to tell me that is it better than Madrid!"

We soon clarified that they were offering Bilbao, not Malabo. Bilbao was definitely better than Malabo and arguably better than Madrid. It is the biggest city in the Basque Country, a region that straddles the Pyrenees on the Atlantic side of France and Spain I quickly concluded that they were indeed offering me something "even better" than Madrid. I liked the idea of going to a tiny Consulate where, instead of being one of many junior officers, I would be THE AMERICAN VICE CONSUL. I knew there was a serious Basque separatist problem, and I found that intriguing. And, unlike Madrid, it had a beach. So, against the advice of friends and mentors, I took it. It was a very good choice. I really loved the place.

At first, I took a very detached approach to the Basque separatist issue. This was, I thought, a Spanish problem that had nothing to do with us. But the problem was all around me and couldn't be ignored – there were assassinations in cafés close to my apartment, bombings were common, and nationalist street demonstrations often led to serious injuries and destruction. A big part of my job was understanding the place, so, soon after I arrived, I launched into a study of the Basques, their history, and most of all, their nationalism.

I was studying on my own, but as the American Vice Consul, I was a very privileged student. I got to talk to just about anybody I wanted to – top business people, politicians, academics, journalists, etc. Only a few years out of the army, I was still an early riser – I did most of my studying in the pre-dawn hours in my beach-front apartment near where the Nervion River flows into the Cantabrian Sea. It was a great place to study – a sea breeze would blow through the apartment and the sound of waves crashing against the rocks would fill the room. When I looked up I could see cargo ships moving through the harbor. I opened computer files on Basque history, on personal observations, and on the Basque language. Soon the files began to fill up and I started to understand what the violence was all about. (Much of this section comes from those files.)

Here it is, in a nutshell: The Basques are probably the descendants of some very early inhabitants of their corner of what is now the Spanish-French Atlantic border region. They have distinctive cultural characteristics and speak – in addition to Spanish or French – what is clearly a very old language: Euskera. But until very recently, they lived within Spain and France as Spaniards or as Frenchmen. Indeed, some Basque intellectuals clearly considered the Basques to be the most authentically Spanish of the Spaniards, the original Spaniards.

But in the early part of the 20th Century, a politician saw opportunity in the vague sense of cultural and linguistic difference felt by the Basques. Sabino Arana decided to turn that feeling into a full-blown national identity. And he would use that new identity as the basis for a new political party, the Basque Nationalist Party, the PNV.

Arana and the PNV did everything they could to make the Basques see themselves not as Spaniards, but as a nation apart. History was re-written. Anything that supported the idea of separation was emphasized, anything that showed the Basques to be Spaniards (or Frenchmen) was edited out. Much had to be invented out of whole cloth. Like the Basque flag. And the name of the country (Euskadi).

Nationalists usually need an "other" some group to distinguish themselves from. Of course, Arana and the PNV chose Spain and the Spaniards. They even came up with pejorative names: The Spaniards became Maketos, and Spain, Maketania. Madrid was presented as the capital of the "other." In the Basque country you will find bars called "New York" or "America" or "Paris" or "London"...but you won't find a single "Bar Madrid." One day, while trying to remember the name of a cafe that I had visited the night before, I told Basque friends that I thought it was called "Cafe Madrid." They all laughed and assured me that – assuming that I had not left Euskadi – it most certainly was not called "Cafe Madrid"!

During the Spanish Civil War the PNV sided with the Republic (i.e. against Franco). Bad move. When it eventually became apparent that they had signed on with the losing team, terrified Basque families put their children on ships and sent them – en masse – to refuge in other countries. (My friend Xavier de Acillona was one of these child refugees.) PNV reps looked out for the exiles, reinforcing loyalty to the party and to its nationalist agenda. Always opposed to Spain's centrifugal tendencies, part of Franco's revenge against the Basques was a harsh crackdown on all things related to Basque nationalism, including the use of the Basque language. Franco's actions helped the PNV in its efforts to convince the Basques that they were not Spaniards, that they were a people apart, that they were not like the supposedly disgusting Maketos.

For decades, nothing much happened. But a generation of Basques was being raised on a steady diet of nationalism, of us-versus-them, of separatism, of hatred for "the other", hatred for Spain. While previous generations had seen themselves as Spaniards with Basque roots, the PNV's nationalist efforts had succeeded in getting them to see themselves as Basques, and to see Spaniards as foreign invaders. By the time I got there, you even had to be careful about how you referred to Spain. You couldn't say, for example, that you hoped to visit other parts of Spain – the nationalists would correct you: "Euskadi is not Spain!" At a reception in Bilbao for the U.S. Ambassador, I watched nationalists play the name game with our boss: "So, how long have you been in our country Mr.

180

Ambassador?" When he said 18 months, they acted confused and asked if he'd really been in the Basque Country for so long. When the meteorologist gave the weather report on Basque TV, he had to be careful about referring to "other parts of Spain." He got around this by referring to "other parts of the Spanish state." (It was acceptable to acknowledge that the Basque Country was in fact currently within the borders of the Spanish *state*, but he'd get into trouble if he implied that the Basques were part of a Spanish *nation*.)

The nationalist zeal to emphasize any and all possible distinctions between the Basque Country and Spain resulted in a weird kind of culture war. When an old picturesque windmill near my apartment was destroyed in a storm, nationalists on the city council refused to have it repaired – windmills were seen as "Spanish." The Basques had been bullfighting for hundreds of years, but now the nationalists rejected bullfighting – too Spanish. The campaign even extended to the trees. The nationalists had preferences for certain trees that were deemed to be native to the region, and disliked other tree species they claimed had been brought to the region by the Maketos.

It all seems silly, but in fact it was deadly serious. It wasn't just a culture war. It wasn't just windmills, bullfights, and trees. Starting around 1968, some of the Basque country's young people, after years of listening to the hateful, us-versus-them dinner time diatribes of their parents and grandparents, decided to go beyond cheap talk. They decided to take action. They formed the terrorist group ETA and they started killing people. In the bloody decades that followed, they killed more than 800 people.

By the time I got to the Basque country, ETA seemed to be a pervasive influence. Everywhere you went you'd see the ETA graffiti. Every morning I'd have to read the pro-ETA newspaper. You'd always watch what you said – you never knew when an ETA sympathizer might be in earshot. After a while this kind of caution became automatic, but visitors had to be warned about the need for discretion – my brother came to visit and raised some worried eyebrows when he asked (a bit too loudly) about the ETA graffiti. Street demonstrations were common, and they were very nasty – nationalist kids with sling-shots and ball bearings took out the eye of a policeman in my neighborhood. Bombings and assassinations were not unusual. ETA's favorite targets were Spanish national policemen. Sometimes they'd put the bomb under the victim's personal car, and blow up the policeman and his children as he tried to drive them to school. After one such atrocity, ETA issued a press release declaring the children to be "legitimate targets" because there was a chance that they might have wanted to follow in their father's footsteps and might have become Spanish national policemen. Two Spanish National Policemen were assigned to protect our Consulate, and I got to know these guys. They were living with this kind of threat. I lost my emotional detachment and came to hate the people who were doing this and the vicious nationalist ideas that propelled the nationalists to violence. I felt sorry for the policemen at the consulate and tried (in vain) to loan them the bullet-proof flak jackets that we had in the Consulate's emergency supplies.

On July 15, 2012 The New York Times ran a story about the human consequences of this nationalist madness:

The day Basque terrorists killed his father in 1980, it was raining, Iñaki García Arrizabalaga recalled recently. His father had offered him a ride to the university. But Mr. García chose his bicycle instead. Even now more than 30 years later, he wonders what might have happened if he had gotten into that car.

Would he also have been found, sitting in a clearing, his arms handcuffed behind a tree trunk, a bullet in his head? Or would his presence have deterred the terrorists who lay in wait that day for his father's car, maybe buying the gentle family man who worked for the phone company one more day of life? Did the assassins look in his father's eyes before they killed him? Did they sleep well that night?.... Mr. García's father was killed because the telephone company was cooperating with wiretaps, a decision he had nothing to do with.

Faced with all this bloodshed, an outside observer might assume that there is some underlying historical justification. But I found none; my study of the history only deepened my disdain. The nationalists had taken a vague sense of identity and had done everything they could to convert it into a full blown case of nationalism and separatism. The nationalist political parties had – for their own partisan purposes – convinced the Basques that they were so profoundly different from Spaniards that they constituted a people apart, that the Spaniards were the hated "other" and that Spanish officials and policemen were foreign invaders. It all seemed quite fake, very cooked up, almost absurd.

There were lots of reminders of how synthetic and contrived this all was: The scene: Three a.m., New Year's Day 1991 in a bar somewhere in the greater Bilbao area. Young Basques greeting the New Year. Much revelry. A girl enters and it is announced that it is her birthday. The crowd breaks into an awkward Euskera version of "Happy Birthday" ("Zorionak to

You!"). Most of the singers can't speak Euskera but they've all learned the song. Well, sort of. The celebration continues. The disc jockey plays a typical Spanish song with the hand clapping, foot stamping beat of Andalusian flamenco – music and dance that is quintessentially Spanish. Immediately, without thinking, about half the group breaks into "Sevillanas" with the girls trying to dance like the Andaluzas and the men stamping and clapping as if they'd been born in Seville. Observing the spectacle, one guy at the bar (with less booze in him) shakes his head and mutters (in Spanish) "Dios mio." There is politico-cultural schizophrenia in the Basque Country.

After the (first) Gulf War the American Pop singer Whitney Houston put the Star Spangled Banner onto American Top Forty. I heard the song on the radio. Later that day, talking about patriotism to some friends in a bar in Las Arenas (Vizcaya), I commented that the song had given me goose bumps. I was a little surprised when one of the people present nodded and said,"Yea I know what you mean." For a brief moment I thought he was going to say the un-sayable and tell me that he had once felt goose bumps upon hearing the Spanish National Anthem, but no... his goose bumps had been inspired by a rendition of the Gernikako Arbola – the Basque National Anthem – his national anthem. I guess to certain extent national identity is determined by things like goose bumps and national anthems. The Basque Nationalist "feeling" is there and it is genuine. They even use our word "feeling" to describe it. "We have this feeling..."

At the time, I was scornful of their feelings, but quite proud of my own. It took me a while to realize that there really wasn't much difference between the two.

A few years later I had another experience with the cynical, political use of nationalism. This time I was in the Dominican Republic, working at the U.S. Embassy's economic section. Our policy goals for "the DR" were fairly straightforward: democracy and development. As we frequently told visitors, we considered it to be in the US interest to see the Dominican Republic – a country just 90 miles from US territory (Puerto Rico) to become "more like Canada and less like Bangladesh." So, we were happily doing whatever we could to help the country move in that direction. I found this to be very gratifying – in the DR poverty was all around us, and I was pleased with the thought that I was using the influence of the United States to help alleviate it.

In 1994, our efforts suffered a major setback when Dominicans went to the polls to elect a President. Joaquin Balaguer, an acolyte of the dictator Trujillo, seemed to have attained President-for-life status. And it was turning out be a very long life. In this election he faced a serious challenge from Jose Francisco Pena Gomez of the Dominican Revolutionary Party (PRD). Pena Gomez – a dark skinned Dominican who had worked as a shoe-shine boy on the streets of Santo Domingo – was the candidate of the downtrodden. The campaign was ugly. Balaguer's people rolled out the nationalistic artillery very early, using Pena Gomez's dark skin as "evidence" that he was of Haitian descent.

Even though they share an island with them, Dominicans have long used the Haitians as their "other." There are, of course, real cultural, linguistic and historical differences between the two groups, but people like Trujillo and Balaguer had over the years deliberately focused attention on these differences, to the point of causing Dominicans to often overlook the human plight of their impoverished neighbors. In October 1937, in response to complaints about cattle rustling in the border area, Trujillo ordered the massacre of Haitians living on the Dominican side of the border. They killed them with machetes. At first they had trouble differentiating Haitians from Dominicans. So they came up with a little test: They knew that Haitians had trouble pronouncing the Spanish word for parsley. So they would hold up a piece of parsley and ask the person to say what it was. If they didn't trill the r's properly or didn't get the j sound sufficiently far back in the throat, they were hacked to death. Over a five day period, Dominican soldiers slaughtered more than 20,000 people. My brother-in-law refers to this event as "our Dominican Holocaust." Balaguer's attack on Pena Gomez's Haitian roots were fully part of this very ugly nationalist mindset.

Many people suspected that Balaguer would use electoral fraud in a desperate attempt to hold onto power. And he did. On election day, PRD voters found that even though they had valid voter registration cards in hand, they were being told that somehow their names were not on the lists of eligible voters (even though the registration cards had been produced by the same computer that generated the lists). It appeared that Balaguer's people had obtained the membership lists for the Dominican Revolutionary Party, and they gone into the voter registration computer files and had run a "delete these names" program.

It was obvious that there had been fraud, and that unless something was done this fraud would allow Balaguer to stay in power, contrary to the will of the Dominican voters.

When the Embassy took a stand alongside those Dominicans who were calling for justice, Balaguer and his supporters responded with nationalism. An organization called the Dominican Nationalist Movement suddenly sprang into existence and began to decry foreign intervention in Dominican

184

affairs. Dominican flags started to appear outside Dominican homes. Demonstrating that patriotism is indeed the last refuge of a scoundrel, Balaguer did everything he could to hide his fraud behind a smoke screen of Dominican patriotism, to cloak his electoral theft in the Dominican flag.

This conflict spilled over into my personal life – Elisa and I were dating at the time, and she invited me to a family social function. After a quantity of Presidente beers had been consumed, Uncle Victor decided it was time to talk politics. He was a construction engineer and a beneficiary of Balaguer's penchant for pouring massive amounts of concrete in public works projects. I tried to change the subject, but Victor wouldn't quit. When he started personally insulting U.S. Ambassador Donna Hrinak, I had to respond. It got fairly ugly.

In the end, justice prevailed. International and domestic pressure caused Balaguer to concede that there had been "irregularities" in the election. A sort of "do-over" vote was organized. It went very smoothly and, although Pena Gomez never became president, at least Balaguer left office.

But of course, us-versus-them sentiments run deep and are very persistent. When we went back to the Dominican Republic in 2012, we were struck by the harsh commentary about Haitians that we heard from our Dominican friends and relatives. "They are coming here to take our jobs!" We pointed out that the rhetoric they were using against the Haitians was almost identical to that used in the United States by those opposed to Latino immigrants, but our friends and relatives were unmoved.

The nationalist attitudes of the Azoreans – more precisely the lack of nationalist feelings in those islands – is for me a reminder of how unnecessary nationalist fervor is. It is the kind of place where you might expect to find nationalist feelings – they are, after all, 900 miles from mainland Portugal, and the islanders have been living very separate lives for more than 500 years. But you really don't find any Azorean nationalist sentiments out there.

This was brought home to me during a visit to the island by Congressman Barney Frank. Frank was one of the Azoreans' only friends in the U.S. Congress, so whenever he visited they rolled out the red carpet. On this particular visit they had organized a tour of economically important areas. I was invited to go along. The Portuguese central government decided to send a fairly senior representative out to the islands for Frank's visit – he was set to arrive on the day of the big tour, on an early morning flight from Lisbon.

At the appointed hour, we all met in the lobby of the Hotel Atlantico. I was standing there with Frank and a few senior officials from the Azorean regional government when the Central Government's rep arrived, stepped into the lobby, and, in an innocent effort to make conversation, immediately put his foot completely into his mouth:

"Wow," he said, "the weather here is even worse THAN IN PORTUGAL."

I thought the Azorean official next to me was going to faint. The man from Lisbon had just given voice to an attitude that the Azoreans found deeply offensive: the mainland Portuguese often seemed to act as if the Azores was foreign territory, not quite fully Portuguese.

"This is PORTUGAL! WE ARE IN PORTUGAL!" they yelled, almost in unison. The poor man looked as if he wanted to head immediately to the airport (to go back to Portugal!).

I remember thinking that the Basques would have loved this kind of remark. They would have seen this as further confirmation of their distinctiveness, of their separateness, of their being from a different country.

****

After a political argument related to some of the themes of this book, my sister threw up her hands and said, in exasperation, "You guys have spent too much time in Europe!"

She was clearly onto something. Living in Europe had changed our views. But this was not simply the result, as my sister may have suspected, of too much hobnobbing with cheese-eating surrender monkeys. It was more complicated than that.

Living in Europe gave us a close look at other peoples' patriotisms, at how Basques, Brits, Azoreans and Italians handle national identity. And living there provided frequent reminders of what happens when people get carried away with their us-versus-them sentiments: You can still see WWII bomb damage in London, and just about every town we visited in Europe had a memorial to the many people destroyed by the World Wars. There was the Basque madness. And there were all those American cemeteries, filled with the bodies of young Americans who'd died on European battlefields.

This was of course quite depressing, but there were reasons for hope: the Europeans are trying to do something about this. They are trying to get beyond nationalism. They are building the supra-national European Union. During my time in Spain they were launching the single market. While we were in Portugal, national currencies were dropped in favor of the Euro, and the Automatic Teller Machines started disbursing the new money. All around us in London we could see evidence of the free

186

movement of European people facilitated by the EU project. In the UK, it sometimes seemed that the main evidence of the EU's existence came in the form of British complaints about it, but it was important to keep the big picture in mind: The EU is an effort to prevent nationalism from ever again carrying Europe back to the killing fields. The goal was to make war between these countries impossible (and in this regard it has been completely successful). The EU's unofficial anthem is, appropriately, Beethoven's "Ode to Joy" – a musical celebration of the brotherhood of mankind.

So in a certain sense my sister was right. We'd spent ten years in a region in which reminders of the bloody the consequences of nationalism are were all around us, in a region that was working hard to prevent future wars by moving beyond nationalism. You'd have to be pretty obtuse to spend a decade in this environment and not come away with some changes in your thinking about nationalism.

MOVING VAN BLUES
DIFFICULT DEPARTURES

"Leaving is a little like dying." Alberto the Trastevere shopkeeper

Over time, we began to suspect that we might not be temperamentally suited to the Foreign Service life. We found it kind of unnatural to always have a departure date looming in front of us. Many people live with the possibility of a move off in their future, but for us, it was not a possibility, it was a certainty. And we always knew exactly when we would go. Our Embassy ID cards had expiry dates that coincided with the month that we would be transferred. Sometimes I felt like a loaf of bread or a gallon of milk. When you met somebody new in the Embassy, you could often catch them glancing at the expiry date, trying to determine if it was worth the effort to befriend you.

Our suspicions about our unsuitability were confirmed when the departure date approached. With about three or four months to go, Elisa would start to get weepy at odd moments. The tears often wouldn't necessarily be associated with someone we'd grown especially close to – we knew we'd stay in touch with them. More often Elisa would get teary-eyed at the thought of saying goodbye to someone who was not really very close to us – a storekeeper, a cafe owner – but who had become part of our daily routine. These were folks we knew we would never see again.

At around this point I would usually have what we've come to call my Foreign Service dream. In this dream, I find myself packing up to leave the house or apartment that we've lived in for the previous three of four years. I find what appears to be a closet door that had somehow escaped my notice. I open it up to find a really fabulous suite of rooms leading to a wonderful beachfront patio... that we had completely failed to take advantage of.

Elisa also has some recurring dreams. In one, she goes back to one of the places that we'd lived before. She has with her a long list of people she wants to see. But time is short and she's afraid that she won't get to see everyone. Another of her dreams is more forward looking: in it, she's in our new house, and she's horrified to find that it is full of bugs (she REALLY dislikes bugs).

Most people with kids have a wall in their house on which the heights of their kids on various dates are marked. "Look how much Johnny has grown since 2006!" We have similar markings, but ours are on a piece of 2x1 lumber that goes into the shipping container every time we move.

Even in the age of cell phones, most people know their home and office phone numbers, but by the time we got to Rome I had so many of these numbers in my head that I started mixing them up and blending them together.

Even though it had in many ways been a very tough post for us, our departure from the Azores was painfully traumatic. We had grown very close to the Azoreans and as we approached the end of our tour we'd start obsessing about all that was about to come to an end: No longer would I walk on the water front with Joao Antonio Mota Amaral. No longer would Elisa bake cakes with Margarida and Paula. No longer would Billy hunt Jimmy-Jimmies with Ivo. No longer would Maria ask Margarida for Ceralaca. Elisa would run into someone in the market. They'd look at each other. One of them would say, "Oh, this may be the last time I run into you here in the market." Both would break into tears. This kind of thing went on for several months. By the time we got on the plane we were emotionally drained.

Our departure from London was made somewhat easier by the fact that Elisa was deeply involved in her garden design studies during our final months at post. She had to focus on her course, and simply didn't have much time to dwell on the fact that we were leaving a place that she really loved. The fact that London (unlike the Azores) is the kind of place that you can easily return to made our departure seem less final. Also, Rome seemed close-by. It was almost as if we were just moving down the road. But still, it was difficult. I took the kids on one final walk through the neighborhood, to Farmer Brothers' Hardware, and to the newsstand of Mrs. Amin... The worldly Londoners took it all in stride. People were coming and going all the time, and everyone knew it was not the end of the world.

But the London departure was made more difficult for me by an awkward injury: On one of our last visits to Hyde Park, Billy and I decided to play a little baseball. His kindergarten teacher, Julie Hannington, was with us that day. The ladies had gone for a stroll around the Serpentine Lake while Billy and I worked on his swing. He was really getting the hang of it. When Elisa, Julie and Maria returned, we were very anxious to show off Billy's batting prowess. I guess I moved the pitcher's mound a bit too close to the plate. I gave him a nice pitch and he really nailed it. The ball hit me right in the mouth. They say it was like one of those slow motion scenes in the cowboy movies where the victim is lifted off the ground by the bullet and falls to the ground in dramatic slow-motion, stirring up a cloud of dust. The Brits in the area were horrified. I was bleeding and – worried about Billy feeling guilty – I was trying my best to keep a stiff upper lip with a split upper lip. You could see my teeth marks on the baseball. I had to go through all the going-away events looking like I'd been in a pub fight or perhaps an ugly domestic dispute.

Packing up from London was very stressful. Elisa was tied up with her studies, so I took charge of the logistics. It's amazing how much junk you can get into a small house when you have little kids. There was a little charity thrift shop on Fulham Road – I made so many deliveries of books and toys and shoes and clothes that I thought they were going to start turning me away. And there was still an enormous amount of junk! I began to fear that we had been close to "hoarder" category. I'd fill up the driveway with stuff, the garbage men would take it away, and I'd immediately start filling the driveway again. I did four driveway loads. But even after all of this, and even after the moving men took 7,500 pounds of stuff away in their van, we still had too much. On the night before our scheduled 5 a.m. departure, at around 1 a.m., as Elisa and I frantically tried to stuff what remained into our luggage, we realized we simply had too much. We surrendered to the laws of physics and decided to leave one large suitcase with our very understanding Australian friends across the street; it was eventually carried to us in Rome by a friend from Brazil.

Leaving Rome was in many ways our most difficult departure. There was, of course, my traditional pre-move injury (this time: Achilles tendon). But there was a lot more to it than that. Italy is such a beautiful place, and we were leaving right at the end of the most beautiful season – the spring. We were leaving Europe, and going far away. Billy and Maria had reached the point where friends were really important to them – for the first time saying goodbye was hard for them.

Auguri Maria! -- Good Luck Maria!

Contributing to the trauma was the Italians' love for drama. They have a well-deserved reputation for bringing elements of theater into real life. For them, life is a stage. Also, with considerable justification they consider themselves to be very fortunate to live in Italy, and feel sorry for anyone who has to leave. They leave very infrequently – for most of them it is simply inconceivable to move far away from family, friends and good food. (Indeed, some Italians seem to harbor a sneaking suspicion that it is impossible to eat well outside Italy – Italian mothers have been known to pack foodstuffs – Italian foodstuffs – when going abroad on vacation.) This all explains the bits of theater that we witnessed each time we told someone we were getting ready to leave: Alberto the storekeeper, for example, threw his hands down, palms forward, and, with his brow furrowed declared, "No! Impossible! But WHY do you have to leave? You just got here!" It was a bit of theater, but it was reality-based theater – he really was sad to see us go. After lamenting our impending departure and sharing the sad news with co-workers and other customers, he summarized the Italian reaction to just about all departures: Shaking his head slowly he said, "Partire e un po morire!" ("To depart is a little like dying" or "Departing is a little like death!") All Italians in earshot put on sad faces and nodded in agreement. Alberto was right. Departure is a little like death. Your daily routine disappears. Lots of things that you have come to enjoy will soon end. As you get close to the end, people start

191

treating you a bit differently – unlike everyone else, soon you won't be around. We said goodbye and shuffled off, dejected, en route to the great beyond.

In Rome, shortly before departure

If you move a lot, it definitely shakes you loose from your moorings. That hometown that you grew up in no longer seems quite so special. The range of your emotional connections to people and places expands. Many people who frequently move at some point stop identifying themselves by their place of birth – they stop thinking of themselves as Bostonians or Iowans. They start to think of themselves as part of a larger entity. When these moves are within national boundaries, that larger entity is usually the country. But our moves took us not just from city to city, but from country to country, so our emotional connections to people and places expanded quite a bit further.

BACK IN THE USA

"Patriotism is your conviction that this country is superior to all other countries because you were born in it." George Bernard Shaw

In the State Department's publications on how to deal with culture shock, they advise that moving back to the USA after a long period overseas can be one of the most difficult adjustments. Their publications on this is entitled "My Passport Says I'm American." You are supposed to be "coming home" but you have been gone so long that it doesn't feel like home anymore. Congress was worried about this, so at some point they had mandated that Foreign Service personnel take "home leave" between assignments. This was apparently intended to keep us in touch with "home" and to prevent us from emotionally drifting away. We found that it didn't really work. We'd been back a couple of times for home leave, but each visit had made us feel more like foreigners – midway through the home leave we'd be yearning to head home… to London or Rome! Sorry about that Congress. Nice try.

How people react when they return to the U.S. depends a lot on where they are coming from. When you return from a long stay in a poor, despotic, conflictive region you are more inclined to look favorably on your prosperous and comfortable homeland. Not long after we came back to the U.S. after a two-week stay in the Dominican Republic, Billy and I were watching a TV report on how dissatisfied Americans are with the direction the country is going. Billy was scornful: "What a bunch of crybabies! At least they can drink the tap water!" I remember an urge to kiss the ground and wave the flag after coming back from Honduras, or El Salvador or Guatemala. But when you come home from the prosperous and democratic countries of Western Europe, well, being able to drink the tap water and vote is not really impressive, and the urge to put lips to dirt is not nearly as strong.

When you go through culture shock overseas, it is understandable: You know you have moved to a weird foreign place, and you expect to go through an adjustment. But when you move back to the U.S. the culture shock can be just as strong, but you can't really understand it. After all, you are supposed to be home. Even our kids seemed to know that returning to the U.S. was supposed to feel like homecoming: During one Home Leave trip, as our plane descended for landing, six year-old Maria – who had left the United States when she was five months old and had never

193

been to Chicago – looked at the skyline of the Windy City and sighed, "Oh, it's so good to be back!"

My first trip to a U.S. supermarket after four years in the Dominican Republic (1992-1996) had provided several of the little cultural collisions that eventually add up to full-blown culture shock. First I inadvertently took my cart with 40 or so items into the Express Check-Out (15 items or less). My fellow shoppers all gave me dirty looks. I couldn't figure out why until the cashier clued me in. I tried to make amends by telling the group that I'd been overseas for four years. The cashier wasn't buying it "Oh, and they didn't have supermarkets where you were?" she asked. I dug myself deeper into the hole when I tried to explain that in the DR, I'd had a housekeeper who did all the shopping. Apparently fearing a possible lynching, the cashier rang up my items as fast as she could. Then came a question: "Paper or plastic?" I really didn't know what she was asking me. I thought she wanted to know about how I intended to pay. "Credit card," I responded. "Paper or plastic?" she asked again. Genuinely confused, I told her that my credit card was plastic. I think by this point the cashier just concluded that I was some sort of crazy person. She loaded my items into bags. PLASTIC bags!

Knowing that we'd all be going through culture shock, we decided to treat our new home as if it were another foreign assignment. As we'd done in all of our overseas posts, we'd try hard to keep an open mind. We'd keep track of the things we liked and didn't like about our new country of assignment, and, as we'd done in Portugal, the U.K, and in Italy, we'd discuss the pros and cons of the new place at dinner time. This turned out to be a very fitting and balanced way to deal with our new (old) posting in the United States of America.

The journey home gave us some very early topics for discussion. The abuse that U.S. airlines heap upon travelers these days, and the police-state treatment doled out by the TSA and the U.S. immigration authorities certainly didn't help engender a feeling of joyful homecoming. As soon as we got done with the authorities ("Sir, turn off that cell phone or I will CONFISCATE it!") United Airlines canceled our connecting flight. We were all exhausted, but were now doomed to six hours of waiting for the next flight. I really knew we were no longer in Italy when, upon finally getting on-board the plane, I asked the stewardess for blankets for our very sleepy and cold kids. "Sorry, sir, blankets are for *First Class* passengers!" Welcome home 99 percenters!

On the other hand, our experiences with ground transportation were much more uplifting. We made several stops before arriving in the Washington area, and in each location we grabbed cabs at the airport.

194

Perhaps subconsciously identifying with their foreign-ness, we struck up conversations with the cab drivers, all of whom were immigrants. We were struck by the deep affection that almost all of these men expressed for the United States and for the cities they had settled in In San Diego and San Francisco, in Denver and in Miami, speaking through thick accents in broken English, almost all of them told us lucky they felt to be living in the USA, how much they liked the city they were driving through, and how pleased they were with their new lives in the United States. One Nigerian cab driver really got all choked up about how lucky he considered himself. This made us feel very good about the USA.

When we finally arrived in Northern Virginia, having escaped the clutches of the airlines and the TSA, we were delivered into the arms... of real estate agents and mortgage brokers. It's a wonder we survived. But we did. In short order we bought a house on a cul-de-sac and started to settle down.

Moving vans began to arrive at our new place. In addition to the much-awaited delivery of our stuff from Rome, it was time for the State Department to return to us the items we had placed in storage. One batch contained items we'd stored when leaving Virginia (2000). There was another batch from the Azores (2003) that included a full-sized swing set, and a third from London (2007). Some of our furniture had been mistakenly sent to Ghana (where it remains – we opted for financial compensation). As we opened these weird time capsules, I found myself wishing that more of it had gone to Ghana. There was stuff that I'd bought when I was still single. There was a TV that I'd had in the army. There was a lot of baby-related equipment. When we finally got around to selling the baby stuff on Craig's list, they guy who bought the crib asked how old our baby was. "Thirteen!" I said. He looked confused. "Thirteen months?" he asked. "No she's thirteen – she's upstairs, on Facebook."

Following the lead of the First Family, we got a dog. We named ours "Cappuccio" – that's what the Italians ask for when they want a Cappuccino coffee. Cappuccio's fur is the color of the foam. He is an English Cream Golden Retriever. The little girl next door (Abbey) always got confused and called him a Cream Cheese Golden retriever. And sometimes (just to goof with people) we'd claim that he was Spanish-speaking. Maria's friend Cecilia taught him how to jump hurdles, equestrian style, forcing us to buy a new, higher fence (thanks a lot, Cecilia). Thus he became known as "Cappuccio, the English Cream-Cheese Flying Latino Retriever."

Our kids adjusted almost immediately. At this point Maria was only eleven and Billy only thirteen, yet they had lived in four different houses, in four different countries – they were ready to settle down. They loved the new neighborhood – there is a wonderful group of kids (and parents) on the cul-de-sac and they loved the fact that for the first time in their lives they could walk to the houses of friends, and hang out in backyards. Billy delighted in finding things that were better in the USA. He even declared that American pizza is better than Italian pizza. Maria frequently tried to defend Italy – she took a firm stand on ice cream, insisting that it was definitely better in Italy. Within days of moving to the new neighborhood the kids effectively put the foreign part of my Foreign Service career to an end by declaring that there would be no more of this moving-around-the-world stuff. They were home, and they intended to stay.

Elisa really missed (misses) Europe, and still, after two years, sometimes has trouble thinking of Northern Virginia as home. The sad fact is that she has encountered a bit of prejudice and racism here. Most people are very nice, but there are those who simply do not like people from Latin America, or people whose skin is darker than their own. That is something she didn't have to deal with in the other places we'd lived. Prejudice is often subtle, but it is definitely out there. In a store, Elisa will notice that the check-out clerk is friendly and joking with all the white women on line. But when she reaches the register, the clerk is suddenly cold. The friendly banter, and joking stops. Most people are nice, buy even if only ten percent of the people in your area are prejudiced bigots, that means that every trip out of your house could turn into an upsetting encounter with some jerk who could ruin your whole day. That makes it hard for this place to feel like home. But we knew that the vast majority of the folks around us were good people. Early on we found the bumper stickers in our neighborhood very encouraging: "WE ARE ALL MEMBERS OF ONE HUMAN FAMILY" and "GOD BLESS EVERYONE – NO EXCEPTIONS!"

I too had a difficult adjustment. I discovered that moving doesn't get any easier as you get older. I found myself once again on the same commuter train that I'd used ten years earlier. The only difference was that it was now in much worse condition – our national infrastructure problem was very apparent. I went to work at the same State Department building as before. The work wasn't nearly as interesting as work in the Consulates and Embassies had been. I felt like I had stepped back to 1999. Walking down the long, color-coded corridors, I'd see many of the same faces I saw ten years earlier. They were older, and most still didn't say hello. It was as if I'd stepped into a weird time warp, like one of those dreams in which you find yourself back in High School. It wasn't a good feeling.

As we were trying to get settled, little reminders of our life in Europe kept popping up. The navigator in our car still spoke with a British accent, gave us distances in kilometers, and would instruct us to "proceed to the

196

motorway." We'd reach into our kitchen cabinet to find drinking glasses that used to be Shrek-themed Nutella jars (in Portuguese). The kids' smart phones would buzz with text messages and Facebook status updates from Italy.

We quickly discovered that medical care in the U.S. had changed quite a bit. The kids' pediatricians were as good as they always had been, but some of the other doctors we visited seemed to have become a lot more focused on profit. As we struggled to understand the deliberately indecipherable "explanations of benefits" from the insurance companies (and the very questionable bills from the doctors that inevitably followed) we often found ourselves yearning for European socialized medicine. What was really striking, however, were the conversations with American friends and relatives who chose to lecture us on how horrible European health care is. In spite of the fact that we'd just come back from ten years in that supposedly horrible system, these folks (apparently having learned all about it on Fox News) were intent on telling us how bad things are over there (death panels, you know) and how wonderful things are here.

After years of being coddled in expensive overseas private schools, we were worried about how Billy and Maria would react to public school in the USA. As it turned out, we had nothing to worry about. They both liked their schools very much. There were of course, some adjustment problems. Billy for example, cried one night, telling us that the new middle school had so many rules and regulations and hall monitors and threats of punishment that he felt like he was in some kind of jail. It was worse than the UK's nanny state. In Maria's elementary school we were kind of taken aback by the way in which the teachers seemed to be trying to almost criminalize normal childhood goofiness – they would issue some sort of "red card" note to the parents for serious misbehavior in school (fair enough), but they used the same red card if the kid didn't do her homework. Billy especially found the contrast between all the rules and all the rhetoric about freedom quite confusing. But we all eventually got used to the cultures of the new schools.

Elisa and I also liked the schools. Ironically, we found the public schools in the U.S. to be far more responsive to us than were the fancy super-expensive private schools overseas. The private schools all seemed to have a "take it or leave it" attitude. If you complained about something, they'd listen for a while, but then they'd subtly remind you that it was their school (not yours) and that if you didn't like the way they were running it, well, perhaps you should look for another school more to your liking. At this point they'd usually also remind you about their long admissions waiting list. We also liked the egalitarian feel of the American public schools – there were no minions skulking about, reserving front row seats at school plays for their upper-crust social superiors. To a far greater extent than was the case in Europe, in the American schools we found a real effort to follow through on the idea that "all men are created equal."

We had worried that our return to the U.S. would mean that our kids would be leaving behind the very international environments that they had enjoyed in London and Rome. But as it turned out, their schools in Northern Virginia are far more diverse and international than their overseas schools.

There were things that surprised the kids. Billy was genuinely shocked by the daily ritual of the Pledge of Allegiance, especially since many of the kids in his class were not U.S. citizens – they just seemed to be going through the motions. We were also a bit taken aback by the adulation of the military – we'd be at a picnic, or a concert and all of a sudden someone would be asking all the veterans to stand up for a round of applause. The kids would elbow me until I was on my feet. It was a bit strange. I'd been in the army for a while some 25 years earlier. And now these people were applauding me for it. This was awkward – it seemed to be part of the kind of chest thumping "we're number one!" militarism that we'd come to feel very uneasy about.

And for a country that is supposed to be defined by its commitment to liberty, we were struck by the heavy handed TSA-like treatment that seemed to have become the norm in post 9-11 America. And not just at the airports. On a trip to New York City, we stood in a long line to get on the ferry out to Liberty Island and the Statue of Liberty. The careless and surly security personnel made my wife so nervous that she left her watch in the tray next to the metal detector. When she went back to retrieve it, the guards all but accused her of trying to steal it. They conducted a little interrogation. They were sarcastic and scornful when Elisa couldn't remember the brand name of her watch. I risked incarceration by telling them that I didn't like the way they had treated her. And this was on the way out to LIBERTY ISLAND.

Our visit to the Virginia Department of Motor Vehicles was another adventure in security theater, but this one ended quite well. Elisa's driver's license had expired while we were abroad, and the DMV insisted that she take a driver's test (within 30 days of arrival). The first obstacle was proof of identity. There was a long list of acceptable documents, but your options narrowed considerably if you hadn't grown up in the United States (no "U.S. high school transcript" for you!) or if most of your stuff (including your original certificate of naturalization) was in a container on a ship somewhere in the Atlantic Ocean. In spite of Elisa having in hand her U.S.

diplomatic passport, we struggled most of a day to convince DMV that she was who she said she was. When we questioned the bureaucratic rigidity, DMV staff trotted out 9-11 and hinted that we were being uncooperative in their heroic efforts to protect the homeland. After of a full day of this, we finally made it to the road test... only to be told that Elisa couldn't take the test because our rental car was in my name (on this the problem apparently was liability, not terrorism). Horrified at the prospect of another day of ID inquisition, we ran out and tried (one hour before DMV closed) to rent a car in Elisa's name. No luck. We were about to give up when I decided to try one more thing. I took a look at the people waiting in their cars to take the road test. There was a young Latino guy there – we later learned he was an immigrant from Honduras. I went up to him and – in Spanish – explained our situation. I asked him if he would lend us his car. (For some reason, that's OK with the DMV.) He consulted with his girlfriend and gave us the thumbs up. Getting an assist from some recent immigrants seemed like a very fitting way to get out of this "us-versus-them" Catch-22. Elisa passed the test, and we escaped the clutches of DMV with our faith in humanity renewed.

So, we had our ups and downs, but just as in our other posts, as time passed we settled in we grew more and more comfortable, and the place started to feel like home. And just as in those foreign places we had lived in, in the USA we found things that we liked, and things that we didn't like, great strengths and difficult problems, good people and bad people. This all reinforced the main lessons that we took away from our ten years abroad, from our ten years with the foreigners.

CITIZENS OF THE WORLD

"Nationalism is the culture of the uncultured, the religion of the commoner and a smokescreen behind which nestles prejudice, violence and frequently racism. The deepest root of all nationalism is the conviction that being part of a certain nation is an attribute, that it is something that distinguishes and confers a certain shared essence with other beings who are equally privileged by their similar destiny. This is a condition that inevitably establishes a differentiation - a hierarchy - relative to other groups. The nationalist argument is the easiest means to stir up a crowd, particularly if the crowd is poor and uncultured and has within it resentments, anger and a desire to vent its bitterness and frustration on something or someone. There is nothing like the great fireworks of nationalism to distract attention from real problems... Nationalism is the path that led us to the killing fields of 1914 and 1939..."
Mario Vargas Llosa, writing in the Spanish newspaper "El Pais" June 2, 1991

On June 14, 2012, two years after we returned to the United States, Maria graduated from Timber Lane Elementary School. At around that time, I was finishing up this book, getting to this, the difficult final chapter, the part in which I would try to pull it all together and lay out my conclusions. As I sat there in that public school gymnasium waiting for Maria's graduation to start, I had time to think about this. What had we learned from our decade abroad? What had those ten years with the foreigners taught us? What was I going to write in the last chapter?

The graduation ceremony provided a lot of food for thought for the final chapter. Up on the stage in front of the podium was a stuffed animal – a Tiger – the school mascot. Alongside the stuffed animal there were two large globes, reminders of Timber Lane's motto, which was emblazoned below: "Citizens of the World, Leading the Future." I was surprised the first time I saw that motto – I knew that there were people who would dislike the world citizenship idea (there were more than a few Tea Party flags in the area). But I was glad Timber Lane was sticking to its guns, boldly preparing its young citizens of the world for future leadership.

The graduates and their families provided many reminders of how appropriate that motto really was. The kids from Maria's class came from just about everywhere: from Nepal and El Salvador, from Bangladesh and Vietnam. There were Muslim kids with last names like Islam and Mohamed. Some of the graduates had walked into that school a few years

200

earlier speaking no English at all. For a moment, I found myself slipping into an "us and them" mindset, thinking that white American kids like Maria were a distinct minority. But wait a second, I reminded myself, my daughter is Latina too, and also the daughter of an immigrant. I realized that these kinds of thoughts were very much old-think – I'm sure some of the other parents also gave some thought to the national mix, but I doubt the kids ever did. They didn't see nationalities – they just saw beloved classmates. So the second part of that motto was also very appropriate: these citizens of the world really are leading the future.

The graduation ceremony began. Awards were given (I'm proud to report that Maria won "Best Writer"), teachers were recognized, speeches were made. I was sitting there, feeling good about the world, thinking of all these little world citizens leading the future, when suddenly the Principal said something that made me fear that the forces of militaristic nationalism we going to intrude on our little celebration of world citizenship. The Daughters of the American Revolution were in the house! Uh oh, I thought, here we go.

As it turned out the DAR lady was very tactful and her speech was nice. She talked about basic democratic values, ideals that every kid (and parent) in that gym would support. But there was an element of nationalism in her comments that sounded out-of-place. I couldn't help thinking that her speech, was – like my focus on the ethnicity of the graduates – kind of outmoded, kind of sad. The DAR lady seemed to be promoting ideas about citizenship and patriotism more appropriate for the 1950s, for a world in which people lived their lives in neat national boxes, ideas similar to those that we had before our ten years abroad. Timber Lane's "Citizens of the World" motto was much more in line with the internet-connected, globalized world these kids will live in, and with the worldview that we brought back from our long sojourn with the foreigners.

In our overseas houses and 'hoods, in the schools that our kids attended and the parks that they played in, with the doctors and hospitals that cared for them, and most of all through all of our "foreign friends," we came to realize that the human elements that unite us with the rest of the world make the nationality-based differences seem insignificant, exaggerated, contrived. Visits to military bases and military cemeteries, and our distant observations of the Iraq war provided sobering reminders of the human cost of the tribal "us versus them" mentality of nationalism and "we're number one" militaristic patriotism.

That nationalistic chip that we had on our shoulders in 2000 was now gone. While before we had seen our U.S. nationality as one of the most

201

important and defining of our personal attributes, we came back realizing that it is our humanity that really defines us. That's who we are.

We came back uneasy about the nationalistic mindset that causes people to believe that they are profoundly distinct, different, exceptional, and perhaps better than people of other nations. American politicians of both parties often proclaim that "we are the greatest nation the world has ever known." Sorry, but we don't walk around thinking that we are better than other people. And we don't believe that that kind of thinking (what some people call patriotism) is a virtue. We wouldn't teach our kids to think of themselves as being inherently better or greater than other kids. And we don't teach them that they as Americans are intrinsically better or greater than other people.

I'm sure there are readers (perhaps including my sister!) who would suggest that if we feel this way, we should go back to Europe. Permanently. But I'd reject the suggestion that we are no longer good Americans. If anything, I'd say that our experiences have made us better Americans. I think we've come back with a clearer, more realistic and balanced view of the world than we had before, with insights and perspectives that might help our country in its interaction with the rest of the world, with a worldview that, if widely shared, might help us avoid a repetition of catastrophes like the Iraq war.

Whenever the subject comes up we try to remind our kids that in addition to being citizens of the United States, they really are citizens of the world, with ties to all the people of the world, ties based on our common humanity. This idea might all seem self-evident, but it marks a big change from the nationalist world-view that we held before we left, and it seems quite at odds with the way that many Americans see things now. We really don't have to remind Billy and Maria of this – they know it, deep in their bones they know it. They know it because of all those *foreigners* who they grew up with in Portugal and England and Italy and all those *foreigner* grandparents and aunts and uncles and cousins in the Dominican Republic. They learned in childhood important lessons about the world that I didn't learn until middle age: that the differences between national groups are superficial, and that what we all have in common as human being is far more important.

INDEX

Other Books by Bill Meara:

"Contra Cross – Insurgency and Tyranny in
Central America"
http://www.contracross.com/

"SolderSmoke – Global Adventures in Wireless
Electronics"
http://soldersmoke.com/book.htm

**The author can be reached at:
bill.meara@gmail.com**